JAPAN AND MULTILATERAL DIPLOMACY

Japan and Multilateral Diplomacy

Edited by
PHILIPPE RÉGNIER and DANIEL WARNER

LONDON AND NEW YORK

First published 2001 by Ashgate Publishing

Reissued 2018 by Routledge
2 Park Square, Milton Park, Abingdon, Oxon, OX14 4RN
711 Third Avenue, New York, NY 10017, USA

Routledge is an imprint of the Taylor & Francis Group, an informa business

Copyright © Philippe Régnier and Daniel Warner 2001

All rights reserved. No part of this book may be reprinted or reproduced or utilised in any form or by any electronic, mechanical, or other means, now known or hereafter invented, including photocopying and recording, or in any information storage or retrieval system, without permission in writing from the publishers.

Notice:
Product or corporate names may be trademarks or registered trademarks, and are used only for identification and explanation without intent to infringe.

Publisher's Note
The publisher has gone to great lengths to ensure the quality of this reprint but points out that some imperfections in the original copies may be apparent.

Disclaimer
The publisher has made every effort to trace copyright holders and welcomes correspondence from those they have been unable to contact.

A Library of Congress record exists under LC control number: 00110700

ISBN 13: 978-1-138-70263-9 (hbk)
ISBN 13: 978-1-138-62947-9 (pbk)
ISBN 13: 978-1-315-20952-4 (ebk)

Contents

Acknowledgements vii
Philippe Régnier and Daniel Warner

Foreword ix
Yoshinobu Yamamoto

Contributors xi

I MULTILATERALISM: A THEORETICAL EXAMINATION

1 Possibilities of Multilateralism: A Regime Theory Perspective 3
   Yoshinobu Yamamoto

2 Constructing International Order: Multilateralism, the United Nations System and International Security 25
   Keith Krause

3 Opening for Omnilateralism: A European View 48
   Wolfgang Pape

II GLOBAL SECURITY, ECONOMIC ORDER AND MULTILATERALISM

4 Multilateralism and International Political Economy: The Global Level 65
   Jean-Pierre Lehmann

5 Multilateralism and International Security: The Global Level 82
   François Heisbourg

III REGIONAL MULTILATERAL ARRANGEMENTS

6 The Eurasian Component of Pan-European Security and Co-operation: The Role of the OSCE in the Caucasus and Central Asia 99
Victor-Yves Ghebali

7 The Regional Level: A European Perspective 126
Fred Tanner

8 Multilateralism and International Political Economy – the Regional Level: An American Perspective 138
David Sylvan

IV JAPAN AND MULTILATERALISM

9 Japan and Multilateralism: The Regional Level 153
Tsutomu Kikuchi

10 Pacifism and the Japanese Attitude toward the United Nations 175
Matake Kamiya

11 Looking Forward – Prospects for Multilateralism: Implications for Japan 185
Reinhard Drifte

Bibliography 200

Index 203

Acknowledgements

In Memoriam

The publication of this book could never have been possible without the lifetime endeavour of Professor Seizaburo Sato to link Japan with the world scientific community for better mutual understanding of international affairs.

With the constant support of his colleague, Professor Yoshinobu Yamamoto, he was the central figure behind a 1996–98 joint academic programmme linking the Graduate Institute of Policy Science (Tokyo) and the Graduate Institute of International Studies (Geneva). We had the immense pleasure to welcome him as a visiting scholar at GIIS in 1996–97 and will ever keep a vibrant memory of both his profile of scientific excellence and his personal convictions and friendship. He was the original source of inspiration of a joint scientific workshop organized in 1998 and from which this book is derived. Professor Y. Yamamoto, who visited us for six months in 1997–98, also played a crucial role in its conception and implementation.

This book is dedicated to the memory of Professor Seizaburo Sato. His regrettably early death in 1999 has been a great loss to both the Japanese and world communities studying international relations.

We take also this opportunity to thank very warmly Professor Y. Yamamoto for his continued co-operation and friendship, and also to express our enormous gratitude for the generous support of the Japanese Consulate General in Geneva and the Japan Foundation in Tokyo.

The Editors

Foreword

After the end of the Cold War, multilateral institutions have increased importance both at the global and regional levels and both in the economic and security areas. The United Nations has been playing a crucial role in keeping peace in a still tumultuous world and the World Trade Organization is only one of the global institutions in the economic area which has been strengthened after the Cold War. In the Asia-Pacific region which had been devoid of multilateral institutions during the Cold War, multilateralism has emerged and been developing positively. In 1989 when the Cold War was about to end, the Asia-Pacific Economic Cooperation (APEC) was established and in 1994 the ASEAN Regional Forum started. Now, the Democratic People's Republic of Korea (North Korea) joined the ARF, which has increased the value of ARF tremendously. Furthermore, ASEAN countries and the three Northeast Asian Countries (China, Republic of Korea and Japan) have started a new regional co-operation called ASEAN 10+3. East Asian countries including Japan have not intended to exclude Europe in their efforts to create regional institutions and fora. The European Union has been a member of ARF, and ASEM (Asia–Europe Meetings) had its third meeting in Seoul in October 2000.

During the Cold War era, Japan kept 'exclusive' relations with the United States, even though it had put rhetorical emphasis on the United Nations and on Asia. However, Japan has been trying to increase its roles in the United Nations and regional institutions to contribute to continuous international community build-up. Thus, it has become an important matter for Japan to seek the ways which it can participate appropriately in multilateral institutions not only at the governmental level but also through academic networks. Free dialogue among scholars may be considered a productive way to pursue this objective.

The Japan Foundation fully supported the project which brought Japanese and European scholars together to provide them opportunities to exchange their views in Geneva in March 1998. This book is the output of that meeting. In this book, a productive dialogue is presented between Japanese and European scholars regarding multilateralism in general, and Japanese attitudes and policies toward various multilateral institutions in particular.

This conference was part of a larger joint academic co-operation between the Graduate Institute of International Studies in Geneva and the Graduate Institute of Policy Science in Tokyo, which was fully supported by the Japan Foundation. The entire project was intended to enhance mutual understanding between Japan on the one hand and Switzerland and the rest of Europe on the other, through joint research and exchange of scholars. I do think that this kind of project is crucial for Japan and Europe to promote mutual co-operation. I would like to express my greatest appreciation to the Japan Foundation, the Graduate Institute of Policy Science, and of course to the Geneva-based Graduate Institute of International Studies, particularly its Modern Asia Research Center and its Program for the Study of International Organizations.

Finally, I must express my deepest regrets that Professor Seizaburo Sato, who had led the entire project on the Japanese side, died before receiving a copy of this book.

Yoshinobu Yamamoto
Tokyo, 25 November 2000

Contributors

Reinhard Drifte: Professor at the Chair of Japanese Studies, Department of Politics, University of Newcastle upon Tyne, Newcastle, UK.
Victor-Yves Ghebali: Professor of Political Science, Graduate Institute of International Studies, Geneva, Switzerland.
François Heisbourg: Professor, Institut d'Etudes Politiques, Paris, France and Chairman, Geneva Centre for Security Policy, Geneva, Switzerland.
Matake Kamiya: Associate Professor of International Relations, National Defense Academy, Yokosuka, Japan.
Tsutomu Kikuchi: Professor, School of International Politics, Economics and Business, Aoyama Gakuin University, Tokyo, Japan.
Keith Krause: Professor of International Politics, Graduate Institute of International Studies, Geneva, Switzerland.
Jean-Pierre Lehmann: Professor of International Political Economy, Institute for Management Development, Lausanne, Switzerland.
Wolfgang Pape: Project Co-ordinator, Forward Studies Unit, European Commission, Brussels, Belgium.
David Sylvan: Professor of International Relations at the Graduate Institute of International Studies, Geneva, Switzerland.
Fred Tanner: Deputy Director, Geneva Centre for Security Policy, Geneva, Switzerland.
Yoshinobu Yamamoto: Professor of International Relations, Department of International Relations, University of Tokyo, Japan.

PART I
MULTILATERALISM:
A THEORETICAL EXAMINATION

Chapter One

Possibilities of Multilateralism: A Regime Theory Perspective

Yoshinobu Yamamoto

The purpose of this chapter is to lay down theoretical foundations for multilateralism and to seek for some implications for Japan's foreign relations after the Cold War. In the late 1980s and into the 1990s as the Cold War came to an end, many multilateral arrangements were formed and/or strengthened in varied issue areas. Multilateral arrangements were strengthened and or formed anew in security areas. The United Nations was revived as a global collective security mechanism and as a provider of peacekeeping operations. While CSCE has been more institutionalized, and transformed to OSCE in 1995, ASEAN Regional Forum was newly created in 1994 and has been discharging an important security function in the Asia-Pacific region. Furthermore, global non-proliferation and 'prohibition' regimes have been strengthened or newly formed. The Nuclear Non-Proliferation Treaty was extended permanently in 1995 and the Comprehensive Test Ban Treaty was signed in the nuclear issue area. Also, the chemical weapons convention was signed, and the prohibition treaty was signed regarding anti-personnel mines.

However, these multilateral arrangements seem widely varied in terms of their basic nature. Some of them are indeed global and non-discriminatory: the total prohibition of anti-personnel mines is an example. Others are discriminatory *vis-à-vis* non-members; and some are discriminatory even among the member-states such as NPT. Moreover, there still exist important bilateral security arrangements such as the US–Japan security alliance.

The major purpose of this chapter is thus to clarify the meaning and possible types of multilateralism by utilizing the concept of the international regime,[1] particularly focusing on the international security area so that we can effectively discuss the merits and limits of multilateralism and the future direction of Japan's foreign policy.

---

[1] Regarding theories and case-studies of international regimes, see, for example, Oran Young (ed.), *The International Economy and International Institutions*, Vols 1 and 2 (Cheltenham: Edward Elgar, 1996).

The Concept of the International Regime in the Security Area

According to the classical definition, 'regimes are defined as sets of implicit or explicit principles, norms, rules, and decision-making procedures around which actors' expectations converge in a given area of international relations. Principles are beliefs of fact, causation and rectitude. Norms are standards of behaviour defined in terms of rights and obligations. Rules are specific prescriptions or proscriptions for action. Decision-making procedures are prevailing practices for making and implementing collective choice.'[2] Even though regimes defined in this way can be bilateral in terms of the number of participants or members, they are usually multilateral and thus the concept of the regime will give us an indispensable insight into multilateralism. As a matter of fact, regimes as defined above can take many different forms. They can be formal or informal. Some cover fairly wide-ranging issue areas and others limit themselves to very specialized fields. They can be very strong and effective in the sense that the members' expectations fully converge around the regime, or they can be very weak.[3]

However varied the regimes are, there seems to exist a set of conditions for creating and maintaining (ideal) regimes. Firstly, there should exist close interdependence among the possible members and the common interests to be achieved by them. Secondly, the common interests cannot be achieved if the nations behave independently. Co-operation is necessary and possible (or at least easy) by creating a set of formal or informal rules. Thirdly, the matters related to a regime usually have externalities and an ideal regime would internalize such externalities within it. This means that a regime has the logic of internalization (inclusiveness) in terms of membership. That is, an ideal regime will expand its members until the externalities are exhausted. Thus, fourthly, an ideal regime is not discriminatory *vis-à-vis* non-members and does not have negative externalities towards the outside.

If we see an ideal regime in this way, it will correspond to what John Ruggie called 'multilateralism in principle'.[4] According to Ruggie, multilateralism in principle must be based on generalized principles. That is, the principles or rules must be applied generally without exceptions. The two examples Ruggie shows are (a) the non-discrimination principle (the most-favoured nation treatment) of GATT and (b) the universal prohibition of, and non-discriminatory sanctions against, aggression in a collective security arrangement. Behind the generalized principle, there exists some kind of indivisibility. For example, the universal prohibition of,

---

[2] Stephen Krasner, 'Structural Causes and Regime Consequences', S.D. Krasner (ed.), op. cit., *International Regimes*, p. 2.
[3] For example, Levy et al. call those regimes which are formal, and in which convergence of expectations is high, full-blown regimes. M.A. Levy, O.R. Young, and M. Zürn, 'The Study of International Regimes', *European Journal of International Relations*, 1:3 (1995), 267–330.
[4] John Gerald Ruggie, 'Multilateralism: The Anatomy of an Institution', in J.G. Ruggie (ed.), *Multilateralism Matters* (New York: Columbia University Press, 1993), Ch. 1.

and non-discriminatory sanctions against, aggression are based on the perception of 'peace indivisible'. One of the ramifications of multilateralism in principle is thus that the members are basically treated as equals and that the members enjoy reciprocal benefits in the long term. Another implication is that multilateralism in principle is directed internally, towards the group of nations, and not directed towards the outside, and that a regime based on multilateralism in principle does not possess negative externalities.[5] Many of the environmental regimes seem to conform to multilateralism in principle. For example, let us assume that a set of nations forms a regime to control acid rain. Usually, such a regime will include all the nations which produce the particles causing acid rain in the region, and those which bear the damage of the acid rain. Even though there will be some conflicts among the members as to the cost sharing, every member will receive reciprocal benefits in the longer term. Such a regime is not directed to the outside and does not have any negative externalities to the outside nations.

However, in reality, there are other forms of multilateral co-operation, as I mentioned above. For example, most of the non-proliferation regimes in the security area (such as MTCR) are formed by the 'haves' against the 'have-nots' so that they are discriminatory *vis-à-vis* the nations outside the regime, even though non-proliferation regimes are typical multilateral co-operation regimes,[6] and even though they will enhance stability and peace in the international system.

Security Regimes and Multilateral Co-operation

When the concept of the international regime was forged in the late 1970s, many thought the formation of international regimes to be impossible in the security area[7] because the relations between nations (particularly between great powers) tend to be conflictual and zero-sum in nature (thus there will be no incentive for co-operation to achieve overall common goals), and because even if the nations perceive that they will gain if they co-operate, defection is possible and if defection

---

[5] As to an interpretation, and application, of Ruggie's general multilateralism, see, for example, Y. Yamamoto, 'Kyochoteki Anzenhosho no Kanousei [Possibilities of Co-operative Security]', *Kosusaimondai*, 425 (1995), 2–20 (in Japanese).

[6] Attempts to categorize security regimes in terms of varied dimensions such as external discrimination and internal inequality include: Antonia H. Chayes and Abram Chayes, 'Regime Architecture: Elements and Principles', and Leonard S. Spector and Jonathan Dean, 'Co-operative Security: Assessing the Tools of the Trade', both in Janne E. Nolan (ed.), *Global Engagement* (Washington, DC: Brookings Institution, 1993), Ch. 3 and Ch. 4, respectively.

[7] Robert Jervis, 'Security Regimes', in Stephen Krasner (ed.), *International Regimes* (Ithaca: Cornell University Press, 1983), pp. 173–194. Charles Lipson, 'International Co-operation in Economic and Security Affairs', *World Politics*, 37:2 (October 1984), 1–23.

occurs, it will instantaneously inflict devastating damage on other nations.[8] In addition, it was widely argued that if a regime were formed in the security area at all, it would be a very special case. For example, Jervis argued that the only case where a security regime was formed was the Vienna regime after the Napoleanic war.[9] However, in the late 1980s it began to be argued that security regimes may possibly be forged, at least as regards some specific areas of security. Thus, many case-studies have been conducted on security regimes between the East and West and between the United States and the Soviet Union.[10] But in the 1990s, while case-studies about specific security regimes have been flourishing, some began to argue that even though security regimes in specific issue areas are important and even though they are effective in regulating state behaviour, they do not concern the overall security relations among nations.[11]

Thus the issue is concerned with what functions security regimes are supposed to play, rather than whether regimes may possibly be forged in the security area. Even when we define security very narrowly (as control of military means and capabilities), it has many different aspects. For example, it is necessary to eliminate or reduce the causes of international conflict. If a conflict arises, we need to solve the conflict without resorting to military means. After the conflict has become serious and after the military alternative becomes a real possibility, then deterrence will become a necessary means to prevent aggression. And, if military means are used, unfortunately, by one side, then the other side will counter it by military means (that is, war). Even after a war occurs, we need some mechanisms to control the horizontal and vertical expansion of war. And after a war ends, we need such mechanisms as peacekeeping operations. Thus, the question becomes what security functions the security regimes will discharge.

In the following, therefore, I would like to examine the security regimes from three different perspectives: (a) what the relations are among the members within the regime (for example, equal or unequal) and what the relationship is of the regime *vis-à-vis* the non-members (for example, discriminatory or non-discriminatory); (b) what security roles the regimes are supposed to play (for example, preventive, deterrent or counter-aggression); and (c) how the security regimes relate themselves to the overall relations between nations.

---

[8] See, for example, Janice Stein, 'Detection and Defection: Security "Regimes" and the Management of International Conflict', *International Journal*, 40 (Autumn 1985), 599–627.
[9] For example, see Benjamin Miller, 'Explaining the Emergence of Great Power Concert', *Review of International Studies*, 20:4 (October 1994), 327–348.
[10] Joseph S. Nye, Jr., 'Nuclear Learning and US – Soviet Security Regimes', *International Organization*, 41:3 (Summer 1987), 371–402. Volker Rittberger and Michael Zürn, 'Regime Theory: Findings from the Study of 'East–West Regimes', *Co-operation and Conflict*, 26 (1991), 165–183.
[11] Barry Buzan, 'From International System to International Society: Structural Realism and Regime Theory Meet the English School', *International Organization*, 47:3 (Summer 1993), 327–352.

Four International Security Systems and Types of Security Regimes

If security is related to the use of military means between nations, national security behaviour is driven by military threats from other nations. If we consider a group of nations, threats will take many different forms. But here I would like to categorize threats according to two criteria.[12] One is whether threats lie within the group or outside the group. The second is whether threats are specific (that is, threats are emanating from a particular nation or nations, or whether they are unspecific or uncertain (that is, we cannot be sure where and when threats come from). By combining these two dimensions, we have four different types of security systems (Figure 1.1).

	The nature of threats	
Location of threats	Specific (threats from particular nation)	Unspecific
Outside of the group	A	C
Inside the group	B	D

Figure 1.1 Types of International Security Systems

Type A: Competitive Balance of Power System

One of the four types of security systems is the one in which there exists a particular threat outside the group and in which the group of nations co-operate to cope with that particular threat. If this situation occurs system-wide, then the international system is very competitive and the security system will be based on deterrence and war preparation against military aggression from a particular nation or a particular group of nations. This system is an adversarial balance-of-power system or a neo-realist international political system. The configuration of national preferences in this system is predominantly zero-sum and thus it is inconceivable that the nations in the system will co-operate to achieve overall common interests. As a matter of fact, even if the game is zero-sum in nature, nations will co-operate to form coalitions. But, such coalitions will never be a grand coalition and are definitely formed against other nations or coalitions. Coalitions in such an international security system serve deterrent functions. Thus, the coalition can be

---

[12] See, for example, Y. Yamamoto, op. cit., and Y. Yamamoto, 'Reisen go no Atarashii Anzenhosho [New International Security]', *Shin Boei Ronshu*, 23:4 (1996), 15–27.

considered to be a public good (or more precisely a club good) to the coalition members. Within the coalition, the nations co-operate to achieve the common good and will develop a set of rules to maintain co-operation, which looks like a regime. The benefits of the coalition will be distributed non-discriminately among the members, and the members are in that sense treated equally even though the cost-sharing may differ depending on individual members, and even though the cost-sharing will sometimes become a contentious issue among members. The game which is played among the members within the coalition (or alliance) will be a prisoners' dilemma game or a suasion game.[13] However, even though an alliance sometimes becomes a regime-like entity such as NATO, it is none the less discriminatory *vis-à-vis* the nations outside. It also possesses negative externalities to the nations which pose threats to the alliance, even though alliance creates stability in the international system as a whole (through establishing a balance of power between itself and the opposing nations). The security functions which alliances play are deterrence and countering military aggression. (Even though the alliances such as NATO during the Cold War are geared toward a specific nation, they sometimes have a function to adjust conflicting interests among members, which is close to Type D regimes, below).

Type B: Controlled Balance of Power System

The second type of international security system is the one in which the threats lie within the group (of nations) and in which the threats are specific in the sense that the threats come from particular nations within the group. The typical example of such systems is the case in which the opposing nations get together in order to control 'mutual' threats. In this system, the overall relations are competitive or adversarial (in this sense, the overall game is a zero-sum game). However, under such an overall conflict structure, the opposing nations (or camps) sometimes move to co-operate partially in order to stabilize the competitive situation, to shun the security dilemma and to avoid inadvertent war. In particular, if war would be unbearable to both sides, it will become a common interest to avoid war (this is a common security). This kind of co-operation can take many possible forms. The opposing nations will develop such 'confidence-building measures' as establishing hot-lines, and the mutual notification of military exercises. Or they will establish arms-control mechanisms in order to avoid the security dilemma. These measures will become systematized and institutionalized well enough for us to call it a 'confidence-building' regime or an arms-control regime.

---

[13] Regarding to the relationship between the structure of games (the distribution of national preferences) and regime formation, see, for example, Arthur A. Stein, 'Co-ordination and Collaboration: Regimes in an Anarchic World', in S.D. Krasner (ed.), op. cit., *International Regimes*, pp. 115–140. Lisa Martin, 'The Rational State Choice of Multilateralism', in J.G. Ruggie (ed.), op. cit., *Multilateralism*, Ch. 3. Andreas Hasenclever, Peter Mayer and Volker Rittberger, *Theories of International Regimes* (Cambridge: Cambridge Univerity Press, 1997), Ch. 3.

As far as the structure of the game is concerned, this type of security system exhibits a nested game structure. To repeat, there exists an overall zero-sum, competitive structure but at the same time mixed motive games are played in some of the security areas. In the areas of mixed motive games, both sides have incentives to co-operate, as well as to compete, and defection is a serious problem. If both try to create an arms control regime, defection would lead to serious consequences. Defection may give a great advantage to the defector and a serious disadvantage to the defected. But co-operation would give more benefits to both than the cases in which they both do not co-operate. This is a typical prisoners' dilemma. However, there are no means to create binding agreements in the international system. But if an agreement is made, then the structure of the game may change.[14] The argument can be made that the agreement must be maintained even in cases in which a short-term national interest may contradict the agreement. Or, one may argue that the nation will lose long-term credibility if it violates the agreement or that the regime itself is considered to contribute to the stability of the bilateral relations or of the international system as a whole. Thus, the probability that those security regimes that are created under the overall competitive situation will be maintained, even without explicit sanctions against violation, is usually fairly high. As a matter of fact, under the competitive international security system, the basic balance of power is usually maintained. Therefore, one may be able to argue that even when the agreement is violated, war could be prevented through the balance-of-power mechanism (that is, the international system is transformed from Type B to Type A).

This type of security regime (for example, the US–Soviet security regime and CSCE) will be based on explicit rules agreed by both sides and will not change the overall balance of power between the two sides. Therefore, the two sides are basically equal and the regime will not discriminate on one side or the other. And, since the violation of the agreement will cause grave consequences, the regime usually has a strict surveillance system through either international or national means, even when sanction mechanisms are not established.

Since security regimes of this type are formed among adversaries, the membership of the regime is usually limited. But the regime does not usually have negative externalities, and is not directed, to the nations outside the regime. The security functions of this type of regime are not deterrence nor use of force, but confidence-building and preventive ones.

Type C: Potential Hegemonic System

The third type of international security system is the one in which threats exist outside the group but in which these threats are not specific. That is, there is no

---

[14] See, for example, Harald Müller,'The Internalization of Principles, Norms and Rules by Governments: The Case of Security Regimes', in V. Rittberger (ed.), op. cit., *Regime Theory*, pp. 361–388.

dividing structural conflict in this international security system but there still exist potential threats which may become realized in the future. The military alliances in the international system of Type A are directed against particular nations (or alliances). In a Type C system, military alliances do exist but they are not directed against particular nations or alliances. They are directed to potential threats and uncertainties outside the group. However, once a threatening nation becomes obvious, then the alliance will be directed against that particular nation. The US–Japan alliance, and NATO after the Cold War, belong to this type. Since this is a military alliance, its function is deterrence and the use of military force against aggression and it is, in this sense, discriminatory *vis-à-vis* non-members and non-inclusive in terms of membership.

Those regimes which are usually called non-proliferation regimes such as the Missile Technology Control Regime and the Wassenar Agreement belong to this category of security regimes.[15] Non-proliferation regimes are intended to prevent some of the weapons and technology from being transferred from the 'haves' to 'have-nots'. Therefore, this type of security regime assumes some kind of hierarchical international system, and one of the functions of non-proliferation regimes is to maintain such a hierarchical international system. Non-proliferation regimes are based on the assumption that proliferation of certain weapons (mass-destruction weapons in particular) would destabilize the balance of power, that the proliferation would thus increase the probability of war occurring, and that if war occurs, the human cost would be devastating in a world with proliferated mass-destructive weapons. As a matter of fact, non-proliferation regimes can be created toward a specific nation or a specific group of nations. COCOM in the Cold War era is a case in point. However, in the post-Cold War era, non-proliferation regimes are not directed to specific nations but the target nations are generally diffused. Security regimes of this type, either military alliances or non-proliferation regimes, are based on the principle of discrimination and non-members will feel alienated, even though the regimes themselves will enhance the stability of the international system as a whole. For example, when faced with the membership expansion of NATO, Russia felt alienated strongly, even though Russia is not the target. And when the United States and Japan made a decision to strengthen functionally bilateral security co-operation in the areas surrounding Japan, China felt alienated and exhibited a strong objection. Non-proliferation regimes may pose concrete economic disbenefits on the 'have-nots' since the 'have-nots' are possibly prevented access to certain technologies. In this sense, non-proliferation regimes may have some negative externalities.

What will be the distribution of national preferences among the members of, say, non-proliferation regimes? It seems that there are two different types of games

---

[15] Non-proliferation regimes usually exclude the 'have-nots' (such as seen in MTCR). The exception is NPT. The reason seems that NPT tries to prevent proliferation not only from the nuclear 'haves' to the 'have-nots' but also from those 'have-nots' which have high technology to the 'have-nots'. One of the recent studies about NPT, is R.G.C. Thomas, *The Nuclear Non-Proliferation Regime* (New York: St Martin, 1998).

in the formation of non-proliferation regimes (or military alliances in a Type C international system). One is, just as in any other regime formation, the game of prisoners' dilemma. Assume that there are several 'have'-nations which would benefit from forming a non-proliferation regime. If all of them co-operate (that is, do not transfer the concerned weapons and technology to the threatening 'have-nots'), then they will gain much more benefits than when they all do not co-operate. However, if everyone co-operates except one, the one who does not co-operate gains much more than when it does co-operate. Then, no one will co-operate and everyone loses (prisoners' dilemma). Thus, some framework (regime) is needed to maintain co-operation, and non-proliferation regimes usually possess some sanctioning measures against violators (say, through the UN collective security measures). However, the compliance in non-proliferation regimes is not only based on possible sanctions but also on a sense of moral obligation. For example, proliferation of weapons of mass destruction, such as nuclear weapons, may be perceived as morally wrong and that sense could be internalized.[16]

We can also discern what is called a suasion game in the formation and maintenance of non-proliferation regimes.[17] Assume that among the 'haves', there exists one nation (or more) (let me call this nation a hegemon) which has strong interests in forming and maintaining a non-proliferation regime and that that nation will take non-proliferation measures regardless of what other 'have'-nations will do. The other nations will gain if a non-proliferation regime is created. But they will gain much more if they free-ride (that is, they do not co-operate, while the hegemon keeps the non-proliferation measures). Then, the outcome will be that only the hegemon takes the non-proliferation measures. If this happens, the hegemon feels very much frustrated and will try to persuade other nations to adopt the non-proliferation measures too. The hegemon tries to change the game structure by employing positive and negative sanctions in order to make the others adopt non-proliferation measures. And if other nations are talked into forming a non-proliferation regime, a regime would be created but fairly strong (informal) compliance measures would be established on the *ad hoc* basis which is employed by the hegemon. Thus, non-proliferation regimes (and alliances in the Type C international system) can be doubly hegemonic. Firstly, they are based on the hierarchical structure between the 'haves' and 'have-nots'. Secondly, there could be some mechanism of domination among the regime members, that is, between the hegemon and the followers.

The security function of non-proliferation regimes does not lie in deterrence nor in use of forces but is to avoid international political instability and to lower the probability of the occurrence of war. If war actually occurs, non-proliferation regimes will serve to limit the human and other damage.

---

[16] See, for example, H. Müller, op. cit.
[17] As to the relationship between the suasion game and regime formation, see, for example, Martin, op. cit.

Security Regimes Based on Generalized Multilateralism

The fourth type of international security regime is that in which threats exist within the group and in which the threats are not specific (Type D in Figure 1.1). This system does not have explicit and enduring cleavages among the nations and thus there exists no friend–foe structure within the group. The relations among the states in this system are either friendly or 'neither friend nor foe' in nature. The distribution of national preferences in this system is not zero-sum even though there could be some manageable conflicts. Thus, the objective of this type of security regime is to maintain peace within the group by a variety of means: internalizing threats, preventing potential conflicts from becoming overt, deterring use of military force within the group, and using collective force against aggression emanating from some of the group members. In other words, Type D security regimes establish co-operation in order to keep peace in the system by all the members. Thus, security regimes of this type are close to the ideal regime which we have talked about before. While this type of security regime can be created as regard to specific security areas (such as confidence-building regimes), it can also be forged as to the overall relations among the nations, which cannot be created in the other types of international system (that is, Types A to C). In the Type B international system in which there are two competing camps, confidence-building regimes can be built between the camps in order to avoid, say, inadvertent war. But confidence-building regimes in the Type D international system become multilateral in the sense that confidence-building measures can be applied to any bilateral, as well as multilateral, relations as a general rule.

In the following, I will present some of the types of the security regimes which fall in this category.

Concert System

A concert system can be defined as a co-operative system among all the relevant nations in which some basic common interests exist among all the members and in which a set of behavioural rules covering the overall relations is established. The set of rules includes: not to take unilateral action; to take concerted actions particularly as to important issues; not to interfere with the vital interests of the other nations.[18] The main characteristic of the concert system is to adjust differing interests among members, and a concert system is not geared against, nor does it alienate, the nations outside the concert system (but in some cases a concert system might take concerted actions *vis-à-vis* nations outside the system).[19] Also, a concert system does not usually have military means of itself. The membership of a concert system is inclusive in the sense that it includes, in principle, all the nations which

---

[18] As to concert systems, see, for example, Jervis, op. cit., 'Security Regimes', Robert Jervis, 'From Balance to Concert', *World Politics*, 38 (1985), 58–79. Miller, op. cit. 'Explaining the Emergence'.

[19] This situation comes close to Type C.

have influence on security matters among themselves (that is, all the security externalities are internalized in the concert system). Historically, such concert systems will include the Vienna system after the Napoleonic War[20] and the Washington Conference system in the Asia-Pacific region in the 1920s.[21] Furthermore, ASEAN can be considered as one of the regional concert systems.[22] ARF is also a concert system in the Asia Pacific region.[23] Besides regional security systems,[24] one can probably predict that a global concert system may be forged among the United States, China, Russia and the EU in the post-Cold War era.

A concert system is, in most cases, informal in nature, even though we can discern a set of behavioural rules which I described above. What is called the 'ASEAN way' is a case in point. The ASEAN way includes such rules as habits of dialogue and consultation, consensus and 'proceed[ing] at the speed which everyone feels comfortable'. The pattern of reaching an agreement seems similar to what Levy called a 'Tote-Board diplomacy' in which everyone co-operates voluntarily and in which an agreement is the sum of voluntary contributions by each of the members.[25]

A concert system is, as far as its security function is concerned, intended to prevent military conflicts within the system through political means. And since a concert system does not have military means of itself, the concert system usually collapses if some of the nations in the system take unilateral action, particularly unilateral military action.[26] If members of the concert system resort to unilateral action frequently and thus if a concert system collapses, then the international system will most probably be transformed into a balance of power system (Type A).

---

[20] See, Jervis, op. cit., 'Security Regimes'.
[21] Regarding the Washington regime. see, for example, Chihiro Hosoya, 'Washington Taisei no Tokushitsu to Henyo [The Characteristics and Transformation of the Washington Regime]', in C. Hosoya and Makoto Saito (eds), *Washinton Taisei to Nihon* [*The Washington Regime and Japan*], (in Japanese) (Tokyo: University of Tokyo Press, 1978), ch. 1. Shinichi Kitaoka, 'Washinton Taisei to "Kokusai Kyocho" no Seishin [The Washington Regime and the Spirit of International Co-operation]', (in Japanese), *Rikkyo Hogaku*, 23 (1984), 68–113.
[22] Regarding ASEAN, see, for example, Susumu Yamakage, *ASEAN: From Symbol to System* (in Japanese) (Tokyo: University of Tokyo Press, 1991), particularly Part III.
[23] As to ASEAN Regional Forum, see, for example, Tsutomu Kikuchi, *APEC* (Tokyo: Japan Institute of International Affairs, 1995), Ch. 7. Susumu Yamakage, *ASEAN Pawa* [*ASEAN Power*] (Tokyo: University of Tokyo Press, 1997), Ch. 9. Michael Leifer, *The ASEAN Regional Forum*, Adelphi Paper 302 (Oxford: Oxford University Press, 1996).
[24] Regarding regional security systems, see, for example, Patrick M. Morgan, 'Regional Security Complexes and Regional Orders', in David Lake and P.M. Morgan (eds), *Regional Orders* (University Park: Pennsylvania State University Press, 1997), Ch. 2.
[25] Marc A. Levy, 'European Acid Rain', in P.M. Haas, R.O. Keohane and M.L. Levy (eds), *Institutions for the Earth* (Cambridge: MIT Press), 1993, Ch. 3.
[26] A good analysis about the fact that a concert system can be destroyed by unilateral actions was conducted by Kitaoka (Kitaoka, op. cit.).

A concert system can coexist with alliance systems (alliances are subsets of the concert members). For example, currently in the Asia-Pacific region, we have an alliance system centring around the United States (alliances between the United States on the one hand and such nations as Japan, South Korea, the Philippines and Australia on the other – what is called the hub–spoke alliance system) and such multilateral security dialogue (concert) system as ARF. These alliances are Type C in nature (that is, they do not have a specific threat, even though they will utilize military means if aggression actually occurs). It seems wise and practical to have alliances along with a concert system just in cases in which a concert system breaks down. But the coexistence of alliance and concert systems sometimes bring about contradictions. That is, while alliances are based on the principle of exclusion and discrimination, a concert system is based on the principle of inclusion and non-discrimination. Thus, as I have mentioned already, those nations of the concert system which are excluded from alliances will feel alienated.

Collective Security System

In some cases, a concert system can be transformed into a collective security system.[27] A collective security system is the one in which the rule of non-aggression is established by consent and in which any aggression will be sanctioned militarily and/or otherwise by all the other members of the collective security system. Thus, a collective security system, just like a concert system, assumes that potential threats lie within the system. The difference between a collective security system and a concert system is that the former possesses military means of itself while the latter does not. It is well recognized that in order for a collective security system to function, there must not be structural cleavages among the major powers and there must be a basic consensus among the major powers about the basic characteristics of the international order. In this sense, collective security predicates upon the basic assumptions of concert system particularly among major powers.

There exist possibilities that a concert system can be transformed into an international system in which use of military force is not conceivable any more. For example, if commercial relations between the members of a concert system increase and if the use of military force becomes counter-productive and irrelevant in solving conflicts, then we will see what may be called a commercial peace. Or, if social communications increase in such a way that the basic (liberal) values become firmly shared at the societal level between and among nations, then the use of military force will never be considered to solve differences of interests among nations. This structure was years ago named a 'pluralistic security community' by

---

[27] Regarding the relationship between concert and collective security systems, see, for example, C. Kupchan and C. Kupchan, 'Concerts, Collective Security, and the Future of Europe', *International Security*, 16 (1991).

Karl Deutsch.[28] This line of argument can be seen in the democratic peace thesis.[29] Note, however, that a pluralistic security community can be created by deepening not only a concert system but also alliance systems of Type A and Type C.

Prohibition Regime

There are some international arrangements which prohibit the production, possession and use of certain weapons. Let us call these arrangements prohibition regimes.[30] A prohibition regime is a regime based on generalized principles in the sense that the rule of prohibition is applied to all the nations without exceptions. There is no internal discrimination (which is quite different form non-proliferation regimes) and prohibition regimes do not have any negative externalities to the nations outside the regime if there are any such nations. Furthermore, the utility of a prohibition regime will definitely increase as the membership expands, and thus a prohibition regime is inclusive in terms of membership.

The weapons which are, or are to be, covered by prohibition regimes are those weapons which cause inacceptable, inhumane damage: chemical weapons, biological weapons, anti-personnel mines and, probably, nuclear weapons. Thus, while prohibition regimes will serve to stabilize security relations among nations and while prohibition regimes will prevent inhumane damage should war ever occur, they are related to moral and human dimensions. Thus, while the use of chemical and biological weapons can be explicitly prohibited by international agreements, their use is also refrained through moral constraints. Therefore, they have been rarely used in war, even though they are possessed by many nations.[31] These observations will imply that a prohibition regime will be formed in the intersecting issue area between security and morality. The weapons such as anti-personnel mines do have military utility but they cause inaccepable human damage. Thus, if and when morality dominates security, a prohibition regime will be forged. That is, viewed from the international system, if prohibition of a certain weapon does not change an overall balance of power, the probability of the formation of a prohibition regime will increase. From the viewpoint of individual nations, if they have alternative security means after prohibition, they will participate in the prohibition regime.

---

[28] Karl W. Deutsch, et al., *Political Community and the North Atlantic Area* (Princeton: Princeton University Press, 1957).

[29] See, for example, Bruce Russett, *Grasping Democratic Peace* (Princeton: Princeton University Press, 1993).

[30] Ethan Nadelmann applies the concept of prohibition regimes to different issue areas such as international crimes (Ethan A. Nadelmann, 'Global Prohibition Regimes: The Evolution of Norms in International Society', *International Organization*, 44:4 (Autumn 1990), 479–526.

[31] See, Richard Price and Nina Tannenwald, 'Norms and Deterrence: The Nuclear and Chemical Weapons Taboos', in P.J. Katzenstein (ed.), *The Culture of National Security* (New York: Columbia University Press, 1996), Ch. 4.

The Game of Stag Hunt

There would be several possible types of distributions of national preferences in forming and maintaining concert systems and prohibition regimes. The distribution of national preferences would not be zero-sum but mixed motive games. For example, it could be, as in many other cases for regime formation, a prisoners' dilemma situation. That is, if all the nations co-operate and make a decision not to produce, possess and use chemical weapons, then everyone will benefit. But, if a nation defects while all the others co-operate, then the defector may benefit since it may be in a better position in balance of power. Then, everyone has an incentive to defect. But if everyone defects, everyone loses. Thus, strong sanctioning measures against defection are needed in prohibition regimes.[32]

In general, the game of battle of sexes (co-ordination game) is one of the basic types of distribution of preferences leading to regime formation.[33] A co-ordination game is one in which the players must select one out of several (two) possible alternative rules. A simple case is whether a car should run on the right hand side of the road or the left. The worst-case scenario is that cars run independently by their own choice. But, if the rule is made as either the right or left, then there will be no problem. And no enforcement mechanism is necessary because if a car violates the rule, it is that car which bears the cost. Of course, some surveillance is necessary in order to check drunken drivers and some measures are necessary to inform what is the rule. While there are many examples of the co-ordination game in regime formation, it seems not many are in security areas. But such agreements as to the routes of submarines and military aircraft to avoid collisions and thus inadvertent wars will be some of the rare examples of security regimes of this type. This type of security regime can be forged in the Type B international system. But in the Type D international system, such security regimes can become multilateral without discrimination.

In the type D international system, one of the typical distributions of national preferences will be what is called the game of stag hunt.[34] In the type D international system, the game is, to repeat, not zero-sum and I have already discussed the cases of mixed motive games such as prisoners' dilemma. If it is crystal clear that they will gain the highest benefits if they all co-operate ('strong harmony'), then there will be no need for them to form a co-operative regime. But, even when the nations will gain the highest benefits if they all co-operate, it may not be clear either due to uncertainties as to the game structure or due to possible changes in the game structure in the future (caused by, say, future changes in the domestic politics). The game of stag hunt is one of such cases. Assume that two hunters are chasing a stag. If they keep chasing, then they will get the stag and will

---

[32] See, Nadelmann, op. cit.
[33] As to the relationship between co-ordination game and regime formation, see, for example, A. Stein (op. cit.) and Martin (op. cit.).
[34] As to the relationship between the game of stag hunt and regime formation, see, for example, Martin (op. cit.) and A. Hasenclever et al., op. cit., Ch. 3.

gain the highest benefits. But, also assume that a rabbit pops up and that one of the hunters defects and chases the rabbit rather than the stag. Since it is impossible to get the stag with only one hunter, the hunter who continues to chase the stag cannot get it and gains nothing. The hunter who defected and who chased the rabbit will definitely get the rabbit, but he will gain less than what he would gain if the two hunters co-operated to get the stag. Of course, the two hunters can chase the rabbit and they can get the rabbit. But, in this case, they will gain much less than when they get the stag, to say nothing of the case in which only one of them gets the rabbit. In this kind of situation, it is necessary to forge some framework which assures that the two hunters continue to chase the stag. The function of the framework (regime) is to enhance confidence that the other player will keep co-operating, to avoid misperception as to the structure of the game including the preferences of the other players (transparency), and so forth. If such functions are to be fulfilled, co-operation will be assured, since mutual co-operation is the best outcome for both anyway. There will be no need for enforcement mechanisms in this kind of regime. ARF seems one of the typical examples of this kind of regime.[35]

Scenography of International Security

Figure 1.2 and Table 1.1 summarize the arguments which have been developed in the previous sections. We categorized four differing types of international security systems on the basis of the two dimensions of threats (Figure 1.1). Figure 1.2 exhibits, for each of the four international security systems, (a) the type of general patterns of international politics (or international security relations), (b) the typical patterns of distribution of national preferences (or the types of the game) and (c) typical security regimes formed in that international security system. Let us consider two of the most contrasting cases, Box A and Box D here. Box A in Figure 1.2 shows that the pattern of international politics is an adversarial balance-of-power system, that the game is zero-sum in nature and that the possible security regimes are those formed within alliances while no regime will be possible for the overall relations among the nations in the system. Alliances in this system are, if they are considered to be security regimes in the sense that they develop a set of rules to enhance security co-operation among the members, discriminatory *vis-à-vis* the nations outside them. In contrast to Box A, the international system in Box D

---

[35] ARF is quite often compared to CSCE(OSCE). The most frequently mentioned difference between them is that the former is uninstitutionalized while the latter has been well institutionalized. One can think of several different reasons for this difference. For example, ARF has been just created while OSCE has a history of more than twenty years. But, within the context of this chapter, ARF was created in the Type D system and is a concert system in nature, while CSCE was created in the Type B system and thus should be formal. If this hypothesized difference is true, then ARF would not be so formalized in the future.

does not have structural cleavages and sometimes even exhibits common interests among the nations, even though there may remain some security uncertainties in the future. Thus, in this system, it will become a common objective to prevent potential conflicts from becoming actual conflicts through concerted behaviour on the basis of general common interests. This is a concert system. A concert system can be transformed into a collective security system in which unilateral military action (aggression) is prohibited by consent and in which unilateral use of force will be deterred or countered by combined forces of all the other nations. The concert system and the collective security system are such regimes, concerned with the overall relations among members, which cannot be seen in the other types of international system. One of the typical game structures is the game of stag hunt. A regime is to be created which enhances multilateral confidence-building and transparency in order to ensure that mutual co-operation is the best outcome for all. In Box D, security regimes could be also created in specific areas. Typical regimes which will be created in this system are what are called prohibition regimes.

	The nature of threats	
Location	Specific	Unspecific
Outside	A Adversarial Balance of Power Zero-Sum Game Regimes within Alliances	C (Potential) Hegemonic System Suasion Game Non-Proliferation Regimes
Inside	B Controlled Balance of Power Prisoners' Dilemma Arms Control Regimes	D Possible Regimes regarding Overall Relations (Concert systems, Collective Security) Stag Hunt Prohibition Regimes

Figure 1.2 Types of International System, Structures of Games and Security Regimes

Table 1.1 Characteristics and Functions of Security Regimes

Regimes	Internal relations	Sanction mechanisms within regimes	External relations	Externalities	No. of members	Formality	Security function
Regime within alliance	equal non-discriminatory	none	discriminatory	negative	too many	formal	deterrence use of forces
Arms-control regime	equal non-discriminatory	none exist	closed group	positive	too many	formal	preventative
Non-proliferation	equal hegemonic	exist	discriminatory	positive negative	many	formal	preventative
Concert system	equal non-discriminatory	none	non-discriminatory	positive	many	informal	preventative
Collective security	equal non-discriminatory	exist	inclusive	positive	many	formal	deterrence use of forces
Prohibition regime	equal non-discriminatory	exist	inclusive	positive	many	formal	preventative

Table 1.1 demonstrates the nature and characteristics as well as security functions of security regimes which will be formed in different types of international system.[36] For example, in the adversarial balance-of-power system, alliances will form, as stated earlier, and an alliance sometimes becomes a regime in the sense that it develops a set of rules to maintain co-operation. If we focus the deterrent function of the alliance, then the benefits of the alliance will be equally

---

[36] Table 1.1 shares similar characteristics to the tables shown in Spector and Dean (op. cit., pp. 152–153, p. 156 and p. 160). However, I deduced the different characteristics of varied security regimes while Spector and Dean created the tables rather in an inductive manner.

shared by the alliance members even though the power relations among the members sometimes become hegemonic rather than equal. But, even when formal and informal rules of conduct within the alliance are not observed, forceful sanctions are usually not taken. Alliance is discriminatory *vis-à-vis* the nations outside and usually gives negative externalities. Alliances can be bilateral or multilateral in terms of the number of the participants and usually take the form of formal arrangements, even though there may exist 'natural alliances' without formal arrangements. The security functions of alliances are deterrence and use of force against aggression.

In contrast to alliances as security regimes, prohibition regimes apply the rule of prohibition to all the members non-discriminatingly and they usually have explicit enforcement rules. They are not geared against the nations outside, and they are based on the principle of inclusion as to the membership since the utility of the regimes will definitely increase as the number of participants increases. Prohibition regimes do have positive externalities to the nations outside. Prohibition regimes are thus multilateral and formal in nature. The security functions of prohibition regimes are usually preventive, and prohibition regimes do not have deterrence and use of military force as their functions.

As seen from Table 1.1, security regimes do not have deterrence and the use of force as their functions except for maintaining alliances and collective security. They are basically concerned with the prevention of conflicts. The security regimes which satisfy the conditions of the ideal regimes are collective security and prohibition regimes and concert systems come close to such ideal regimes.

The Roles of Security Regimes: Scenography of International Security

The types of international system and the types of distribution of national preferences (the types of games) determine significantly whether security regimes are forged or not, and what kinds of security regimes will be created if they are ever created.[37] How, then, do security regimes influence the security and political relations among the nations? As a matter of fact, a security regime which was created under a certain type of national preference distribution will contribute to stabilizing the international system of that national preference distribution in general as well as to fulfilling the specific roles given to the regime, such as arms control. For example, as I have already stated, the arms control regimes which are created in the controlled balance of power system (Type B) will contribute to avoid security dilemmas and thus reduce tension, and to promote the stability of the

---

[37] However, the distribution of national preferences and the structure of the games are not sufficient conditions for regime formation, while they are necessary conditions and determine what kinds of regimes will form. For example, even when the structure of the game is a prisoners' dilemma, a regime may not be forged. In order for a regime actually to form, we would need, for example, the occurrence of visible events and a diffusion of knowledge about the issue around which a regime to be formed (see Hasenclever et al., op. cit., *Theories*).

international system, even though the arms control regimes do not have a military deterrent function by themselves. Furthermore, arms control regimes and confidence-building regimes under overall competitive situations will allow time to change the adversarial situation, or will reduce the adversarial competition directly and thus change the international system itself. Even though non-proliferation regimes are predicated on the principle of exclusion and on the hierarchical system, they not only stabilize the international system by preventing proliferation of dangerous weapons but also could become a stepping stone to prohibition regimes. By stabilizing the international system in which basic common interests exist but in which there still loom uncertainties, a concert system will prevent the international system from moving to a competitive system on the one hand and will provide chances to transform the international system into one in which the use of military force is inconceivable. Even though prohibition regimes do not ban the use of military force generally, they will enhance the moral foundations of the international system and contribute to the stability of the international system, of any type, and to the avoidance of inhumane damage, should war ever occur. Therefore, in most cases, security regimes in any form will contribute to the stability of the international system, even though they do not directly deter or prohibit the use of miliary force.

We have analysed several types of security regimes as 'ideal types'. However, as I have already mentioned, these different types of security regimes coexist or are mixed in the real international system.[38] In addition, the distribution of national preferences, which has a determining impact on regime formation, can change over time depending on internal and international factors and the interaction between these two factors.[39] Therefore, if the current international system exhibits a general

---

[38] As to the fact that different security regimes coexist in reality, see, for example, Morgan, op. cit., and Sheldon W. Simon, 'International Relations Theory and Southeast Asian Security', *The Pacific Review*, 8:1 (1995), 5–24.

[39] How the distribution of national preferences (and thus the structure of games) is determined (and transformed) is the great issue in international politics. Such neo-realists as Kenneth Waltz argue that the distribution of national preferences is determined by the interactions among the states (Kenneth Waltz, *Theory of International Politics* [Reading: Addison-Wesley, 1979]). However, recently, it is often argued that the national preferences relevant to international politics are determined domestically, and thus that the distribution of national preferences is the sum of national interests determined domestically (See, for example, Andrew Moravcsik, 'Taking Preferences Seriously: A Liberal Theory of International Politics', *International Organization*, 51:4 [Autumn 1997], 513–553). If we follow the neo-realist thesis, the zero-sum nature of international politics will be permanently reproduced. If we follow the 'liberal' perspective which argues that national preferences are determined domestically, we do not know what types of distributions of national preferences will appear in the future. I think that the national preferences relevant to international politics are determined by both international and internal politics, and by the interaction between these two. It will be one of the central issues in international politics to develop a theory which endogenously tells us the distribution, and transformation, of national preferences relevant to international politics.

harmony of interests among nations, we may see some adversarial relations regionally and there may exist some possibility that the international system would move back to an adversarial system. Thus, even though a concert system is currently developing, we may have to create a controlled balance-of-power system regionally. And if a competitive international system is far away from the current system, we must not ignore the possibility that the international system might turn into a competitive one in the future. Conversely, even if the current international system is adversarial, we have to think about how to alter the adversarial system and to create a harmonious system, even though a harmonious system looks quite far removed from the current system. Thus, wherever we are, we have to think about measures to stabilize the current system and to strive for creating a peaceful future international system, and to avoid falling into an adversarial system. In taking this kind of scenography of international peace, varied security regimes will give us some concrete measures and alternatives to forge and maintain international peace.

Implications for Japan: Concluding Remarks

In the Cold War era, Japan's security policies were based on two pillars – the Self-Defense Forces and the US–Japan Security Treaty. Therefore, Japan leaned heavily toward bilateralism in the security area. However, when the Cold War was over, Japan added multilateral components to its security policies. Japan made a decision to undertake peacekeeping operations under the auspices of the UN after the Gulf War (1992). It also participated in the ASEAN Regional Forum in 1994. These multilateral moves by Japan were historic. Japan came to have four pillars in its security policies: national Self-Defense Forces, the US–Japan Security treaty, regional security arrangements such as ARF, and global security arrangements such as the United Nations. Up until 1995, Japan had moved toward multilateralism, while the US–Japan security arrangements have not been strengthened partially because the American policies toward East Asia had not been settled. The United States tried to withdraw from the Asia-Pacific region in stages according to the East Asian Strategic Initiative issued in 1990. The first stage (1990–92) was implemented according to plan. In the second stage (1993–95), a reduction in ground forces in Korea was planned but was postponed due to North Korean nuclear issues. In what is called the 'Bottom-up Review' in September 1993, it is stated that the United States would continue to maintain the forward deployment forces at about 100,000 in North-East Asia. In February 1995, the United States issued the East Asian Strategic Review in which it declared its strong commitments to East Asian security – for example, the forward deployment of 100,000 forces.

Japan tried to reformulate its security policies after the Cold War on the basis of this strong US commitment to East Asia. In late 1995, the Japanese government issued the *Bouei Keikaku no Taiko*. In this document, the Japanese government formally stated that it will commit itself to a variety of regional and global security activities, while it will enhance the efficiencies of the SDF and while the US–Japan security alliance is considered to be the cornerstone of Japanese security policy. Since 1996, the United States and Japan have agreed to deepen their defence co-operation in the surrounding areas (the US–Japan Defense Guideline).

Let me discuss briefly a few points which are essential in order to understand the future directions of Japan's multilateral security diplomacy. Firstly, how is Japanese multilateral security diplomacy related to the Japan's bilateral security relations with the United States? The question is whether the bilateral security relations with the United States and participation in multilateral (regional) security arrangements are complementary or contradictory. This question is raised in four different contexts. One is between the United States and Japan. When the Higuchi report was issued in Summer 1994 which laid down the basic directions for the Japanese security policies, it put multilateral security before the US–Japan security treaty as far as the composition of the report is concerned. The United States had some anxiety that Japan might shift its priority from the bilateral security relations to multilateral security. And, in Japan, the relationship between bilateral and multilateral security frameworks has not been well thought out while some hoped that Japan could gain independence from the United States in the security areas through participating in multilateral security frameworks. But, the priority of the US–Japan security relations has become clear over time. The North Korean nuclear issue (1994) and the Chinese military exercise over the Taiwan Strait (spring 1996) made the Japanese recognize anew the vital importance of US–Japan security relations. This feeling led to the strengthening of US–Japan security relations, while the Defense White Paper of 1997 clearly stated that regional multilateral security arrangements supplement the US–Japan security relations and SDF.[40]

Secondly, the bilateral and multilateral security arrangements are considered to be complementary in the following way. Regional multilateral security arrangements such as ARF are very important in the post-Cold War era since they provide chances to maintain and promote multilateral confidence-building. Military presence of the United States in East Asia is crucial in maintaining stability in the region, and the US–Japan security treaty will give an assurance of the American presence. The US–Japan security treaty gives convergent expectations as to not only American behaviour but also Japanese behaviour in this region, on the basis of which the nations in this region can develop multilateral security dialogue systems. Furthermore, from the Japanese perspective, a multilateral security dialogue system such as ARF does not have its own military means and will not help if military aggression actually occurs. Thus, it is essential to maintain and strengthen the US–Japan security alliance, while it is worthwhile to forge multilateral security dialogue systems.

Thirdly, some nations may feel contradictions between the US–Japan security alliance and multilateral security arrangements from their own national interests.

---

[40] *Nihon no Bouei* (Defense White Paper), 1997, p. 102.

When Japan and the United States began discussing strengthening the bilateral security relations (via defence co-operation guidelines in the surrounding areas), China has made strong objections. Of course, China is afraid that a functionally expanded US–Japan security framework would have grave implications as to the Taiwan Strait. But China has argued that while it would admit the US–Japan security treaty if it is maintained within the scope established in the Cold War era, bilateral security alliances are outmoded since there exist no enemies to cope with in the post-Cold War era through military alliances, and that multilateral security arrangements which do not assume any explicit enemies should be the way that post-Cold War international security is to be established.

Fourthly, the relationship between the bilateral and multilateral relations should be examined at the global level. Japan was one of the last nations which signed the anti-personnel land mines treaty. The reason is that the United States had no intention of signing it, and that Japan had paid serious attention to the American position. It was after the Nobel Prize was given to the NGO which had pushed the land mines treaty that Japan made a decision to sign the treaty. This implies a possibility that bilateral security relations would sometimes prevent the formation of multilateral regimes. However, the relationship between the bilateral and multilateral security can be complementary at the global level. For example, one of the reasons why Japan decided to send peacekeeping operations overseas is that Japan strove to maintain confidence within the United States (and the World community) regarding Japan's contribution to international peace. The United States and Japan revised the ACSA agreement so that it now covers non-peacetime co-operation in UN peace and security activities.

As a matter of fact, Japan's participation in regional and global security frameworks has been increasing. Japan has been sending personnel from SDF to the Chemical Weapons Convention and served the chairmanship of MTCR. Since Japan is constrained from using forces overseas due to the Constitution, Japan must refrain from fully participating in, say, UN-led international security activities. But, because of that, Japan has strong incentives to participate in regional and global security frameworks (regimes) which do not require the use of military force and whose security functions are preventive in nature.

Chapter Two

Constructing International Order: Multilateralism, the United Nations System and International Security

Keith Krause

> Multilateralism is a word for policy wonks, so let's not use it anymore.
> *Madeline Albright*[1]

Multilateral approaches to international security have had a chequered, and to a great extent, marginal, history in twentieth-century world politics.[2] The failure of both the League of Nations and the United Nations experiments in collective security has given rise to general scepticism or outright suspicion about the practicality or desirability of any generalized multilateral arrangements to achieve security. As John Ruggie puts it, 'the term multilateralism has never had much appeal in political circles to describe security relations'.[3] It matters little whether one attributes failures in multilateral security projects to flaws in institutional design, to the caprice of history, or to a lack of a sufficient 'commitment' on the part of great and lesser powers; the result is that most scholars and analysts have treated security affairs as the supreme realm of *realpolitik*, in which the scope for co-operation to overcome the security dilemma is extremely limited.[4] On these accounts, the scope and prospects for international security can best be captured by the workings of balance-of-power and alliance systems, both of which can be

---

[1] Cited in John Ruggie, 'Third Try at World Order? America and Multilateralism after the Cold War', *Political Science Quarterly*, 109:4 (Fall 1994), 559.
[2] Thanks are due to Michael Barnett for comments on a previous draft of this chapter.
[3] Ruggie, 'Third Try', 558. It is, of course, misleading to treat 'multilateralism' as coterminous with the United Nations, especially since many of the most interesting experiments in multilateralism are currently taking place outside of its ambit, and at the regional or sub-regional level.
[4] For a representative, if somewhat caricatured, statement of this see John Mearsheimer, 'The False Promise of International Institutions', *International Security*, 19:3 (Winter 1994/1995), 5–49. See also Robert Jervis, 'Co-operation under the Security Dilemma', *World Politics*, 30:2 (1978), 167–214.

multilateral, but in a very restricted sense of the term.[5] In the contemporary period, multilateralism in the security realm can be reduced to American hegemony.

On the other hand, the end of the Cold War reinvigorated the 'liberal' or utopian strand of multilateral scholarship, most of which has concentrated in recent years on the role of the United Nations and the Security Council in the maintenance of international peace and security, and in particular on the Chapter 'six-and-a-half' innovation of peacekeeping and the expanded use of Chapter VII of the UN Charter for a range of multilateral peace and security operations since 1989.[6] More than fifteen operations have been authorized since 1989, and at the peak in 1993, there were more than 78,000 military and related personnel engaged in UN operations. But the flush of post-Cold War optimism that was evident in the early 1990s has faded since the Iraqi, Somalia and Rwanda crises, and has been replaced with a more sober assessment of the possibilities for multilateral action. Most thinking today concentrates on incremental or managerial solutions to perceived shortcomings in multilateral peace operations (such as clarifying mandates, subcontracting to regional organizations, or creating limited rapid reaction forces), and does not tackle many of the deeper issues underlying the multilateral security system.[7] On this account, multilateralism boils down to managing security co-operation among great powers.

I want to approach the topic of 'multilateralism and international security' from a more oblique and broader angle, in order to break out of this 'realist–utopian' (or 'neorealist–neoliberal') dialogue to highlight some shortcomings in the literature on multilateralism and international security, and to shed some light on contemporary trends in multilateral diplomacy and practice. My central claim is

---

[5] As Steve Weber argues, if states balance power and seek to preserve autonomy, then multilateralism is not an obvious institutional form to adopt (as opposed to unilateralism, bilateralism, isolationism, neutrality, and so on). Steve Weber, 'Shaping the Postwar Balance of Power: Multilateralism in NATO', in John Gerard Ruggie (ed.), *Multilateralism Matters: The Theory and Praxis of an Institutional Forum* (New York: Columbia University Press, 1993), 235–238. On this contrast between neo-realist and neo-liberal rationalist accounts see Thomas Risse-Kappen, 'Between a New World Order and None: Explaining the Reemergence of the United Nations in World Politics', in Keith Krause and Michael C. Williams (eds), *Critical Security Studies* (Minneapolis: University of Minnesota Press, 1997), pp. 257–262.

[6] Recent literature on this has been voluminous. For a recent sample see: James Mayall (ed.), *The New Interventionism: 1991–1994* (Cambridge: Cambridge University Press, 1996); Tom Weiss (ed.), *Collective Security in a Changing World* (Boulder: Lynne Reinner, 1993); Daniel Warner (ed.), *New Dimensions of Peacekeeping* (Martinus Nijhoff, 1995); Adam Roberts, *Humanitarian Action in War*, Adelphi paper 305 (London: IISS, 1996).

[7] See http://www.un.org/Depts/dpko/rapid/ for details on the current standby arrangements. For details of the Canadian proposal for a rapid reaction force, see 'Towards a Rapid Reaction Capability for the United Nations', Department of Foreign Affairs and International Trade, 1995 (available at: http://www.dfait-maeci.gc.ca/english/news/newsletr/un/rap1.htm). See also Thomas Weiss (ed.), *Beyond UN Subcontracting: Task-Sharing with Regional Security Arrangements and Service Providing NGOs*, special issue of *Third World Quarterly*, 18:3 (1997).

that the global multilateral security order is based upon a set of generally understood norms and principles (including a restricted understanding of who or what deserves to be 'secured') that can be characterized as 'liberal interventionism'. In order to sustain this claim, I will draw upon a more critical conceptualization of multilateralism to emphasize issues that have been largely neglected in the literature on international security. I will first briefly outline two different understandings of multilateralism (loosely labelled 'rationalist' and 'critical'), then sketch how both of these have been used in the international political economy literature, and finally discuss what this implies for 'multilateralism and international security'.

Critical Versus Rationalist Understandings of Multilateralism

The various different definitions of multilateralism can be grouped (and contrasted) into two visions, with radically different implications for thinking about multilateralism and international security.[8] The first and most restricted vision ('rationalist') regards multilateralism as simply a larger-scale extension of self-interested inter-state interactions. Multilateralism is 'an institutional form that co-ordinates relations among three or more states on the basis of generalized principles of conduct,' and it is contrasted with 'bilateralism' (a set of relations between two states) or 'imperialism', (co-ordination of relations between dominant and subordinate actors).[9] This state-centric and contractarian vision treats states as autonomous (and functionally equal) actors operating in a self-help system under the security dilemma, and following the logic of instrumental rationality. It gives rise to the familiar neo-realist versus neo-liberal debate over the potential for co-operation between states (and draws extensively on rationalist or game theoretic modelling), with the neo-realist concluding that international institutions are 'basically a reflection of the distribution of power in the world ... based on the self-interested calculations of the great powers, and [having] no independent effect on state behaviour'.[10] The neo-liberal accepts the underlying premises of the neo-realist, but attempts to show that under certain (fairly restrictive) conditions states can create and participate in multilateral institutions to avoid dilemmas of common aversion (such as major or nuclear war), solve co-ordination dilemmas (such as

---

[8] This discussion parallels, in schematic form, the distinction between 'new' and 'old' institutionalism developed by Alexander Wendt and Raymond Duvall, 'Institutions and International Order', in Ernst-Otto Czempiel and James Rosenau, *Global Changes and Theoretical Challenges: Approaches to World Politics for the 1990s* (Lexington: Lexington Books, 1989), pp. 51–73. See also Risse-Kappen, 'Between a New World Order and None', pp. 255–297.

[9] John Gerard Ruggie, 'Multilateralism: The Anatomy of an Institution', in Ruggie, *Multilateralism Matters*, p. 11. See also Robert Keohane, 'Multilateralism: An Agenda for Research', *International Journal*, 45:4 (Autumn 1990), 731–764.

[10] Mearsheimer, 'False Promise', 7.

creating enough confidence for arms control to work), reduce transaction costs, and supply costly information.[11]

The implications for multilateralism and international security are straightforward: it is virtually unthinkable that multilateral arrangements (such as UN peace operations) could be effectively put in place unless they are in the narrowly-defined interest of the major powers. As Robert Cox puts it, 'international institutions are a public ritual designed to legitimate privately determined measures'.[12] In practical terms, this would mean that multilateralism and international security is reducible either to a study of American policy in the unipolar moment (the realist view), or to a study of co-operation among Western great powers (Britain, France and the US, with occasional input by Russia): several analyses of the Gulf War and the UN embargo against Iraq adopt this argument. Interestingly enough, although some of this work does deal directly with security issues, it almost never mentions the United Nations, and focuses overwhelmingly on institutions such as NATO and European security more generally.[13]

A 'critical' understanding of multilateralism, by contrast, shifts the focus to the underlying structures and processes of world politics, and highlights the 'reciprocal relationship between global structural change in all its dimensions and the development of multilateralism'.[14] It emphasizes five things, the first of which is shared with the rationalist perspective:

– power: it accepts that power relations are embedded in all multilateral arrangements, even those based on diffuse reciprocity and formal equality;
– ideas: it sees these arrangements, however, as reflecting not just the interests of major or superpowers, but also a particular 'social purpose' that helps determine how states define their interests;

---

[11] For general statements of this see Robert Keohane, 'Multilateralism: A Agenda for Research', *International Journal*, 45:4 (Autumn 1990), 731–764; Lisa Martin, 'The Rational State Choice of Multilateralism', in Ruggie, *Multilateralism Matters*, pp. 91–121; David Baldwin (ed.), *Neorealism and Neoliberalism: The Contemporary Debate* (New York: Columbia University Press, 1993).

[12] Cox, 'Multilateralism and World Order', 168.

[13] See, for example, Weber, 'Shaping the Postwar Balance of Power'; Patrick Morgan, 'Multilateralism and Security: Prospects in Europe', in Ruggie, *Multilateralism Matters*, pp. 327–364; John Duffield, 'International Regimes and Alliance Behavior: Explaining NATO Conventional Force Levels', *International Organization*, 46:4 (Fall 1992), 819–855; Gunther Hellmann and Reinhard Wolf, 'Neorealism, Neoliberal Institutionalism, and the Future of NATO', *Security Studies*, 3:1 (Autumn 1993), 3–43.

[14] Robert W. Cox, 'An Alternative Approach to Multilateralism for the Twenty-first Century', *Global Governance*, 3 (1997), 105. As argued elsewhere by Cox, 'to define a meaning of multilateralism ... we must begin with an assessment of the present and emerging future condition of the world system, with the power relationships that will give contextual meaning to the term'. Robert W. Cox, 'Multilateralism and World Order', *Review of International Studies*, 18:2 (April 1992), 163. For background on his approach see Robert Cox, 'On Thinking about Future World Order', *World Politics*, 28:2 (January 1976), 175–196; 'Social Forces, States and World Orders: Beyond International Relations Theory', *Millennium*, 10:2 (Summer 1981), 126–155.

– institutions: it argues that 'institutions matter' in the sense that outcomes are not determined purely by the diplomacy of powerful states, but that multilateral arrangements can affect how choices are framed and outcomes reached;
  – agency: it treats all arrangements as constructions, not inevitably determined by the anarchic structure of world politics, but as the product of the conscious actions of policy-makers in particular historical circumstances;
  – actors: it draws attention to social, politico-military and economic forces operating not just above and below, but across the state, forces that disregard or efface the importance of state boundaries.[15]

On this account, multilateral action to maintain or restore international peace and security (such as UN operations), however effective or weak it may be, is the concrete expression of the power relationships and social purposes of post-1945 international society, conditioned by the political, economic, social and military structures that define world politics. Although what this means in practical terms will be developed below, I can state here my two theses. First, even if a rationalist approach to multilateralism can explain relatively easily such operations as the 1990–91 war against Iraq, the American invocation of Chapter VII in the Haitian crisis, or the non-intervention in Rwanda, a critical perspective is needed in order to make sense of the wide range of operations that have been undertaken since the end of the Cold War (such as the Cambodian, Angolan, El Salvadoran and Somalian operations), many of which cannot be explained in a satisfying way by the simple logic of self-interested states acting occasionally in concert.[16] Second, multilateral actions to ensure or restore international peace since the end of the Cold War have been based upon a particular understanding of 'international peace and security' that, while it goes somewhat beyond the simple self-interest calculations of states ('stability'), reflects a conservative commitment to perpetuating the Westphalian order and existing multilateral arrangements, rather than incorporating a broader understanding of security with human and societal dimensions.

This way of thinking about multilateralism has been hardly developed at all in the study of international security. It has, however, received some attention in

---

[15] These five points are elaborated in, respectively, Cox, 'Multilateralism and World Order'; John Ruggie, 'International Regimes, Transactions and Change: Embedded Liberalism in the Postwar Economic Order', *International Organization*, 36:2 (Spring 1982), 379–415; Alexander Wendt, 'Anarchy is What States Make of it', *International Organization*, 46:2 (Spring 1992), 391–425; Keith Krause and W. Andy Knight, 'Introduction: Evolution and Change in the United Nations System', in Keith Krause and W. Andy Knight, *State, Society and the UN System* (Tokyo: UNU Press, 1995), pp. 1–33.

[16] Of course, one can always retrospectively construct a rationalist/realist argument that states were pursuing their narrow, even short-term, interests in each of these operations. My argument is not that such accounts are wrong, merely that they are incomplete in important ways on which I hope to shed some light.

analyses of the world economy. For John Ruggie, for example, the particular form that multilateral arrangements take reflects a fusion of power with social purpose. The overwhelming preponderance of American power after 1945 helps explain why the current multilateral system was an American one, but not what was distinctively 'American' about it (as contrasted, for example, with a hypothetical British or Nazi German construction of international economic order based on imperial preferences and spheres of influence, or on exploitative bilateralism). He argues that the underlying principle was one of 'embedded liberalism' based on a normative consensus that emerged from Western industrial states after the experience of the Great Depression, and which advocated welfare liberalism and a regulated market system. Anne-Marie Burley expands on this, by showing how the post-war multilateral arrangements to govern the world economy not only accommodated the need for domestic economic intervention (that is, Keynesianism), but were also the outward projection of the 'New Deal state'. In many cases (such as the FAO, WHO, ICAO) the institutions that were established directly mirrored American ideas and experiences of the Roosevelt era.[17]

For scholars such as Robert Cox, this overly-benign view must be sharpened by a critical analysis of the interests and power of other economic, social and political actors. He (and the so-called 'Italian school' of neo-Gramscians) examines the ways in which multilateral arrangements such as the World Bank, IMF, GATT/WTO, G7 and OECD regulate and structure the world economy in ways that serve the interests of global capitalism and entrench the neo-liberal project at the expense of different visions of the proper relationship between economy, state and society, and the local, national or international interventionary schemes which these visions can generate.[18] In a sort of internationalization of the logic of Karl Polanyi's *Great Transformation*, these scholars analyse the emergence of global civil society as a defensive response against the massive upheavals in everyday (international and national) life and social order that are wrought by the attempts to realize in practice the ideal of the self-regulating, *laissez-faire*, global market. Domestically, such a 'double movement' reshaped both the state and civil society,

---

[17] Ruggie, 'International Regimes, Transactions and Change: Embedded Liberalism in the Postwar Economic Order'; Anne-Marie Burley, 'Regulating the World: Multilateralism, International Law, and the Projection of the New Deal Regulatory State', in Ruggie (ed.), *Multilateralism Matters*, pp. 125–156. As Burley put it, the 'international law of co-operation and the international regimes it created grew out of the same transformation in the philosophy of government that spawned new domestic regimes', p. 129.

[18] Representative contributions would include: Robert W. Cox, *Power, Production and World Order* (New York: Columbia University Press, 1987); Stephen Gill, *American Hegemony and the Trilateral Commission* (Cambridge: Cambridge University Press, 1990); Craig Murphy, *International Organization and Industrial Change* (Oxford: Oxford University Press, 1994); Mark Rupert, *Producing Hegemony: The Politics of Mass Production and American Global Power* (Cambridge: Cambridge University Press, 1995). For an overview of some of this scholarship, see Randall Germain and Michael Kenny, 'Engaging Gramsci: International Relations Theory and the New Gramscians', *Review of International Studies*, 24 (1998), 3–21.

eventually producing, in the late nineteenth and first half of the twentieth century, the regulatory welfare state. Internationally, it generated a dense web of multilateral governance arrangements, and an increasingly well-organized and articulated global network of forces opposing the more extreme versions of global neo-liberalism.

While not attempting to assess the claims of these scholars, it is worth pointing out that for Ruggie, Cox, et al., the focus of attention is not on the interaction of states and their foreign policy apparatuses, but on the sets of ideas that shape their actions, and on the broader social forces that are at work within and across states. Hence neither the project of embedded liberalism, nor that of contemporary neo-liberal economics, is simply a projection of American hegemony – they are, rather, the expression of a particular view of the proper relationships between state and market, between state and citizen, between market and society (in the global as well as domestic realms). Overall, this is a different way of looking at multilateralism (in the WTO, for example) than simply seeing outcomes as the product of inter-state bargaining power, and it has interesting implications for how we might conceive of multilateralism and international security.

A Critical Perspective on Multilateralism and International Peace and Security

An extension of the logic of scholars such as Ruggie and Cox to the sphere of international security would require us to answer the following sorts of questions:

- What dominant ideas of 'governance' are embedded within the current multilateral arrangements (or lack thereof) for ensuring international peace and security?
- How restrictive or open are these arrangements, and what scope for interpretation and adaptation exists?
- How has the recent practice of multilateral peace and security reflected these ideas of governance?
- Whose interests (and not exclusively 'which state's interests') are served by such arrangements, and whose are sacrificed (explicitly or implicitly)?

I will take up the first three of these in turn, and discuss them in the context of several post-Cold War multilateral security operations. I will briefly address the fourth question in my conclusion.[19]

---

[19] A fifth question that I do not treat would be 'what, if any, forces of change are at work today in the arena of multilateral peace and security?'

Ideas of Governance and International Security

The UN constitutional order contains three different conceptions of the nature of the international community over which it is meant to exercise 'governance': this community is sometimes understood in terms of individuals (the human rights discourse), in terms of peoples (the self-determination discourse), or in terms of states.[20] These different visions are all reflected in the first three paragraphs of Article 1 of the UN Charter, and they coexist in an uneasy tension in the UN 'constitutional' documents. There is a complex interplay between the Charter, other foundational documents (such as the Universal Declaration of Human Rights and related Covenants), and significant resolutions (such as those concerning decolonization and the rights to self-determination). In principle, any of these three senses of 'international community' could serve as the foundation for a multilateral security order; in practice, the tilt has been largely (but not exclusively, as I will note below) towards the state-centric conception.

The rhetorical goal of saving 'succeeding generations from the scourge of war' placed the Security Council at the heart of the multilateral system for maintaining international security (Article 24(1)). Its structure and powers reflect several ideas about the appropriate scope of multilateral action. To begin with, it is a modified collective security system that seeks to make the idealist aspiration of collective security compatible with the practice of balance of power politics and the acknowledged self-help nature of world politics.[21] Although the organization was to respond to threats to or breaches of the peace and acts of aggression (Article 39), the presumed automaticity of the League collective security mechanism was abandoned, the right of states to use force in self-defence was reaffirmed (Article 51), and virtually unlimited discretionary power was given to the Security Council to determine when a 'threat to international peace and security' existed.[22] The explicit recognition of the legitimacy of great power governance, expressed in the veto of the five permanent members and the primacy of the Security Council over the General Assembly (Article 12), matched well the post-1945 configuration of power but owed as much to the nineteenth-century concert system as to ideas about collective security.

Somewhat more subtly (and despite the rhetoric of sovereign equality) the system was premised on a compromised notion of sovereignty that included a great

---

[20] These three are from Michael Barnett, 'The UN Security Council, Indifference, and Genocide in Rwanda', *Cultural Anthropology*, 12:4 (1997), 565.
[21] Ruggie, 'Multilateralism: The Anatomy of an Institution', 26.
[22] The issue of unrestricted scope came to the fore in the debate over Security Council actions in the Libyan extradition case. See the International Court of Justice decision on provisional measures in 'Questions of Interpretation and Application for the 1971 Montreal Convention arising from the Aerial Incident at Lockerbie', (Libyan Arab Jamahiriya vs. United States of America), 14 April 1992, and UN Security Council resolutions 731 and 748. See also Martii Koskenniemi, 'The Police in the Temple: Order, Justice and the UN: A Dialectical View', *European Journal of International Law*, 6 (1995), 325–348.

degree of latitude in how 'threats to international peace and security' were interpreted, latitude that has been used by the Security Council. On the one hand, a hard version of sovereignty is presented in Article 2 (sovereign equality, non-intervention in domestic affairs), and in the terms of membership for the UN. On the other hand, the subordination of the non-intervention provisions of Article 2(7) to Chapter VII of the Charter allowed the Security Council to override sovereignty when a threat to international peace and security was deemed to exist.[23] The discretionary power of the Security Council to determine what constituted a threat to international peace and security meant that sovereignty (understood here as the ultimate adjudicative authority) was thus compromised for the overwhelming majority of states. Although throughout the Cold War Chapter VII was seldom invoked (in Korea and South Africa, most notably), the opening provided by this compromised notion of sovereignty allowed (when circumstances had changed) the Security Council to stretch to the breaking point the notion of 'threats to international peace and security' in order to justify interventionary acts.[24] The logic that this stretching seemed to follow will be outlined below.

A third cluster of elements that followed from both of these underlying norms could be called the ethic of 'liberal interventionism'. There are three elements to this idea of liberal interventionism. The first is a commitment to the state system as the most just resolution to the problem of global political order.[25] Rather than opposing 'order' to 'justice' it makes more sense, as Martii Koskenniemi has argued, to see the two as existing in an uneasy dialectical relationship.[26] Of course, not all visions of order and of justice are compatible, and the Westphalian commitment to order restricts the kind of justice that can be pursued to a liberal one, in the sense of both 'live and let live' *laissez-faire*, and in a relatively narrow conception of international rights and obligations (rights and obligations confined principally within political communities; the relative downplaying of ideas of economic justice). This in turn was linked to a latter-day 'standard of civilization' by which great powers determined the terms on which states were allowed to participate in international society. Formerly, this was expressed in terms of 'civilization' versus 'barbarians'; post-1945, it was articulated in terms of the 'free world' (a standard which demonized other political forms and justified authoritarianism in the name of a higher good); today, it is oriented around notions of 'democracy' and free markets.[27]

---

[23] As Article 2(7) says with respect to the non-intervention principle: 'this principle shall not prejudice the application of enforcement measures under Chapter VII'.
[24] I am obviously using 'intervention' loosely here, in a more political than legal sense.
[25] See Michael Walzer, 'The Moral Standing of States: A Response to Four Critics', in Charles Beitz, et al. (eds), *International Ethics* (Princeton, 1985), pp. 217–237; Roberts, *Humanitarian action in War*, p. 19.
[26] Koskenniemi, 'The Police in the Temple'.
[27] See Gerrit Gong, *The Standard of Civilization in International Society* (Oxford: Clarendon Press, 1984). For the contemporary variants, see Larry Diamond and Mark Plattner (eds), *The Global Resurgence of Democracy* (Baltimore: Johns Hopkins

The last element was 'intervention' itself. Despite the impression that a legalist or textual reading of the Charter might suggest, one can easily argue that intervention has been a far more common state practice than non-intervention since 1945.[28] Of course, the issue is not 'intervention versus non-intervention' *per se* (how much intervention must occur before the norm is challenged?), but rather the explicit and implicit understandings of states of the terms on which intervention can or should be undertaken.

The Scope and Potential for Change: Narrow Adaptation to the Cold War[29]

One common, but mistaken, argument holds that the ideas underpinning the multilateral security system remained dormant during the Cold War, and that they were only resuscitated and translated into more concrete form by the burst of UN and multilateral activity that characterized the immediate post-Cold War world. Although the wartime expectation that the victorious powers would remain united to preserve a stable international security environment and collectively punish defectors proved false, and although bipolar East–West tensions and rivalry, the concern with spheres of influence, and the nuclear balance of terror dominated global politico-military relations, pressures for multilateral action in the peace and security arena did not vanish entirely. In fact, despite being made a marginal actor in most security issues, the various adaptations of the multilateral peace and security apparatus of the UN throughout the Cold War (however minor) translated the ideas sketched above into 'normal' multilateral responses to conflict and crisis.[30] These practices were entrenched, however, only with the explicit approval of the great powers (or at least of the superpowers), and were part and parcel of the 'order-making' logic sketched above.

The first response was an attempt to shift decision-making power for peace and security matters away from the paralysed Security Council to the General Assembly, via the 1950 Uniting for Peace resolution (Resolution 377 (V), 3 November 1950), which empowered the Assembly to address breaches to international security if the Council failed to do so, and projected the General Assembly into the security domain that had been hitherto reserved for the Security

---

University Press, 1993); Samuel Huntington, *The Third Wave: Democratization in the Late Twentieth Century* (Oklahoma: University of Oklahoma Press, 1993).

[28] According to data compiled by Jennifer Milliken, there have been more than 170 'interventions' in conflicts (any non-neutral action by external parties in conflict that was not sanctioned by all combatants) since 1945. While many of these would not be classified by international lawyers as formal interventions (since they were not dealing directly with matters of domestic jurisdiction), and many were part of the decolonization process, the non-adherence to a strict norm is overwhelming.

[29] This section draws upon a discussion in Krause and Knight, 13–16.

[30] See W. Andy Knight and Mari Yamashita, 'The United Nations' Contribution to International Peace and Security', in David Dewitt, David Haglund and John Kirton (eds), *Building a New Global Order* (Toronto: Oxford University Press, 1993), pp. 284–312.

Council. What is important to note, however, is that the Uniting for Peace resolution was American-sponsored, and was designed not to empower the Assembly, but rather 'to put the United Nations in a position to tell the United States and its allies that they may act, to confer its official blessings upon such action as the Western bloc may choose to undertake'.[31] Although the resolution has only been used ten times, and occasionally against the interests of major powers (most recently in the 1997 emergency special session on the West Bank and Occupied Territories, in response to vetoed Security Council resolutions), the idea behind it – that the role of the UN is to confer legitimacy on acts that are undertaken by the great powers and their allies – enjoys great currency today (in, for example, the Gulf War, the restoration of democracy in Haiti, Operation Turquoise in Rwanda, and arguably the NATO operation in Kosovo).

A second response was the establishment of a number of institutions to address the problem of nuclear weapons and the arms race, including the Atomic Energy Commission (1946), International Atomic Energy Agency (1957), the Nuclear Non-Proliferation Treaty (1968), and a host of lesser disarmament and arms limitation treaties (most notably the 1993 Chemical Weapons Convention). Again, however, the UN was a subordinate forum for arms control, to be used either to entrench global bans (such as on chemical weapons), or discriminatory ones that acknowledged great power legitimacy (such as the NPT). More importantly, it was completely unable to advance towards disarmament, or towards the control of the flow and accumulation of conventional weapons around the world.

The third response, peacekeeping, deviated somewhat further from the post-1945 vision of the UN, but remained within the order-maintenance logic and has proven to be perhaps the most important global multilateral security arrangement. Although only thirteen peacekeeping and observer missions were created during the Cold War, the institution of peacekeeping became a durable feature of multilateral life. But the invention of peacekeeping was not a substitute for the inoperable collective security mechanisms of the Security Council; it was rather a more benevolent multilateral version of the ongoing great power practice of interventionary 'order making'. Other situations, which were deemed to require either greater force or less consent, were left to the great powers, who did not hesitate to intervene widely.

The UN understanding restricted 'peacekeeping' to a minimalist form of intervention (consent-based, interpositionary, impartial, non-forceful) designed to prevent conflicts from spilling over beyond fairly narrow bounds and threatening the nuclear peace between Cold War blocs.[32] More importantly, it was based on a

---

[31] Inis Claude, *Swords into Ploughshares*, 3rd edition (New York: Random House, 1964), p. 247. See also Adam Roberts and Benedict Kingsbury, *United Nations, Divided World: The UN's Roles in International Relations* (Oxford: Clarendon Press, 1988), p. 34.

[32] A good summary of this is the distinction between first- and second-generation peacekeeping. See John Mackinlay and Jarat Chopra, 'Second Generation Multinational Operations', *The Washington Quarterly* 15:3 (Summer 1992), 113–131. See also Ramesh Thakur, 'International Peacekeeping, UN Authority, and US Power',

particular vision of political communities that saw them as self-contained, territorially-demarcated, and easily recognized entities. This was most clearly reflected in the logic of interposition: in order to place UN forces between warring parties, there has to be a place on which a border can be inscribed and enforced, and relative homogeneity on either side of it. The UNFICYP operation in Cyprus, or the UNEF operations in the Middle East, illustrate this logic perfectly. The structural limitations that this conception of peacekeeping suffered from were illustrated well in the Bosnian war, with its ideas of safe havens, ethnic enclaves, and so forth. As Michael Williams has polemically argued, 'if the identity of territoriality and sovereignty is central to successful peacekeeping ... in effect ... this makes the heinous process of "ethnic cleansing" a precondition for successful peacekeeping'.[33] This is not to argue that peacekeeping implied ethnic cleansing, but simply that it was unlikely to be successful in situations that had not been so (tragically) 'clarified'.

Restricted Reinterpretation in the Post-Cold War World

There is nothing novel about the observation that the Cold War kept the development of multilateral arrangements to maintain international peace and security restricted within fairly narrow parameters that privileged order-maintenance and the discretionary judgement of the great powers. What is more interesting is how little has changed since the end of the Cold War. Despite the short-term expansion of peace and security operations in the period from 1989 to 1994, and despite a significant change in their orientation towards a range of disputes short of war (ethnic, cross-border, tribal and other civil conflicts) that were not fully anticipated by the framers of the Charter, the underlying approach to multilateralism and international security has hardly changed at all.[34] It still privileges unaccountable great power governance, is based on a 'compromised sovereignty' that condones (or encourages) intervention, acts to reinforce the Westphalian sovereign order, and promotes a liberal vision that is consistent with this Westphalian order. This claim is only reinforced by the alacrity with which

---

Alternatives, 12 (1987), 461. For an official elaboration of the role which UN Observer Missions and Peacekeeping operations have played, see the second edition of *The Blue Helmets: A Review of United Nations Peace-keeping* (New York: United Nations Department of Public Information, 1990).

[33] Michael C. Williams, 'Peacekeeping and the Politics of Post-modernity', unpublished paper, 1992. That this is a 'realist' logic is revealed clearly by Chaim Kaufmann's argument for ethnic separation (or 'cleansing') in 'Possible and Impossible Solutions to Ethnic Civil Wars', *International Security*, 20:4 (Spring 1996), 136–175. Arguably the same case can be made for the Serbian/Kosovo conflict.

[34] For the expansive vision, see *An Agenda for Peace*, report of the Secretary-General pursuant to the statement adopted by the summit meeting of the Security Council on 31 January 1992. General Assembly Document A/47/277, 17 June 1992.

great powers have abandoned the UN in recent years, and in particular in its complete disregard of NATO's use of force in Kosovo.

Great Power Autonomy and Unaccountability

Perhaps not surprisingly, the empowerment of the Security Council was accompanied by a precipitous decline in the transparency of its decision-making. Until the mid-1960s, the deliberations and debates of the Security Council were open to the public, whereas today, they are usually set-piece speeches followed by a preordained vote (and often not even speeches are given, as a perusal of the provisional verbatims will attest). In many Gulf and post-Gulf War cases, drafts of resolutions were negotiated in capitals, with hardly any discussion around the Security Council itself until sufficient agreement had been reached.[35]

Parallel to this, the great powers have used the opening provided by the Charter to expand tremendously the scope of their actions under Chapter VII of the Charter. Riding the tide of sentiment for a broader conception of security after the Cold War, the Security Council declared in 1992 that 'non-military sources of instability in the economic, social, humanitarian and ecological fields have become threats to peace and security'.[36] Although many observers welcomed this broader understanding of security as an improvement over the restricted emphasis on interstate stability that characterized Cold War multilateralism, the problem is that without consistency or accountability in its application the legitimacy of Security Council actions in this domain can be questioned. In fact, the Security Council has used this expanded conception to invoke Chapter VII in an unusually wide range of circumstances, but with no discernable concern for its consistent application. As Koskenniemi rhetorically notes, the Security Council may have been 'in fact making a *carte blanche* declaration of the limitlessness of its powers'.[37]

Several examples of this can be given, but perhaps the two most interesting concern the use of Chapter VII against acts of alleged state terrorism, and to establish war crimes tribunals in the Yugoslav and Rwandan conflicts. With respect to terrorism, Chapter VII was invoked to impose sanctions against both Libya and the Sudan in order to force the extradition of suspects in different terrorist attacks, the first time in connection with the downing of the Pan American airliner over Lockerbie, Scotland; the second with the attempt on Egyptian President Mubarak's life during a state visit to Ethiopia.[38] In both cases, the

---

[35] Helmut Freundenschuß, 'Between Unilateralism and Collective Security: Authorizations of the Use of Force by the UN Security Council', *European Journal of International Law*, 5 (1994), 492–531.

[36] See *The Responsibility of the Security Council in the Maintenance of International Security*, UN document S/PV.3946 (31 January 1992).

[37] Koskenniemi, 326.

[38] See Security Council Resolutions 1044, 1054, and 1070 in the Sudan case, and Resolutions 731 and 748 in the Libyan case. The latter was taken to the ICJ for a ruling on provisional measures (which were refused), and although a final judgement on the

punitive action (which implies a determination of guilt of the state in question as a sponsor of terrorism, and comes awfully close to a determination of the guilt of the suspects without a judicial process) was imposed with extremely little concern for due process.[39] Concomitantly, the discretion of the Security Council not to act in other perhaps equally egregious cases of state terrorism (Israel's attempt on Hamas leaders in Amman comes to mind, for example) has meant that no coherently applied principle of justice can be discerned behind the authorization and non-authorization of Chapter VII actions. With respect to the war crimes tribunals in Rwanda and Yugoslavia, despite the explicit linkage made between grave breaches of human rights, threats to international security, and possible enforcement action by the UN, states have hardly enthusiastically supported them in ways that lead us to believe that this linkage was taken seriously.[40]

Compromised Sovereignty Encouraging Intervention

Most observers who have commented upon the Council's expanded notion of what constitutes a threat to international peace and security have argued that it forces a reconsideration of the justifiability, necessity or scope of humanitarian intervention.[41] They usually point to Resolution 688, which was used as the basis for the creation of a protection zone for the Kurdish population in northern Iraq,[42] and to Resolution 794, which authorized the intervention by the American-led

---

legality of the Resolution has not come down, it appears that the court is reluctant to rule Security Council actions as *ultra vires*. See the International Court of Justice decision in 'Questions of Interpretation and Application for the 1971 Montreal Convention arising from the Aerial Incident at Lockerbie' (Libyan Arab Jamahiriya vs. United States of America), 14 April 1992.

[39] Koskenniemi, 345–346 also discusses the weak 'due process' involved in the UN sanctions committees for Iraq, Yugoslavia, Libya, Somalia and Angola.

[40] The Yugoslavia tribunal, established under Resolution 827 (25 May 1993), determined that 'continuing reports of widespread and flagrant violations of international humanitarian law occurring within the territory of the former Yugoslavia' constituted a 'threat to international peace and security' (preambular paragraphs 3 and 4, operative paragraph 2). The Rwanda tribunal (Resolution 995) used the same preambular language.

[41] See, *inter alia*, Barry Benjamin, 'Unilateral Humanitarian Intervention: Legalizing the Use of Force to Prevent Human Rights Atrocities', *Fordham International Law Journal*, 16 (1992–93), 120–158; Adam Roberts, 'Humanitarian War: Military Intervention and Human Rights', *International Affairs* 69:3 (July 1993), 444–449; Nigel Rodley (ed.), *To Loose the Bands of Wickedness: International Intervention in Defense of Human Rights* (London: Brassey's, 1992); Fernando Teson, *Humanitarian Intervention: An Inquiry into Law and Morality* (Dobbs Ferry: Transnational Publishers, 1988); Kelly Kate Pease and David P. Forsythe, 'Human Rights, Humanitarian Intervention and World Politics', *Human Rights Quarterly*, 15 (May 1993).

[42] Resolution 688 stated that 'repression of the Iraqi civilian populations ... led to a massive flow of refugees towards and across international frontiers ... which threaten international peace and security in the region'. On the Kurdish operation in general see Roberts, 'Humanitarian War', 436–439.

Unified Task Force (UNITAF) in December 1992,⁴³ as representing the incorporation of humanitarian ideals (protection of civilians) into Chapter VII operations (several cases during the war in the former Yugoslavia would also fit this analysis). Without entering into the debate surrounding humanitarian intervention, one can note that those scholars who admit some right of intervention seem most comfortable with it being multilateral, and conducted under Security Council authorization.⁴⁴

But two points are worth making about the legal and normative bases of the concept of intervention invoked here. First, it does not reflect a subordination of the latitude of action assumed by great powers to a determination by the Security Council of the legality of their action. In other words, the great powers still preserve the margin of manoeuvre for intervention (on whatever terms and for whatever reasons) that they assumed throughout the Cold War, and indeed, throughout the nineteenth and twentieth centuries. The military actions of the United States, Britain and France to establish protected enclaves in northern Iraq were in fact not explicitly authorized by the Security Council (and were condemned by some member-states).⁴⁵ One might also note the declaration by President Clinton that the United States reserved the right to resort to force to compel Saddam Hussein to co-operative fully with UNSCOM (or to punish him for non-compliance).⁴⁶

Second, even if actions are multilateral, the issue of who decides (which is what makes sovereignty 'compromised' in the sense I have used it here) is resolved in favour of the Permanent Five. They have invoked Chapter VII in resolutions more than seventy times between 1993 and 1998 (nineteen times authorizing the use of force since 1990), and have been conspicuously careless in the way in which they have done so. All attempts to make the use of force genuinely multilateral (by reactivating the operational elements of Chapter VII) have been pushed aside, in favour of language that authorizes individual states or

---

⁴³ Resolution 794 stated that 'the magnitude of the human tragedy caused by the conflict in Somalia, further exacerbated by the obstacles being created to the distribution of humanitarian assistance, constitutes a threat to international peace and security', and, invoking Chapter VII, authorized action (including the use of force) 'to establish a secure environment for humanitarian relief operations in Somalia'. S/RES/794, 3 December 1992.

⁴⁴ See Laura Reed and Carl Kaysen (eds), *Emerging Norms of Justified Intervention* (Cambridge, Mass.: American Academy of Arts and Sciences, 1993); Jarat Chopra and Thomas Weiss, 'Sovereignty is no Longer Sacrosanct', *Ethics and International Affairs*, 6 (1992), 95–117.

⁴⁵ Secretary-General Perez de Cuellar thought that a new resolution would be required to justify the creation of safe havens (and he refused to allow the force to wear blue helmets); the Chinese threatened to veto any resolution that authorized Chapter VII action to enforce Resolution 688, the British, French and Americans finally declared their action 'consistent with' resolution 688. Peter Viggo Jakobsen, 'National Interest, Humanitarianism or CNN: What Triggers UN Peace Enforcement after the Cold War?' unpublished paper, 1995.

⁴⁶ *Le Monde*, 5 March 1998.

groups of states to 'take all necessary measures,' and to use force. But since the states taking the forceful action are also the ones granting the authorization, it is fair to see the role of the Security Council as providing in many cases 'international political cover' for the interventionary actions of great powers.[47] There is little new to celebrate in this.

Reinforcing the Westphalian Order

One could draw from these two features of recent multilateral security practice two diametrically opposed conclusions. On the one hand, one could conclude that rationalist multilateralism is correct, and that states act multilaterally in the realm of international security only to achieve narrowly defined aims (such as securing access to cheap oil or cementing strategic gains). On the other hand, one could argue that 'we are clearly witnessing what is probably an irresistible shift in public attitudes towards the belief that the defence of the oppressed in the name of morality should prevail over frontiers and legal documents,' or that 'the time of absolute and exclusive sovereignty ... has passed'.[48] Some scholars have even gone so far as to argue that as a result the international community is moving 'beyond Westphalia' towards new political forms that crack the hard shell of state sovereignty.[49]

But the former view is too narrow, for it misses the rationale behind the interventions in Somalia, Northern Iraq, the former Yugoslavia and elsewhere. The latter view is also mistaken, since the form that multilateral security activities have taken do not necessarily undermine the foundations of the Westphalian state system. In fact, multilateral peace and security operations have systematically acted to reinforce the sovereign state system, rather than to undermine it. Again, several examples can illustrate this careful circumscribing of multilateral security operations. In the case of Somalia, the Security Council's logic was best laid out by the delegate from Djibouti, who argued that 'Somalia ... is a land with no effective mechanism for governance ... [It] is in key respects a non-State ... Perhaps our role in Somalia is at bottom to provide a secure basis for its re-

---

[47] Lawrence Freedman, 'The Gulf War and the New World Order', *Survival*, 33 (1991), 195, 197.

[48] Former Secretary-General Javier Perez de Cuellar's 24 April 1991 speech at the University of Bordeaux, cited in Gene Lyons and Michael Mastanduno, *Beyond Westphalia? International Intervention, State Sovereignty and the Future of International Society*, summary of a conference held at Dartmouth College, May 1992, 2; Former Secretary-General Boutros-Boutros Ghali, *An Agenda for Peace*, paragraph 17.

[49] Gene Lyons and Michael Mastanduno (eds), *Beyond Westphalia: State Sovereignty and International Intervention* (Baltimore: Johns Hopkins University Press, 1995); W. Andy Knight, 'Towards a Subsidiarity Model for Peacemaking and Preventive Diplomacy: Making Chapter VIII of the UN Charter Operational', *Third World Quarterly*, 17:1 (1996), 31–52.

emergence institutionally.'⁵⁰ The goal is to restore empirical sovereignty to a single entity in the juridically sovereign territory of 'Somalia'; it is not to allow the people to freely determine their political destiny in ways that might fracture this sovereignty. As a result, northern Somalia, which declared its independence (as the Republic of Somaliland) was not recognized or supported internationally, nor was its independence even acknowledged as a possible outcome of the reconciliation process. Similar difficulties were part of the complex debates on the appropriate resolution to the war in the former Yugoslavia.

That the political project is bounded in this way can also be demonstrated by the difficulties the UN faced in situations in which restoring empirical sovereignty encountered strong local resistance. In the case of humanitarian intervention in the Sudan in 1989 the UN, because it was forced to deal with the government in Khartoum on an ongoing basis, was unable to break out of a framework that put a high priority on maintaining Sudan as a single state (and which therefore limited its ability to aid the south and gain the trust of the people). '[Operation] Lifeline paradoxically illuminated the extent to which the world organization itself may be one of the last bastions of national sovereignty as traditionally understood', and 'the nature of the UN's primary constituency and accountability helps explain a number of problems associated with its effort to respond to a humanitarian crisis involving an insurgency as well as a recognized government'.⁵¹ In the case of El Salvador and the Central American peace process, 'the state-centricity of ... international organizations like the UN ... [left] the irregular forces in the region outside the formal negotiation framework on establishing a peacekeeping mission', making peace-building difficult.⁵² In the case of the mandated referendum on the independence of the former Spanish colony of Western Sahara (Resolution 690), relative inaction by the UN to implement the terms of the Resolution in the face of Moroccan resistance is in part explained by the realization that 'a referendum which favours Morocco might prove to be the best means of resolving the problem in human and institutional terms', since the alternative would be the creation of yet another juridically sovereign but empirically weak micro-state.⁵³ And in the case of the genocide in Rwanda, the Secretariat persisted, well into the genocide, in portraying the conflict as a civil war between the Rwandese army and the Rwandese Patriotic Front (RPF), deciding to withdraw most UNAMIR forces on

---

⁵⁰ Security Council document S/PV.3188 (26 March 1993), 8.
⁵¹ Thomas G. Weiss and Larry Minear, 'Do International Ethics Matter? Humanitarian Politics in the Sudan', *Ethics and International Affairs*, 5 (1991), 214, 208.
⁵² Stephen Baranyi and Liisa North, *Stretching the Limits of the Possible: United Nations Peacekeeping in Central America*, Aurora papers 15 (Ottawa: Canadian Centre for Global Security, 1992), 7.
⁵³ Armand Roy, 'The Western Sahara', in *Peacekeeping: Norms, Policy and Process*, 1993 Peacekeeping Symposium (Ottawa: York University, 1993), 62. Major-General Roy is a former force commander of MINURSO. As the Secretary-General argued in the *Agenda for Peace*, 'if every ethnic, religious or linguistic group claimed statehood, there would be no limit to fragmentation, and peace, security and economic well-being for all would become ever more difficult to achieve' (para. 17).

21 April (two weeks after the aircraft carrying President Habyarimana was shot down above Kigali, and well after the massacres had started) because it could not fulfil its mandate of maintaining a ceasefire between these two parties. Protection of innocent people was not part of the picture.[54]

This formulation of the scope of multilateral security activities as 'maintaining order' and continuing the state-building project of the Westphalian state system goes beyond the narrow first-order 'self-interest' of states, and incorporates the shared interest of major actors in preventing the collapse of the part of the Westphalian edifice from which they derive their own legitimacy. But it is tightly bounded by a concern to design actions so that they do not at the same time threaten those foundations. Thus although 'nation-building is becoming an essential aspect of peace-operations', the goal of UN operations remains to create relatively strong state structures to fill the void created by the collapse or weakness of existing structures.[55]

Liberal Laissez-Faire Democratization

A final, and somewhat novel, element of this order-creation exercise is the use of the marker of 'democracy' – the holding of internationally supervised elections – as a means to certify the legitimacy and success of a peace and security operation. Although the strongest rhetoric of the 'right to democratic governance' has come from the EU and OSCE as part of the process of integrating former Eastern bloc states into a wider Western community, it has also been used to justify (and terminate) multilateral security operations by the UN and the Organization of American States (OAS). This has been attempted in a wide range of consensual and non-consensual (that is, Chapter VII) contexts, from Angola, Cambodia, Namibia and El Salvador to Bosnia and Haiti.[56] Perhaps the most dramatic has been the Chapter VII operation to restore democracy in Haiti, which (in Resolution 940, 1994) authorized member-states 'to form a multinational force under unified command and control and ... to use all necessary means to facilitate the departure from Haiti of the military leadership' and the restoration of the elected government.[57] Even at the time, this was seen as a controversial extension of the

---

[54] Howard Adelman and Astri Suhrke, 'Early Warning and Conflict Management', study no. 2, *The International Response to Conflict and Genocide: Lessons from the Rwanda Experience* (March 1996), chapter four.

[55] *Reform of United Nations Peacekeeping Operations: A Mandate for Change*, staff report of the US Senate Committee on Foreign Relations (August 1993), 11.

[56] The OAS has also 'started to intrude into the national affairs of members states and has adopted resolutions with respect to democracy ... [in] Nicaragua, Panama, Guatemala, Peru and Haiti ... [such that] according to OAS practice, sovereignty can only be recognized in countries with democratically elected governments', Joaquín Tacsan, 'Searching for OAS/UN Task-Sharing Opportunities in Central America and Haiti', *Third World Quarterly*, 18:3 (1997), 497–498.

[57] This followed several other resolutions (in particular, 875 and 917) that imposed sanctions on Haiti.

logic by which situations were considered 'to constitute a threat to peace and security in the region'.

It is almost too easy, however, to point out how selectively this principle has been applied beyond Europe. The international community did not 'restore' democracy in Algeria (after the annulation of the December 1991 elections before the second round could be held) or 'impose' it in Indonesia, for example, and in countless other cases the international community has been content to rubber stamp flawed electoral processes. Of course, democratic experiments work out well in some places, and badly in others, but success or failure is seldom connected to multilateral action *per se*. What is perhaps more important, however, are the two rationales behind this emphasis on democracy. In the first, the international community uses the formal ritual of a democratic 'election' to eschew greater (and ongoing) responsibility for the difficult, long and costly task of post-conflict rehabilitation and reconstruction, preferring to leave that to the informal and development communities. This makes the organization and holding of elections more of a public relations exercise to mark 'success' than a genuine implantation of democratic institutions and sensibilities. As Michael Barnett put it:

> few genuinely believed that one election at the end of a peacekeeping operation was enough to institutionalize 'democratic' practices, but the ritual of the election symbolized how peacekeeping operations were to help rehabilitate fallen members of the international community.[58]

Second, in cases where democratic experiments were taken more seriously (such as Angola, El Salvador and Cambodia), the design and logic of democratic institutions resonates poorly, if at all, with local social, political, historical and economic realities.[59] Under both rationales, 'democracy' is treated as the new 'standard of civilization' and as a cornerstone of international security, reflecting the belief that democratic states are both more legitimate, and less likely to go to war with each other.

Conclusion

The last element of a critical analysis of multilateralism and international security – a discussion of whose interests are served by this form of 'global governance' – cannot be dealt with in any detail here. But a few reflections on where I agree and disagree with other scholars who are attempting to go beyond rationalist accounts of multilateralism will highlight key aspects. One can distinguish three general

---

[58] Barnett, 'The UN Security Council, Indifference, and Genocide in Rwanda', 567.
[59] For the Cambodian experience, see Pierre Lizée, *Building Peace: The Challenges and Contradictions of the Cambodian Peace Process*, unpublished doctoral dissertation, York University, 1995. Arguably the same could be said about the Dayton Agreement's attempt to impose a form of democratic governance in post-war Bosnia. This claim requires a bit more support than I can give it here.

lines of argument about the scope and nature of multilateralism and international security that I find somewhat unconvincing. The first, from scholars such as Thomas Risse-Kappen, characterizes the current situation as one of 'faint-hearted multilateralism' in which the dominant liberal great powers (Britain, France and the US) find it increasingly necessary to use force inside of a multilateral framework, but whose 'liberal' values also make it difficult to use force for other purposes than to respond to imminent threats to national security. Arguably, NATO's willingness to use force in Kosovo puts paid to this argument.[60] The second, articulated by scholars such as Peter Jakobsen, argues that in humanitarian cases where a clear 'national interest' rationale does not also exist, 'the CNN effect is a necessary condition to mobilise pressure on (the western) governments to act'. The third, from jurists such as Helmut Freundenschuß, is that Security Council practice has been careless, haphazard and completely inconsistent, to the point where 'the only sensible conclusion is that the *opinio juris* is that ... words do not really matter'.[61]

All of these views, while correct to some extent, seem to obscure which interests are served by the current multilateral arrangements, and which interests are sacrificed. They make the logic of security operations appear *ad hoc*, driven by media and public opinion pressures, or completely subordinate to narrow understandings of national interest. But on my account, the principal 'beneficiaries' of current multilateral arrangements are not only particular states (great powers, or the sole superpower), but the sovereign state in general, whose status and role is reinforced rather than undermined by recent multilateral security operations.[62] There are a multitude of forces challenging the sovereignty of states (or changing the meaning of sovereignty), but post-Cold War multilateral security operations have consistently shored up both the legitimacy of the sovereign state as the principal means by which to achieve security, and the legitimacy of the hierarchy of states that grants great powers unconstrained discretion to 'order' world politics as they see fit. This parallels the argument of scholars such as Michael Barnett, who argues that multilateral action has been directed towards reinforcing or restoring the empirical sovereignty of states, often through the use of means that derogate from a strict understanding of juridical sovereignty.[63]

A second, more indirect, 'beneficiary' of the current arrangements may be the UN itself. The most striking evidence of this appeared in the case of inaction in the

---

[60] Of course, the 'faint-heartedness' is manifest in the refusal to entertain casualties, but that is a different matter.
[61] Thomas Risse-Kappen, 'Faint-Hearted Multilateralism', unpublished paper, 1994: Jakobsen, 29; Freundenschuß, 523. Freundenschuß was the alternative Austrian representative on the Security Council in 1991–92.
[62] This does not mean that great powers' interests are not served by these arrangements, only that other interests are also at work.
[63] Michael Barnett, 'The New U.N. Politics of Peace: From Juridical Sovereignty to Empirical Sovereignty', *Global Governance*, 1:1 (February 1995). His argument in turn leans on Robert Jackson, *Quasi-States, Sovereignty, International Relations and the Third World* (Cambridge: Cambridge University Press, 1990).

genocide in Rwanda. In addition to the reluctance of states to get involved in another operation in the wake of the Somalia debacle, a clear rationale for inaction was the perceived need to protect the reputation of the UN from further damage. This led to what Barnett has called the 'bureaucratization of indifference':

> the UN had more to lose by taking action and being associated with another failure than it did by not taking action and allowing the genocide in Rwanda. The moral equation was: genocide was acceptable if the alternative was to harm the future of the UN.[64]

As a result, the UN has subsequently incorporated a criteria of 'winnability' into its judgement of when or how operations should be launched, usually resorting to the traditional peacekeeping logic that stability on the ground is a precondition for intervention. The problem is that this places the initiative in the hands of the men with guns who can ensure that there is no peace to keep, and hence no multilateral intervention to stop the killing.

A third, more occluded, set of beneficiaries are those interests that take their sustenance from the perpetuation of the existing order. It has been widely noted, for example, that the Permanent Five members of the Security Council, charged with upholding international peace and security, are also the vendors of approximately 80 per cent of the world's armaments.[65] In virtually all of the conflicts in which the international community intervened – most notably in the Gulf War, the Somalia conflict, and the Rwanda genocide – the arms used by warring parties came from Security Council permanent members. In the case of the genocide in Rwanda, there is even some (albeit unclear) evidence that France continued to supply the Rwandese army (and perhaps indirectly the Hutu militias) after the genocide had started.[66] This is not the old, crude, and misleading 'merchants of death' argument. But the continued reliance on institutions and instruments of organized violence to create and perpetuate state power cannot be ignored or treated as incidental. To have the international community take as its principal goal the creation of 'strong' states, yet to be paralysed into inaction

---

[64] Barnett, 'The UN Security Council, Indifference, and Genocide in Rwanda', 561–562. Barnett was a political officer at the US mission in New York during 1994–95. See also Adelman and Suhrke.

[65] For details, see US Arms Control and Disarmament Agency, *World Military Expenditures and Arms Transfers, 1996* (Washington: ACDA, 1997); Keith Krause, *Arms and the State: Patterns of Military Production and Trade* (Cambridge: Cambridge University Press, 1992).

[66] The French government launched in 1998 an inquiry into these allegations. See also Stephen D. Goose and Frank Smyth, 'Arming Genocide in Rwanda', *Foreign Affairs*, 73:5 (September/October 1994), 86–96; *Rearming with Impunity: International Support for the Perpetrators of the Rwandan Genocide*, a Human Rights Watch Arms Project report A704, 1995; Joost Hiltermann, 'Post-Mortem on the International Commission of Inquiry (Rwanda)', *Bulletin of Concerned African Scholars*, available at http://www.prepcom.org/low/pc2/pc2b4.html.

whenever violence is threatened, effectively empties multilateral action in the peace and security realm of virtually all content.

Perhaps more significantly, the failure of successive UN operations to incorporate effective post-conflict disarmament and arms control (regional or national) measures into their operations has been a serious shortcoming that points up the limitations of existing multilateral arrangements. As Robert Jackson points out, a commitment to building strong states in Africa, Asia and now the former Soviet Union ignores the 'paradox of the state', in which the most important threats to security in the Third World (and often elsewhere) arise from states and regimes, and are directed against individuals and communal groups.[67] The creation of strong states that are not constrained within a broader security-building process (which necessarily involves such things as arms control) hardly represents a solution to 'threats to international peace and security'.

It is not difficult to see whose interests are sacrificed in all of this: those of countless millions of people whose states fail (actively or passively) in their fundamental duty to provide them with minimal security from force and violence. Although recent multilateral practice has adopted a definition of international peace and security that goes slightly beyond a purely state-centric focus on inter-state wars, its vision of community still treats the state as the central object and guarantor of international peace and security. The notion that it is ultimately individuals who are being secured is occluded. But in a century in which the greatest number of 'political' deaths have been perpetrated by states against their citizens, rather than in inter-state (or even internal) wars, the practical impact of this conception of how to achieve international peace and security is clear.[68]

The current resting point for multilateral action in the realm of international peace and security is inconsistent, weakly legitimate, and ultimately unsustainable. There are, however, three different directions in which matters could develop. Any of these three might provide more acceptable (that is, effective and legitimate) multilateral mechanisms, although there is no guarantee of this. The least radical move would retain the emphasis on shoring up the Westphalian order, but make the link between peace and good governance more explicit, and devote greater resources to creating states that do not diminish the security of their citizens. This would mark a fairly dramatic reinterpretation of Article 2(7), and would require the linking of peace and security operations to development and post-conflict disarmament processes. It would also require that Security Council operations be more accountable, transparent and consistent. The second approach would follow the lead of jurists such as Koskenniemi, and advocate a 'retreat' from activism, since the current operations and decision-making procedures have upset the balance between order and justice, originally captured by a division of powers (and

---

[67] Jackson, *Quasi-States*, 140.
[68] Rudolph Rummel estimates that more than 170 million deaths by 'democide' have occurred in this century. This can be compared to between 20 and 40 million deaths in warfare since 1945. See Rudolph Rummel, *Death By Government* (New Brunswick, Transaction Publishers, 1994).

a system of checks and balances) between the Security Council, the General Assembly and the International Court of Justice. According to his metaphor, the 'police' (who are responsible for maintaining order) have increasingly usurped the role of judges, metaphorically arresting, trying and punishing 'suspects' according to a great power logic that is illegitimate and unaccountable. The third (and most radical) approach would shift the understanding of security in 'threats to international peace and security' away from states and towards the international community of individuals over whom the multilateral order exercises some 'governance'. Of course, this would even more dramatically overturn the sovereignty paradigm, by formalizing the multilateral right of humanitarian action and intervention. But an analysis of whether (and how) any of these alternatives might emerge must be deferred for another time.

Chapter Three

Opening for Omnilateralism: A European View[1]

Wolfgang Pape

In the mass media we are used to seeing neologisms spring up every once in a while to describe new phenomena as they evolve. Recently, we thus have experienced the shift from geo-politics to geo-economics and now even to '*geo-psychology*'[2] in order to better understand what is happening in the world from France (from de Gaulle to soccer) to India (from disregard to the bomb). Rather than depict a situation of past or present, I have dubbed as 'omnilateralism' an appeal for a better 'geo-future.'[3]

Just consider: Japan has been repeatedly exposed to *uni*lateral American measures (victimization?). It has negotiated numerous treaties with other countries on a *bi*lateral basis (zero-sum games?). Japan is also a member of most of the so-called *multi*lateral institutions (passive listener?). Is it not time that it finally contributes to an all-comprising *omni*lateral system (commensurate with its economic power)?

As the logic of Europe as *Weltkind in der Mitten* (Goethe) indicates, there has to be some balance of weight on both sides, in the east as well as in the west of Europe. Without any doubt, America on the western side of Europe has contributed enormously to the setting-up of the multilateral system.

The multilateral system as it has evolved over recent decades can also be seen as a product of the Cold War[4] insofar as it has been very much influenced by the confrontational bilateralism between East and West in the ideo-political sense. With the fall of the Berlin Wall, it is therefore high time now to allow growth beyond the icy attitudes and warm up to new ideas, such as omnilateralism.

---

[1] This presentation reflects only the personal view of the author and cannot be attributed to any institution.
[2] See Flora Lewis, *International Herald Tribune*, 10 July 1998.
[3] The concept of 'omnilateralism' was first developed by Wolfgang Pape in *World Affairs* (July–Sep 1997), 94–109, following his fellowship at the Brookings Institute, Washington DC.
[4] Chalmers Johnson (JPRI Working Paper No. 22, July 1996, p. 15) even writes that 'for most of the Cold War, GATT was part of an American grand strategy against the USSR in which the U.S. traded access to its market and technologies in return for the support of nations such as Japan, South Korea, and Taiwan against communism'.

With regard to the main institutions such as the United Nations, the GATT/the WTO and the so-called Bretton-Woods system,[5] it is of course difficult – if not impossible – to imagine their creation without the proactive participation of the US. Similarly Western Europeans have contributed to the establishment of these organizations, for instance through the Atlantic Charter with the UK. These contributions can be tracked to a point that the multilateral system easily appears as not only Western-inspired, but even as an outgrowth of almost pure Western thinking, including of course its tolerance of otherness in pluralism.

For the average newspaper reader and non-expert it is hard to make out the influence of non-Western and in particular Asian countries on the setting up and even on the working processes of these institutions. Although some of those countries have been members or even founding fathers of the institutions, the Asians' impact on these multilateral institutions so far seems to have been minimal.

Often in the past, this was explained by the Asian countries' economic backwardness and poverty, until Japan caught up with the West after having joined the IMF in 1952 and GATT in 1955 (OECD in 1964) and subsequently benefited considerably from that multilateral system.

Most of the EC countries early on applied Art. 35 of GATT against Japan, thus denying to the country relations that were assured to the other contracting parties. As these restrictions were gradually lifted over the following years, Japan's trade partners perceived the need to at least partly replace those restrictions by Voluntary Restraint Agreements and similar arrangements.

In doing so, the question evidently remains even after decades of membership: has Japan also adapted its internal economic patterns to the basic principles of this Western-made multilateral system?[6]

Following the debate on Japan's industrial policy[7], some critics argued that GATT's traditional market-based and non-discriminatory orientation showed weaknesses and thus needed modification. The West then demanded that Japan play a more active role on the international stage 'commensurate with her economic might.'

---

[5] It is symptomatic that currently in the aftermath of the Asian Crisis there is a growing call to overhaul 'the architecture of the global financial system' (R. Rubin, US Treasury) and to bring the Bretton Woods institutions up to date. Even Japan's Sakakibara is quoted as saying that the IMF's 'checks and solutions are insufficient' (FT, 5 March 1998).

[6] Lei A. Nefiodew (*Der fünfte Kondratieff* (Wiesbaden, 1991), p. 201, bluntly denies such adaptation by describing 'Japans Unangepasstheit an die internationale Wirtschaftsgemeinschaft'.

[7] Cf esp. Chalmers Johnson's concept of Japan as a 'developmental state' (see his book *Miti and the Japanese Miracle* [Stanford, 1982], *passim*) and the ensuing discussion.

As a matter of fact, the Japanese mainstream understanding of internationalization or *kokusaika* is still too passive to lead to any proactive input into the multilateral system which would help it also to encompass the particularities of the internal workings of their naturally very Japanese society. The process of so-called deregulation might render the country's legal basis seemingly more similar to Anglo-Saxon concepts.

However, it will hardly or at least only in the long term alter ingrained patterns of behaviour on the Japanese islands. '*Kisei kanwa: soron sansei, kakuron hantai!*' or 'Softening of regulations: agreeing in principle, but opposing the details'. This slogan was recently confirmed when 80 per cent of the Japanese wanted further deregulation, while at the same time 70 per cent believed that certain areas with implications for their daily lives, like public security, welfare and culture, should be deregulated only 'with caution'.[8] Phrases taken from models elsewhere like 'Big Bang' (from First of April!) and the like often sound hollow when checked for actual substance of implementation and measured against the original idea.

One is sometimes tempted to compare this slow process with the speedy adoption of continental European laws during the Meiji period (for example, German BGB). Those alien rules were also without roots in the country's social culture which thus in many instances remained on the surface of the burnished dualism of *tatemae* and *honne*.[9] The German scholar Josef Kohler once explained law as a cultural phenomenon. Hence, if it is alien in a given society, such incompatibility creates friction or might even lead to forms of schizophrenia.[10]

Also the OECD points out in its 'Vision 2020' that the prospects for the New Global Age, in which all countries can be active players, depend on the ability to adapt to changes and emphasizes first the many 'behind-the-border' barriers which need to be tackled.[11]

There is now reason for some to fear a similar dualism could sharpen in a China which under outside pressure precipitately and superficially adopts Western rules,[12] but internally still cannot equally fast adapt her traditional patterns of behaviour.[13]

---

[8] See *Yomiuri Shimbun*, 27 June 1997.
[9] Time and again Japan used 'cultural differences' against 'universal fairness' as an argument in WTO, GATT, ISO and so on to defend particular rules in Japan from 'culturally different snow' demanding divergent standards for skis (see for details W. Pape, 'Nichttarifäre Handelshemmnisse in Japan', *Recht der Internationalen Wirtschaft* [Heidelberg, September 1990]) and recently alcohol as a 'social lubrication' justifying a lower tax on Shochu than the 'more moral stance' allows in the West (cf. *Tokyo Shinbun*, 22 February 1997).
[10] The increasing importance of cultural issues in international relations is exemplified by the fact that ethnic and religious strife figured prominently in all but three of the thirty-one major armed conflicts under way in 1994, according to studies by the Stockholm International Peace Research Institute (SIPRI), see Michael T. Klare, 'The New Global Schisms', www.mfa.gov.tr/NEWS/selti/11-96/04.htm, 1 November 1996.
[11] OECD Document 'Towards a New Global Age', C(97) 80, Paris 1997.
[12] According to the Director-General of the WTO, Renato Ruggiero, 'by the year 2005 all developing countries in the WTO will have the same degree of protection for

That for some – young people especially in China – the reception of western thinking has already gone too far finds its expression in the recent list of the *'No!'*-shouting bestsellers from first 'Japan that can say No' to similar titles for China and Asia as a whole. From the experience with *gaiatsu* in opening up Japan since the mid-nineteenth century,[14] to similar pressure from the outside on other countries, one might easily conclude that civil liberties in a state are inversely proportional to the impact of such external pressures.[15] Others go even farther in drawing up a worst-case scenario arguing that the economic determinism of the West could well cause 'violent efforts to throw off, to master, or to revenge, the invasive influence ... of disruptive Western ideas and values'.

According to this view of William Pfaff 'The internationalisation of any non-Western economy automatically undermines social practices, and religious and cultural norms. It is a literally subversive force.... There will sooner or later be a reaction.' On this timing, I should like to qualify Pfaff's analysis, as we in Europe and America also first had to develop these concepts: one of the major problems for East Asia is the incomparable speed of development.

First in Japan, followed by the 'Four Tigers' and then South-East Asia, the acceleration to reach industrialization and subsequently beyond has dramatically progressed with each 'wild goose' following Japan and now even the 'Dragon.' Social advances that have taken centuries in the UK to grow internally are now pushed into those countries within a few years. Backlashes, at least, cannot therefore be avoided, even in well-controlled societies such as South Korea (consider the New Labour Law, at issue with OECD standards, the government hardly disowning – if not even guiding – anti-import bids as 'frugality campaigns' for reasons of trade balance, thus possibly violating the basic principles of the WTO). Furthermore, there is a growing realization not only in Asia that nowadays modernization does not necessarily mean Westernization any more.

---

intellectual property as the United States' (*International Herald Tribune*, 27 November 1996). However, thereby he neglects the considerable gap in most countries between the Western-inspired international law and its actual implementation in culturally divergent societies. It has taken Japan, for instance, decades and the realization of Sony's trademark being copied in Latin America in the mid-1980s in order to effectively act against counterfeiting at home in Japan itself.

[13] Cf. *International Herald Tribune*, 2 January 1997: 'China's Legal Reforms May Backfire for Some, Little Effect Seen on Abuse by Police'.

[14] Partly as a reaction there is already talk of a 'reverse *gaiatsu*' by the EU and Japan that is 'multilateralised' against the US to see US policymakers forswear a negative hegemony and short-term unilateralism (cf. Susan Strange, EUI Working Paper RSC No. 94/10, p. 4).

[15] Such a conclusion is drawn also in the context of NATO enlargement by Ernst-Otto Czempiel, in Dieter Senghaas (ed.), *Frieden machen* (Frankfurt am Main, 1997); cf. also EU Ambassador E. Wilkinson, 26 March 1998 at the European Parliament.

Against superficial appearances, the recent Asian Crisis has only exacerbated these tendencies, as can be seen in particular in Indonesia. US-made medicines prescribed by the IMF ('social-engineering') – although heavily sweetened with a sugar coat of billions of dollars – are not easily swallowed even by the sick economies of the region.

The imposition of harsh and ruthless austerity policies by the IMF, as well as undifferentiated pushes for deregulation without regard to regional or national particularities, could aggravate a growing Asian backlash. Negative sentiments resulting especially from the so-called Rubin Doctrine in favour of (Western) banks having lent only in dollars to Asia, are already growing.[16]

'Some Asians are beginning to perceive such Western participation as nothing more than blatant exploitation.'[17] A new breed of financial professionals in Korea have taken up jobs as Shark-Watchers, helping companies to fend off hostile takeovers by foreigners as legal changes make hostile bids much easier.[18] These reactions might add to mob opposition to sharply rising prices, thus stirring up more ethnic and nationalist violence.[19] 'As more people lose their jobs, and once-regular purchases become unaffordable, the temptation to blame foreigners will become more acute.'[20] As a consequence, warnings of virulent anti-Americanism are growing louder, from Henry Kissinger and also others in Asia itself.

Leaving aside the more recent example of the Asian financial crisis, the reoccurrence of such direct clashes of domestic and international models cannot be entirely ruled out for the future. Their impact, however, can and should be mitigated by involving the non-Western countries much more as proactive stakeholders in the international system.

For instance, returning to the experience with Japan in GATT/the WTO, such unmitigated discrepancies between inside and outside in the case of China would not only cause much greater problems for the West than in Japan's case in view of

---

[16] Cf. *The Economist*, 10 January 1998.
[17] See *International Herald Tribune*, 20 January 1998: 'Think Twice About Forcing Change in Asia' in particular in view of increasing unemployment in those economies; cf. also the danger of China becoming less open as indicated by Rone Tempest in *International Herald Tribune*, 26 November 1997 'China's Trade Barriers Provide Shelter in Asia's Storm', and *The Economist*, 24 January 1998, p. 76 'China is now likely to learn from its neighbours' experience and proceed more slowly in opening up its own financial system and making its currency fully convertible.' Also Taiwan plans 'to tighten the country's financial regulatory environment' (Oxford Analytica Brief, 27 November 1997) and its 'Currency Controls May Be Kept Beyond 2000', *International Herald Tribune*, 19 January 1998.
[18] See *International Herald Tribune*, 5 February 1998.
[19] Cf. *International Herald Tribune*, 10 February 1998 'Suharto Talks up Economy as Unrest Spreads' in Indonesia where protesters carried national flags and vented their anger on the richer minority of Chinese descent.
[20] See *The Economist*, 24 January 1998, p. 64 ; but already before the Asian Crisis, David A. Hitchcock described how 'positive images of the US are beginning to fade in that region' based on 100 interviews in seven East Asian countries ('Factors Affecting East Asian Views of the United States', CSIS Report, Washington DC, 1997).

China's size.[21] But they would also create even more problems, because China is clearly more assertive internationally, as the re-emerging self-styled 'Middle Kingdom' (in its own naming)[22] supported by a highly active overseas network of another 50 million.[23] China is already the world's second largest holder of foreign exchange reserves, after Japan.[24]

This fundamental attitude of the Chinese seeing themselves still in the centre is clearly coming to the fore again. 'What interests China with regard to foreign countries is above all the resources and methods of enrichment. Yet the Chinese are hardly more interested than before in cultures and lifestyles. Modern-day China does not experience the tremendous cultural curiosity which Japan has always felt for the West ever since the Meiji era'.[25]

Unless China joins as an integral 'stake-holder', and not merely a passive listener, in the existing multilateral system,[26] this system remains only 'multilateral Western'. That claimed-for 'world order' would not be truly all-comprising and thus would remain unable to claim genuine universal values for all.

Without going into details of underlying philosophies, there are good reasons to shed doubt on the absolutism that we have reached the 'end of history'. Rather, we can see culturally divergent identities increasingly re-emerge, after the contentions of the hot and cold wars of our century had covered them up under

---

[21] With its trade surplus with the US expected to be greater than that of Japan's in 1997, China has already bought a sizable amount of US Treasury bonds exceeding that of Japan in 1996. 'China could jolt the US financial market as well as the world economy by dumping those bonds ... such a danger involving China is much greater compared with Japan's holding of US bonds' (see *Mainichi Shinbun*, 24 February 1997).

Harou Shimada, who advises the Japanese government, fears: 'If you bring in 1.2 billion workers at those wages, that can destroy the global trading system' (*International Herald Tribune*, 7 March 1997).

[22] Prof. Yuan Ming of the Chinese Academy of Social Science expressed this sentiment during an international conference in Beijing in early November 1996 with the traditional saying: 'China changes the world by changing itself!' Cf. Also the recent campaign in China for a 'spiritual civilisation' (*Washington Post*, 30 January 1997). The China expert Prof. Lucian W. Pye of the Massachussetts Institute of Technology sees a 'xenophobic nationalism and combative pragmatism' move into the country's spiritual wasteland at present (*International Herald Tribune*, 27 November 1996).

[23] This network is most obviously spearheaded by Singapore which seems to have served as a model not only for the late Deng Xiaoping (see Andreas Huber, *Die wirtschaftlichen und politischen Beziehungen der VR China zu den ASEAN-Staaten am Beispiel Singapurs* [Hamburg 1995], pp. 86–89).

[24] *Financial Times*, 4 March 1997, p. 4: 'China joins forum on forex'.

[25] See Jean-Luc Domenach, '*China and the World: Uncertainties and Ambivalences*', IFRI (Paris, December 1997), p. 3.

[26] David Shambaugh (*International Herald Tribune*, 31 January 1997) similarly calls for China to be a 'productive partner in the community of nations'.

superficial layers of ideologies. Not only in terms of geopolitics, there is a multipolar[27] constellation emerging.

The mobile individuals of today are seeking their personal roots more and more in regional and even local cultures in order to balance their loss of identity in the globalizing economies. This is the case in Europe as well as in Asia where even Anglo-Saxon pop music is losing ground to local or regional hits.[28] Thus eroding the American and British dominance, a new group of singers like Eros Ramazotti and Andrea Bocelli reflect today's 'Eurotaste' to a degree that even *The Economist* of London elevates them to 'pan-European stars'.[29]

In order to balance such reorientation towards regional and even local cultural phenomena (compare also the American bestseller *Jihad vs. McWorld*), world bodies rightfully deserve their name only if these organizations fully encompass the proactive partnership of all players on this globe, from Occident as well as Orient.

The absolutism of neither Hegel, nor more recently Fukuyama, claimed 'the End of History', but the forces of pertinent, traded cultural notions and new patterns of communication (for example 'death of distance' through the Internet) are too strong to be any longer neglected in global governance. These divergent cultural presumptions have to be understood first in order to establish a sense of 'co-ownership', and an inclusive approach for international institutions which could provide an additional source of legitimacy. The need for such legitimacy has become obvious again particularly in the recent Asian Crisis when IMF measures on occasions were opposed as being solely Western-made. Therefore, only stakeholding through proactive contributions by all members would allow the international system to evolve into a modern form of participatory governance, to be dubbed omnilateralism.

One example where Eastern concepts might greatly contribute to world-wide problem-solving can be derived from their more holistic approach to nature, and consequently more direct comprehension of the interdependence in our common ecological system.[30]

---

[27] Multipolarity pops up frequently now in international declarations without US participation; especially cf. Russo-Chinese Joint Declaration of 23 April 1997 in Moscow on the 'multipolar world' for example the reinforcing role of the UN and promotion of the dialogue with the Third World, particularly in view of amending the world trading system.

[28] Cf. for instance the recent phenomenal growth of ethnic music, particularly in East Asia with the 'Queen of Dangdut' selling 500,000 records across Asia (far more than the Spice Girls, the most popular Western group) where now 70 per cent of record sales are generated by local artists (see *International Herald Tribune*, 30 May 1997). This trend of localization of music balances the globalization of visual communications in the computer age where symbols from icons to *kanji* increasingly cross cultural borders (for details see Wolfgang Pape, *Shaping Factors in East Asia by the Year 2000 and Beyond* (Hamburg 1996), pp. 29–32).

[29] See *The Economist*, 21 February 1998, p. 81.

[30] One concrete manifestation of the holistic approach is the long-established Japanese horticulture of minaturising in scale an intact whole landscape (Sansui; Bonsai also for

On the highly topical issue of the protection of the environment, it is the old Buddhist principles of interdependence in nature and cycles of reincarnation that lend themselves much better to understand the need for recycling of materials than our Western concept – or rather illusion – of creation from zero. Holistic views of nature tend to conserve, whereas our analytical approaches often tend to divide before conceiving common elements.

If some East Asian economies have not yet manifested these holistic values as much as could be expected from their religious background, this can be explained mainly by the rapid speed of development and the resulting social transformation that presently does not yet fully allow the reflection of traditional values. In general, poor countries have the world's worst environmental problems. They cannot afford to put up with them.[31] With the stabilization of a broader middle class in society, there will re-emerge a stronger identification with original values, as we have seen already in Japan since the late 1980s.

Concrete examples of how the Chinese have practised for over a thousand years the concept of recycling can be found in their traditional – now called 'bio-intensive' – techniques of agriculture. Normally, several life-systems are co-ordinated in sequence: for instance, rabbit excrement falls into a pool of ducks and fish to fertilize it, and the pool then irrigates fields for rice and vegetables, the waste of which in turn feeds the rabbits. Many people might think that this might be good only for the Chinese. But the surprise lies in the fact that it seems to be truly good for all, that is, 'omnibus'. For example, basically the same techniques are now applied by John Jeavons and his colleagues of 'Ecology Action' in their 'bio-intensive mini-agriculture' in Willits, Northern California.[32]

China), whilst gardening in the West traditionally amounts to systematic cutting down into geometric separation of the elements and sorts of plants (for example, the Parc de Versailles). Seeing 'nature as the mother' (Takeshi Umehara, *Voice* [Tokyo July 1995], 166; in Japanese) is now perceived as one of the reasons for Japan's success to go beyond modernisation. Not by accident, the Worldwatch Institute gave Japan ('an impressive record') and China ('one of the most elaborate, ambitious national Agenda 21 plans') relatively good marks on their environment policies; see 'State of the World 1997', New York 1997.

[31] See *The Economist*'s 'Survey of Development and the Environment', 21 March 1998, p. 3.
[32] see 'Factor Four – Doubling Wealth, Halfing Resource Use' by E. von Weizsäcker, A.B. Lovins and L.H. Lovins, Earthscan, pp. 131–132: 'Many techniques of bio-intensive agriculture and horticulture are known since over thousand years in China ... Normally, several life-systems are co-ordinated on top of each other: Rabbits excrements fall into pool of ducks and fish to fertilise it, and the pool irrigates fields for rice and vegetables, the waste of which in turn feeds the rabbits.' Similar techniques are now applied by John Jeavons and his colleagues of Ecology Action in their 'bio-intensive mini-agriculture' in Willits, Northern California.

Another concrete manifestation of the holistic approach that could serve 'omnibus' and enrich all our lives can be seen in the long-established Japanese horticultural art of only reducing in scale an otherwise intact whole landscape (cf. Sansui; Bonsai also for China), whilst gardening in the West traditionally amounts to systematic cutting down into geometric separation of the elements and sorts of plants etc. (as in the Parc de Versailles). Seeing 'nature as the mother'[33] is now perceived as one of the reasons for Japan's success to go beyond modernization. Not by accident, the Worldwatch Institute gave Japan ('an impressive record') and China ('one of the most elaborate, ambitious national Agenda 21 plans') relatively good marks on their environment policies.[34] The fact that Chinese cities have relatively few polluting motorized bikes, mopeds, and so on, but rather millions of human-driven non-polluting bicycles, nowadays seems to be the result less of technical and economic backwardness, but the intended outcome of a strict license system. Apparently, it is 'very difficult to get a license for a motorcycle and frequently it is refused'.[35]

Looking for other examples of possible Oriental contributions to mend extreme, and in the long-term harmful, behaviour in the international and also internal contexts, one is tempted to cast a critical eye also on exaggerations of the 'private' (cf. *privare*, Lat.= robbed from the public) individual centring on a relationship with an absolute 'god of the book' which often leads to righteousness and overdone litigation (hence the new trend in the US towards more arbitration).[36]

This contrasts in Confucian-Buddhist Asia with the idea of *messhi boko* (Japanese for self-sacrificing for the public good). Similarly indicative is the basic understanding of humans being in-between (Japanese *ningen* as woman in-between) and the strong identification with the *ie* or house as a group rather than only the individual in isolation.

Not entirely unrelated is the generic nexus of *guanxi* or connections in China which is increasingly seen as a traditional version of the modern concept of networking, be it in person or only virtually through the Internet. Some go even farther and suggest the linked verses in dialogue of the Japanese *renga* tradition of multi-dimensional unity as the possible structure for networking in the information age. For them there is a need for 'synthetic' perspectives with a concept of 'circulation' (or 'recycling') and 'symbiosis' instead of the Western analytic methods with an extreme belief in (linear) progress through competition of individuals.[37]

There must also be numerous further examples for the comparative researcher in the Arabic world. For instance, it would be perhaps instructive to study the concept of interest-free loans as prescribed under Sharia for Islamic banking which

---

[33] See Takeshi Umehara, *Voice* (Tokyo July 95), 166; in Japanese.
[34] See '*State of the World 1997*' (New York, 1997), p. 9.
[35] Prof. Lijun WANG, EUVP, Bruxelles, 22 May 1997.
[36] See *International Herald Tribune*, III.97.
[37] Cf. Kenichi Ito, 'Non-European Civilizations Rediscovered', Symposium at the JDZ Berlin, 1 June 1996.

is clearly on the rise now.[38] 'Money cannot make more money. Money must be used productively. And risk has to be shared.' These are the slogans of the Islamic banker that might be worth considering, in particular in the wake of the so-called Asian Financial Crisis.

Of course, Muslims too recognize that interest plays a very important role in the modern economic system in the Western world. It has been viewed not only as an integral part of the price mechanism, but also as an important policy instrument for governments' control over the economy.[39] Samuelson defines interest simply as 'the price or rental for the use of money'. Keynes goes a step further in stating that the 'money rate of interest is the percentage of excess of a sum of units of money contracted'. Seen from the perspective of Islamic economics, Abu Saud also emphasizes the aspect of excess when he regards 'interest as the excess of money paid by the borrower to the lender over and above the principal' for its use over a certain period of time.[40]

Muslims consider the excessive nature of interest (*riba*) to breed exploitation and inequalities that run counter to the egalitarian objectives of Islam. Hence lending money for interest was deprecated, and in most cases prohibited, by all the biblical religions.[41]

Islamic banking is based on equity (*musharakah*) in a profit/loss-sharing system (*mudarabah*) which aims at more stability and efficiency in allocating resources. Such partnership-financing makes the financier participate in the risk together with the entrepreneur in the business venture.[42] However, in spite of more than two decades of Islamic financial institutions working in the field of banking with a world-wide growth now of 15 per cent, 'interest-free techniques and the specifications of basic ratings are still under discussion'.[43]

We have seen the failure of the systems of state planning and become increasingly aware of the great burden levied upon major parts of the population in the name of the market economy. Therefore, it is not only for Muslim experts that the Islamic systems seem to be the only credible alternative concept not yet discredited by practical experience.[44] The debate on these systems should also be

---

[38] See *International Herald Tribune*, 22 September 1998, 'Not for Muslims Only: Islamic Finance on the Rise'.
[39] Cf. Saad Abdul Sattar Al-Harran, '*Islamic Finance*', *Malaysia*, 1993, p. 5.
[40] Cf. Abu Saud, M.'*Money, Interest and Qirad in Islam*', in: Studies in Islamic Economics, Leicester, 1983, p. 64.
[41] Cf. Saad Abdul Sattar Al-Harran, '*Islamic Finance*', *Malaysia*, 1993, p. 6.
[42] Cf. Dr.Saad Al-Harran, 'Leading Issues in Islamic Banking and Finance', *Malaysia*, 1995, p. vii; Western investment banks that take up equity of the recipient of the loan in a similar fashion share at least part of the risk of the entreprise to be financed.
[43] See Volker Nienhaus, 'Islamische Wirtschaftsordnungen', *Internationale Politik* (Bonn August 1997), p. 17.
[44] *Idem*, p. 14.

pursued by non-Muslims in an open spirit with a view towards enriching the omnilateral system with appropriate elements from Islamic economics, not at least also in order to avoid clashes of 'the West against the Rest'.

There are certainly other elements to be drawn not only from Asian cultures not yet explored here like for instance India, but also from other continents that could enhance global governance, 'omnibus' as co-owning and thus proactive stakeholders.

The search for such constructive elements in emerging societies as contributions towards building a truly omnilateral system will, of course, remain an ongoing task that will never be finished as long as history flows and does not end, which is our basic axiom and starting point.

If omnilateralism – in contrast to the merely multilateral system of today – cannot be realized, there is a danger at some point in the future that China, in view of its own importance,[45] either will not see any more a need to join the 'Western-made' institutions, or if entering as only a 'passive member' (like Japan into GATT in 1955), China might sooner or later break up the inculcated purely Western concepts from the inside like an alien and outgrown cuckoo in a nightingale's nest.

Admittedly, such omnilateralism seems to be a rather idealistic vision which underrates the urgent need and this year's window of opportunity to 'constructively engage' China into the world trading system. However, it is precisely the constructive nature of the engagement (that is, building together) which should reflect China's input to build an omnilateral system. Otherwise, there is clearly a risk of taking non-Westerners only into the existing system *tel quel*, like in a conservative club which accepts a new member who just happened to move into the 'neighbourhood' of the club, in terms of development (like South Korea into the OECD) or have grown sufficiently important as the new boy on the block (Russia into 'Group of 8' and China into WTO etc.?).

The multinational organizations, however, are expanding their geographical and thereby also cultural reach, and hence should likewise encompass their new members' particularities. This, of course, does not at all exclude the existence of universal fundamental values, as agreed upon by all 'omnilaterally'.

When I quoted Goethe's *Weltkind in der Mitten* at the beginning to locate a European in-between America and Asia, I wanted to indicate the relative distance and nearness of Europe to both. As we physically, or the electrons on the Internet, travel over the continents nowadays, one might start to wonder if there is really anybody 'unique' in this world: the Japanese islanders at the periphery of Asia who have often so pretended, or the pioneering Americans now as 'cultural creatives'[46] on their seemingly endless mainland with their exceptionalism?

---

[45] China is already now the world's second largest holder of foreign exchange reserves, only after Japan (*Financial Times*, 4 March 1997, p. 4: 'China joins forum on forex').

[46] See Paul Ray, 1995 (24 June 1997 at Cdp, Bruxelles) pointing out the fast growth of this new idealistic group of people in the US.

Seymour Lipset in his book *American Exceptionalism* indirectly confirmed us in the belief that we Europeans are in many respects somewhere in the middle between the extremes at both ends of this shrinking world.

If one accepts Europe as *Weltkind in der Mitten*, then naturally there evolve opportunities for us Europeans to assume a role as mediator.[47] This is a role Europe can should play much more often. But its preoccupation with its own integration process (now in particular with its East) has hitherto prevented it fulfilling that function. The Cold War had strengthened the alliance with America, but left the 'missing link 'with East Asia. It is time the '*Weltkind* regained its balance and opened up to omnilateralism!

One important step in that direction was taken with the establishment of ASEM, the AsiaEurope Meeting, which took place in Bangkok 1996 for the first time and has become a point of crystallization in recent European policy towards East Asia. In view of the second ASEM summit in early April in London, it is certainly timely to explore its background somewhat more in detail.

The traditional 'leanings' of the United Kingdom towards Asia and in particular Germany's evolving enthusiasm for the increased opportunities in that region (Bonn's *Asien Konzept* of 1993) had already prepared a fertile ground upon which the European Commission in early 1994 had planted its comprehensive policy paper *Towards a New Asia Strategy*. The goals of this basic document were, in a nutshell, twofold: to raise the EU's profile in Asia and to promote better mutual understanding.

With this strategy, co-operation had become the keyword in EU–Asia relations, and unlike US Secretary of State Christopher in November 1996 in Shanghai, Europeans do not regard it as too hackneyed or even lacking credibility to link it with the term 'partnership'. The word 'co-operation' is now omnipresent in the 'Communications' of the EU on Asia.

These so-called 'Communications' in general reflect a consensus for recommended policies as reached among the currently fifteen member-states upon a proposal by the European Commission, the executive branch of the Union.

For instance, in the main EU Communication on Japan of March 1995 the word '*Co-operation*' comes up almost thirty times, and in the Communication on China more than thirty times. In the case of Japan, you could easily say that it was a fast road 'from confrontation to co-operation'. Some people even feel the change was too fast, more like speeding in a Porsche on the Autobahn. That is: beyond the recommended speed of 130 km/h, but still in a rather safe vehicle.

---

[47] Such mediation by Europe is also of importance, for instance, in Japan's dealing with Africa where EU countries are more experienced, or even in South-East Asia where the Japanese are burdened with history and appreciate the assistance of a third party.

However, for the first AsiaEurope summit, 1996 in Bangkok, both sides clearly considered co-operation necessary from the outset, because through complementary 'strategic alliances' closer ties could better be established between the two regions.

For that purpose, ASEAN had invited China, Japan and South Korea to participate in the first ASEM, thus forming an Asian side of 'ASEAN plus 3', that is, ten Asian countries.

It is interesting to note that the self-chosen format of the participating countries, 'ASEAN plus 3', coincides with the membership of the East-Asian Economic Caucus (EAEC, or 'Caucus without Caucasians') proposed by Malaysia's Prime Minister Dr Mahathir.

In spite of pre-Summit uncertainties and earlier scepticism about ASEM, the Bangkok meeting of leaders at the highest level in March last year was regarded as a 'success beyond expectation'. It has marked a historical turning point in the relations between the two regions, as a new dialogue among equals between Europe and Asia has begun to replace the notion of the 'missing link' in the Triad.

This first ASEM confirmed the clear will on both sides to develop further a genuine partnership among equals. It has laid the basis for a strengthened political and economic dialogue. It opened new avenues for co-operation, in a wide range of areas including global issues such as environment and crime, and in particular in strengthening mutual awareness and cultural links between Asia and Europe. It confirmed the interest of expanding our dialogue on human values, in a constructive climate and respecting our cultural diversity.

To list a few examples of the follow-up actions: there are Business Fora, Meetings of Ministers of Finance and the Economy, an Environmental Technology Centre, an AsiaEurope Foundation, Youth and University Exchange Programmes, but also co-operation in the multilateral framework like dialogues on the reform of the UN and meetings on Trade and Investment which have contributed to the consensus-building in the WTO last autumn in Singapore.

A surprising reaction after the meeting came from Malaysia's Prime Minister, as he was one of the most sceptical at the outset: 'Dr Mahathir prefers Asem to Apec'[48] read the headline in Kuala Lumpur of an article including the following soundbites:

> [Asem] has been more successful than [Apec]

---

[48] Cf. *Sunday Star*, Malaysia, 3 February 1996; Apec's difficulties in relying merely on peer pressure for liberalization because of the misunderstandings between the Americans and the Asians are exemplified most recently by the call of Mexico to clarify the forum's basic plans for free trade: 'Free trade for lots of countries has a very different meaning', the country's trade minister said recently, pointing out that any question 'What do you mean by free trade?' in Apec 'is seen as a spoiler' (FT, 12.2.97). More optimistic was still Y. Funabashi 'Asia Pacific Fusion', IIE, Washington DC, 1995.

> European leaders acknowledged that Asia should not be expected to follow European standards immediately as Europe had taken a long time to be where they are.
>
> Europe had avoided thorny issues that would have caused confrontations and had instead stressed on development.

Most unexpected was not so much the partly condescending criticism from major third countries, but the surprising reaction from some countries to discuss as a quasi-counterbalance the grouping of a so-called 'JUSCANZ'. This initiative to bring together *J*apan, the *US*A, *C*anada, *A*ustralia and *N*ew Zealand in response to ASEM is very flattering. It shows that ASEM, in its early stages, is taken much more seriously by outsiders than originally predicted. In particular, the reported endeavours of JUSCANZ to also include Norway and Switzerland as EU outsiders might give rise to new theories of anchoring or even containment.

Such moves – sometimes perhaps smiled upon as desperate in fear of being left out (cases of 'geo-psychology'?) – only underline the necessity for the overarching international system to comprise all members as proactive stakeholders. Thus also their institutions are further legitimized in a more participatory form of governance towards true omnilateralism.

Not the private[49] car, but the 'omnibus', for and by all, might be the right vehicle for a better 'geo-future'.

---

[49] *privare* (Lat.) = to rob (from public).

PART II
GLOBAL SECURITY, ECONOMIC ORDER AND MULTILATERALISM

PART II

Chapter Four
Multilateralism and International Political Economy: The Global Level

Jean-Pierre Lehmann

Globalization: So What's New?

Globalization has become a buzz-word that can mean everything and anything. It has positive connotations in certain quarters – especially among multinational corporations (MNCs) – and pejorative connotations in other quarters, including the French (for whom *mondialisation* equals *américanisation*), most NGOs, trade unions, and left-wing political parties, movements and journals.

So we should be clear from the start, that in our lexicon 'globalization' is not necessarily synonymous with 'McDonald-ization'! 'McDonald-ization' may be a side-effect of globalization, but it is not a driving force or a key feature.

Globalization refers to the intensification of the economic interdependence of the world-economy primarily through the movement of capital in various forms. That movement of capital consists of the following: trade in bonds and equities, currency transactions, cross-border bank lending, foreign direct investment (FDI) and the capital transactions carried out from trade in goods and services. Globalization means that these flows of capital can occur more or less in unimpeded fashion: that is, there are no major barriers. This in turn arises from the fact that in the 1990s, most trading nations have fully or partially abolished those means of control that would have inhibited the process. Global norms are adhered to.

Interdependence is illustrated in many forms. One is the growing global integration of production. In a non-protectionist trading environment, it is possible – indeed highly desirable – to have various levels of the chain of production distributed in different parts of the world. Assembly is done on a global basis and a great deal of the production process is 'virtual'. Interdependence is acutely illustrated by both the herd and the contagion effects that occur in the movement of capital, as has been witnessed in the Mexican debt crisis of 1995 and more recently by the Asian financial crisis. Global contagion can be seen from the fact, for example, that the price of copper is falling precipitously because Chile has become much more dependent on trade with Asia (about 35 per cent of exports). Herds move (stampede) in, herds move out, contagion spreads.

One should always be suspicious of buzz-words and all forms of jargon and avoid using them so far as possible. Among the 'globo-sceptics' (have I coined a term?), there is a fairly prominent school which says, in essence, 'yes, globalization there may be, but it's nothing new, it was all happening at the end of the nineteenth century'.[1] Certainly, it is true that, as the IMF puts it, 'by some measures, international economic integration increased just as much in the 50 years before World War I as in recent decades, and reached comparable levels'. Furthermore, the driving forces were somewhat comparable: 'then, as now, integration was driven in large part by the proliferation of markets and rapid technological change'.[2]

A good history comparing Globalization-I (late nineteenth century) and Globalization-II (late twentieth century) remains to be written. It is a fascinating subject, which includes many of the same actors, but not without twists in the tale. During Globalization-I a prominent British merchant bank called Baring's was, among other things, instrumental in financing railway development in the Argentine. If in Globalization-I, however, Baring's was a major force, in Globalization-II it re-emerged as a major farce, played out through its dramatic collapse in Singapore. There are many strands indeed to this good story.

Whether the denouement of Globalization-II occurs in a manner comparable to the way it occurred at the end of Globalization-I, that is, through carnage, war, destruction and fascist ideologies, remains to be seen. We will touch on this briefly in a later section of this chapter.

For now, however, having said that one should be a priori and adamantly suspicious of buzz-words, it is certainly the view of this author that the term 'globalization' has meaning and that it is indeed appropriate to use it. There has taken place in the last decade or so a phenomenon that is quite powerful, extraordinary and new. Globalization may not be the most felicitous term to describe this phenomenon, but for lack of a better alternative it will have to do.

The most fundamental feature that distinguishes Globalization-II from Globalization-I is that in the latter version, the term 'globalization' has a much greater ring of credibility – in three respects.

The first is that is that in the late nineteenth century the players were barely a score of Atlantic countries (with Japan as a latecomer, but operating in a primarily regional space), whereas today virtually all countries of the globe either are players

---

[1] See, for example, Paul Bairoch and Richard Kozul-Wright, 'Globalization Myths: Some Historical Reflections on Integration, Industrialization, and Growth in the World Economy', UNCTAD paper no. 113, March 1996.
[2] IMF, *World Economic Outlook*, May 1997, Annex, 'Globalization in Historical Perspective', p. 112.

or aspire to be players.³ Although by no means is global wealth or opportunity evenly divided across the globe – indeed very far from it, a point we shall return to – nevertheless the second respect in which globalization today connotes greater credibility is that although the dominant players remain primarily entities (MNCs) emanating from Atlantic powers, there has been a shift to competition emerging from the Pacific, initially Japan, but increasingly including globalizing firms from other countries of the East Asian region. An illustration: Latin America now trades more with the five leading trading entities of East Asia (China, Hong Kong, Taiwan, Korea and Japan), than it does with the countries of the EU.

The third is in the nature of the technology. Peter Drucker has said that what is currently going on in information technology is not another industrial revolution, but a fundamental intellectual revolution, the likes of which has not been seen since the invention of Johann Gutenberg half a millennium ago. The advent of information technology will ultimately totally revolutionize the organization, usage, communication and diffusion of information. As exciting as the technological advances of the late nineteenth century were and as formidable in opening up new geographical horizons, these were nothing in comparison with the pace of current scientific discovery and the very vast horizons of cyberspace!

As the IMF report remarks:

> The process observed before 1914 could hardly be called 'globalization', however, since large parts of the world did not participate and also because the speed of transport and communication was such that it was much less feasible than it is today to organize markets, or to operate firms, at the global level. Furthermore, international financial markets today are characterised by much larger gross flows, with a much larger variety of financial instruments being traded across borders.

Globalization and the Prospects of Peace and Prosperity

By no means is the world perfect. The obscurantist forces of religion still prevail, as can be seen anywhere, but most poignantly perhaps in Algeria, Israel and Northern Ireland.⁴ The terrifying tenacity of man's inhumanity remains tragically visible in former Yugoslavia, Cambodia and Rwanda, to name only three of many possible examples. The remarkable economic growth that has occurred in recent decades notwithstanding, an enormous degree of poverty remains, including

---

³ I have written in more detail about this in two recent articles: Jean-Pierre Lehmann, 'The Millennium: New Century, New Prospects', *World Today* (January 1998), and 'Government and Business in Global Markets', *Financial Times* (27 March 1998).

⁴ One could hardly avoid being amused by the audacity, or astonished by the hypocrisy, of the pope recently telling Fidel Castro that he should allow more dissent in Cuba. Will Castro get a chance to convey the same message in the Vatican?

among those very countries that have experienced high growth rates. Persistent discrimination against and abuse of women, world-wide, continue to stand out as an indictment of our times. There are other tragedies and anomalies.

Nevertheless, it is also true that never in recorded history has there been such fantastic peace and prosperity, never have the opportunities been greater. The phenomenon of globalization is intimately connected with this glorious perspective.

The three central pillars of globalization are the business strategies of firms – primarily their willingness to invest their resources (men and money) abroad – the supporting technologies, and the international economic order. Reference has already been made to the importance and extraordinary prospects of technology. For the purposes of this paper, not too much attention needs to be paid to business strategies. It can be taken as a given that most firms have and will retain globalization strategies. Here, greater consideration needs to be given to the international economic order.

From the vantage point of 1998, it can be stated, and stressed, that never has the world seen a truly global economic club of members adhering, or aspiring to adhere, to the same rules and regulations of an open, multilateral trading system, as it is experiencing at present. In the nineteenth century there were the colonizers and the colonized. During four-and-a-half decades after World War II, the world-economy was divided vertically – between a capitalist West and a communist East – and horizontally between a rich North and a poor South. These divisions were both driven by and bred diverse economic doctrines and systems, including some pretty insane ones. The order of the day was mutual suspiciousness across all axes. An investor from the North might be permitted in the South, but only as a necessary evil.

All this has changed dramatically. In 1990 there were just over 100 nations which were members of the WTO. By October 1997 there were 132 members and 30 observers, all of which (with the exception of the Holy See) are currently negotiating to join the WTO. This is one of the most admirable consequences of the collapse of the Soviet Union on the one hand, and a brilliant sign of the sea change that has taken place in the policies and attitudes of most developing countries in respect to trade liberalization and the multilateral system on the other. The outliers – Iraq, Iran, Libya, Syria, North Korea, Cuba – can hardly be counted on the fingers of two hands and, on the basis of current trends, it is a reasonably safe bet that in the course of the next few years they too will be applying to join.

The trends in membership are reflected in the evolution of laws and regulations. For example, in 1996 there were 138 changes in 144 trade measures that were implemented in 65 countries. Among these changes, 89 per cent were conducive to trade expansion and facilitation, with only 11 per cent imposing more constraints and controls.⁵ Financial services, telecommunications, agriculture and direct investments are among the many items that are being or will be increasingly brought under the multilateral, transparent global system.

The two key geopolitical forces for change, not by any means unrelated, in this direction have been the end of the Cold War and the redefinition of policies (and ideologies) among countries of what was formerly known as the Third World. Attitudes and policies among Third World countries have changed, from autarky and import substitution to becoming more open and outward-looking, for a number of reasons.

For one thing, it became abundantly clear by the 1980s that the more closed the economies the more paltry the economic results, the more open the more abundant the results. As economies opened, the view also increasingly prevailed that foreign direct investments were not a bad thing – especially if they created jobs, added value, transferred technology and boosted foreign earnings through exports – and that MNCs might be given a red carpet rather than a raspberry (or worse). Indeed, by the early 1990s, so forceful and so plentiful had this positive movement towards FDI become, that the operative paradigm of the international economy became one whereby corporations compete globally for market share – increasingly through investment, rather than just exports – while countries compete globally to attract investment share.⁶

In the global age of freer trade, the driving force of FDI that prevailed in the 1970s and 1980s – to overcome protectionist barriers – is no longer as important or as operative. Also with MNCs having become far more global, their local loyalties erode. In some countries, for example Sweden, domestic companies are moving abroad not just the lower end of their manufacturing operations, but their R&D and head offices as well. Thus countries need to compete not only to attract foreign investment, but also to retain domestic investment, and countries compete in many cases for similar investments across continents. When, say, the Japanese firm NEC decides it will set up a new semiconductor plant, the competition to attract the investment may range across Alabama in the US, Scotland in the UK, Penang in Malaysia, Kitakyushu in Japan and Monterey in Mexico. Since competition between areas seeking to attract investment is also increasingly determined less by crude labour costs than by quality of infrastructure, education, productivity, and so on, by and large the nature of current global competition between states and between firms is virtual rather than vicious. It is a good thing.

The changed policies of Third World countries also arise from geopolitical considerations. In the days of the Cold War, the USSR and the USA competed to

---

[5] See, Richard Blackhurst, 'The WTO and the Global Economy', *The World Economy* (1997); and Michael Hart, 'The WTO and the Political Economy of Globalization', *Journal of World Trade* (1997).

[6] See John Stopford and Susan Strange, *Rival States Rival Firms* (1991).

attract allies. This was done in great part by hand-outs. To secure the balance of power in a particular region of the world, or even to secure a vote at the General Assembly of the UN, Washington and Moscow would pay off targeted countries, or rather the tyrannical rulers of the targeted countries. The famous CIA memo referring to Mobutu: 'he may be a son-of-a-bitch, but he's our son-of-a-bitch' says it all, as does the lavish amount of 'aid' that was transferred into his Swiss bank accounts. That has now changed. Mobutu died a lonely man and had a lonely burial.[7]

The end of the Cold War is not quite yet the end of history. Conflicts still occur and will continue to occur. They are exclusively regional conflicts at present, but there is no law that stipulates that global conflict will not reoccur for whatever reason. An important force lying behind the peaceful and prosperous reality and prospects associated with the globalization of the late twentieth century has been the presence and power of *Pax Americana*. It is perhaps more than just a happy coincidence that the leading economic power and the leading political power should be one and the same.

Although most signs of the 1980s seemed to point to the fact that the famous Paul Kennedy thesis[8] would indeed become prophesy, by the early 1990s the economically disastrous Reagan years came to an end and the American economy enjoyed a very spirited comeback. It is difficult to envisage how globalization could have occurred without the twin engines of American economic and geopolitical power. It follows that the future of globalization will be closely tied to the future course of *Pax Americana*. We will return therefore to this question later.

Concerns of Globalization

Globalization has its supporters and it has its enemies. It also counts people who (like myself) are basically in favour, but worry that some of its features and consequences may get out of hand. Let us go through some of these concerns, not all of which, by any means, I sympathize with, but all of which are nevertheless part of the public policy and public opinion debate.

---

[7] For example, although Mobutu attended the funeral of the Japanese Emperor Hirohito, no member of the Japanese imperial family reciprocated by attending Mobutu's funeral.

[8] Paul Kennedy, *The Rise and Fall of the Great Powers: Economic Change and Military Conflict, 1500–2000* (1987). In an oversimplified nutshell, the 'Kennedy thesis' was that as powers grew, their vested interests spread; they therefore increased military expenditure to defend these interests, resulting in due course in being overextended, hence no longer having the economic resources to meet their commitments and defend their interests, which would in turn lead to decline. This pattern of history was occurring with the US. The thesis seemed all the more valid during the late 1980s as the American economy appeared fated to be overtaken by the Japanese economy.

The quotation from the IMF noted that in this phase of globalization both the scale and the scope of global financial transactions are without parallel. This is not a new innings, but an entirely new financial ball game. One set of figures should suffice to illustrate the point: according to the Bank of International Settlements, in the period 1980 to 1996 average annual growth in different areas of international economic activity was as follows:

trade in bonds and equities – 25%
currency trading – 25%
bank lending – 10%
FDI – 8%
trade – 6%
GDP – 2.5~3%

Dr Mahathir is by no means the only person on this earth who is concerned about the size and power of finance. In terms of perception, there seems to be a growing cleavage between the 'real' economy and the never-never land of runaway global finance. The differences in the sums are astonishing. There is a feeling, held not only by politicians but also by managers of the more 'mundane' companies that engage in the production and exchange of goods and services, that all their effort can be dissipated by the push of a button of some smart-Alec computer nerd.

A sense of what may be a growing cleavage between the world of industry and the world of finance can be garnered from a press release jointly issued by UNCTAD and the ICC (International Chamber of Commerce), entitled 'Leading multinationals vote their confidence in Asia' (18 March 1998). The main message was that 'multinational companies find that overall confidence in East and South-East Asia as a destination for foreign direct investment remains unshaken, despite the financial crisis in the region'. Throughout the two-page text, the distinction between direct investments and portfolio investments is frequently drawn.

Thus, as the ICC Secretary General Maria Livanos Cattaul stresses, for those 'multinational corporations that are keenly interested in the region for direct investment in the production of goods and services ... this is a resounding vote of confidence in the economic fundamentals of East and South-East Asia and the region's long-term prospects'. To ensure no one fails to understand what Ms Cattaul is saying, in the next paragraph (and on several other occasions in the text), emphatic reference is made to the fact that 'foreign direct investment by its nature requires commitment over the long haul'. This is in contrast to 'capital investments by portfolio investors (which) focus on shorter term financial gains and tend to be volatile'. On the other hand, 'direct investors are mainly concerned with visible economic transactions, such as the establishment or expansion of plants, the operation of internationally integrated production systems, the international transfer of technology, and the distribution of intermediate and final products in world markets'.

The idea of the twenty-first century witnessing a good old-fashioned class conflict between portfolio investors and direct investors is intriguing. Leaving zanier thoughts aside, there is the concern that globalization is driven by herds of juvenile analysts with fantastic skills in manipulating international money transactions, but no depth and no sense of responsibility.

Globalization has also extended to other nefarious areas of activity. The internationalization of the drugs trade has been around for a while, but it too is now catching on to and benefiting from the information technologies and open borders that accompany globalization. Extremist parties operate on the internet. The arms trade has been globalized. The Russian mafia, the Japanese *yakuza*, the Chinese triads, and so on, play across the globe. Global management and the usages of information technology serve the purposes of the pornography and prostitution industries, including their entire 'range of services', notably paedophilia.

There are cultural concerns about globalization, some of which may appear to be silly, but not all of which should be summarily dismissed.

Globalization is in good part driven by the globalization of information and communication. Apart from the fact that some of the global media moguls are highly unsavoury characters, by and large a global source of information is not a bad thing. So long, however, as it is counterbalanced by some local source and interpretation of information. In the antediluvian days when CNN did not exist, finding out news in a foreign country required making the effort of finding and interpreting local sources. The news might be biased, censored, or whatever, but it did give a local flavour. There are many executives one meets today, operating in 'global' markets, who read only the *Wall Street Journal* and watch only CNN.

There are two advertisements on CNN, both in respect to 'global communications', that vividly reflect a stinging indictment of our age. One is for the MCI telephone card where the message is pounded away ('subtlety' is not a word CNN would know how to spell) that the great thing about this card is that its user when abroad not only does not have to worry about having to speak a foreign language (heaven forbid!), but indeed that he/she will not even have to have contact with natives. In your sanitized, global hotel room, you just press a few buttons, and, Bob's your uncle, you've got an American operator! Wow!

The other is for the ATT card. You hear this eager-beaver bozo American male voice calling various parts of the world and at one point Paris, where, after the dring-dring, he says, 'Hey, Marcel, I'll be in Paris tomorrow, let's set up a presentation'! Why not: 'I'll be in Paris tomorrow, I hear there's a great representation of *Phèdre* at the Comédie Française. Do you think you can get us some tickets?' Or variations along these lines, even at a baser level: 'I know this excellent little restaurant on the rue Jacob, where we could try to get reservations after which we can swing with the bands and check out the talent at La Huchette'.

It is the image of these Bozos running around the world with their MCI and ATT cards, speaking only nasal American and calling up the Marcels of this world at all hours to set up presentations, that gives globalization such a very distressing aura. Cultural wasteland on a global scale.

The concern arises that a purely business-driven (and presentations-driven) global environment ultimately creates a vacuum. The MBA is a good thing, but if the trend continues it will gain overwhelming supremacy, as the disciplines of political science, history, sociology, international relations, political economy and the humanities flounder – or only recruit the third rate – and then we will have troubles. Globalization sometimes sounds like a tree whose trunk grows and grows and whose branches proliferate, but that has no roots: what will happen when the wind comes?

There are two other concerns in regard to globalization. At a speech opening a symposium sponsored by the WTO to engage in dialogue with NGOs on trade and the environment,[9] the Director-General of UNCTAD, Rubens Ricupero, stated that historians in the future will credit the third quarter of the twentieth century with two major themes, that of human rights and the environment. For many NGOs, the WTO is their *bête noire*. Many NGOs are fired by the belief, shared by many ordinary people, that globalization is responsible for the trampling of human rights on a global level and the destruction of the environment on a comparable scale. These concerns border occasionally on alarm. This may not be justified, but the concerns none the less remain real and must be addressed.[10] Globalization may be sowing the seeds of its own destruction.

Globalization: Exclusion and Backlash

The forces of globalization are forces of both integration and polarization. These contradictory forces can be illustrated at many different levels. For example, take Shanghai. It is an amazing place and perhaps the latest flamboyant case of the East Asian 'miracle' story. Shanghai is all about contemporary architecture, fast-

---

[9] The symposium was held at the WTO conference hall in Geneva on 17 and 18 March 1998. I am grateful to Gary Sampson, Director for Trade and Environment at the WTO for having invited me to participate.

[10] In this context, there are responsible bodies that are seeking to address the concerns and respond to them in a serious manner. Two reports published by the European Roundtable, *European Industry: A Partner of the Developing World. Foreign Direct Investment as a Tool for Economic Development and Cooperation – Suggestions of Future Improvement* (1993) and *European Industry and the Developing World: For a Global Framework of Mutual Interest and Trust* (1997) are in this category. The aloofnessof many enterprises, however, and their arrogant disregard for the concerns of their critics may ultimately prove very costly.

moving business, rising young professionals (who employ servants, Mao!), luxury German cars, Italian fashion, French wine, mobile phones and the latest computer wizardry. You go 100 (or less) kilometres down the road, however, and hello Pearl Buck.

My late friend and great globo-enthusiast, Gerald Segal,[11] insisted this phenomenon, namely the cyclically growing gaps between haves and have-nots, has always existed and is no more alarming now than it was in the past. I believe that while the phenomenon *per se* has indeed existed before, under globalization it is gaining different features and manifestations. The polarization effect of globalization operates at two levels.

At one very macro level, the globalized world is increasingly divided between developing economies and societies and stagnating or underdeveloping societies and economies. In the former category one would include Western Europe, North America,[12] a number of the countries of East Asia (including China) and some of the countries of Latin America and Central and Eastern Europe, such as Slovenia. In the latter category and at the opposite extreme, there are the orphan nations of globalization, in the Middle East, Africa, Central America, the CIS and the South Asian continent. In more than half the sub-Saharan countries of Africa, the population is growing faster than the economy, thus recording a negative *per capita* GDP growth. Since the end of the Cold War, official state aid to developing countries has substantially decreased. Private capital, on the other hand, is not compensating for the fall in state aid as private investors find these economies an understandably unattractive proposition. Hence, arguably these countries are worse off as a result of globalization and, on the basis of current trends, they could be going from bad to worse.

No matter what measure of economic activity one cares to use, North America, Western Europe and the Asia-Pacific account for anywhere between 70 per cent at a minimum to 90 per cent of the world. This is true of total GDP, it is true of trade, of foreign direct investment, of mobile telephones, of antibiotic consumption, and so on. The 400 million people of the Middle East and North Africa receive less

---

[11] His many publications include a recent highly-acclaimed book co-authored with Barry Buzan, *Anticipating the Future: Twenty Millennia of Human Progress* (1998) in which, among other things, the term 'mondo culture' is coined and presented in a very positive light as in essence encapsulating at the values level the globalization of the best of the West. This theme is further elaborated upon in the development of the civilizing phenomenon the authors define as 'westernistic' to distinguish from 'western', as 'Hellenistic' is different from Greece; see Gerald Segal and Barry Buzan, 'A Western Theme', *Prospect* (February 1998).

[12] This is admittedly somewhat different from the conventional usage of the term 'developing'. North America and Western Europe however are developing, not simply because they continue to grow, even if in the case of Europe on a relatively modest scale, but also because there remains a brisk pace of development of new technologies, new kinds of services, and so on.

than 1 per cent of current flows of FDI. There is of course an element of vicious circle here. The disruptive political movements and terrorist groups in some of the countries of the Middle East and North Africa are in part caused by the absence of investments, domestic and foreign, the pressures of rapid urbanization, growing populations and extremely high levels of unemployment.[13] The level of violence that occurs, however (such as in Algeria), or the uncertainty induced (such as in Egypt), further deter foreign investors.

From a broader and longer-term perspective, this facet of the polarization of globalization need not be a cause for alarm. Conceivably, the contrary could be the case. Globalization can be likened to a theatre that includes three types of actors: those that are on centre stage, those that are in the wings and getting dressed for their parts, and those that are off-stage. 'Getting dressed' involves privatization, liberalization and generally aiming to provide an environment that will be conducive to market-driven economic activity and attractive to investment. The economic and social benefits of such policies should, in principle, be positive. The trend, as noted earlier, has been to see the direction increasingly taken by almost all actors and potential actors of the world-economy moving towards the theatre. It may nevertheless be the case that some will not make it, for whatever reason, and that the globe will be left with a cluster of nations that may form a category of *lumpenstadt*.

What is perhaps more vivid in the current landscape are the differences within countries, regions or continents. The example of Shanghai and the hinterland was mentioned above. In fact, globalization is manifested primarily through the global integration of urban metropolises. There is more in common, from virtually every viewpoint, between Shanghai and Boston, than between Shanghai and the provinces. Not only is there a good deal of communication and trade between Shanghai and Boston, but people in both cities increasingly speak the same kind of language, or rather on similar subjects. A comparable picture could be drawn in respect to Jakarta and Frankfurt, Sao Paolo and Rotterdam, and so on.

What is happening in so-called Third World countries is also occurring in the developed world. The pace of competition of globalization is increasingly bringing about a class of people who are and feel ousted, who cannot keep up. In the West and Japan, these pockets of *exclus*[14] can be found in rural districts, but mostly in the rising number of urban ghettos of Third World-like conditions. In the US they tend to be primarily in the inner cities, in France they are in the suburbs. The phenomenon is the same, vagrancy and hopelessness. In American inner cities,

---

[13] Ibrahim A Karawan, *The Islamist Impasse*, Adelphi Paper 314, International Institute for Strategic Studies, London, 1997.

[14] The term *les exclus* has become increasingly common in usage in France to refer to the long-term unemployed, who more often than not become homeless, and come to constitute people who have no stake in society. In English the term would be translated as 'the excluded'.

such as Washington or Detroit, life expectancy is considerably lower than it is in Bangladesh, while the incidence of diseases such as tuberculosis is considerably higher.

Although it is true that this is not new, a point made by Tony Judt,[15] among others, is that in the past the poor were held together by communities. What one is seeing now – and the British film *Brassed Off* does an excellent job in bringing the phenomenon to light – is the disappearance of communities that are replaced by nothing. There is little solace in this world for the *exclus*.

In much of the West the proletariat is disappearing. Those who succeed move on to white-collar service jobs, those who fail join the ranks of the *exclus* and come to constitute a lumpenproletariat. This will prove a destabilizing factor in societies, though one that might be contained.

While the lumpenproletariat may be at an extreme end of the social scale and may also be effectively disenfranchised, there are also the increasing ranks of perceived 'victims' of globalization: for example less well-skilled employees of corporations and the small and medium-sized enterprises who find the struggle to survive more and more a losing battle. They are not disenfranchised; indeed they are politically vocal. This is where extreme right-wing racist politicians, such as Jean-Marie Le Pen in France and Shintaro Ishihara[16] in Japan, gain their following.

The benefits of globalization may be exaggerated by its supporters; its costs and evils are certainly exaggerated by its critics and detractors. There is, however, a very strong risk that there might be a strong backlash that could prove ugly, disruptive, or even worse. The combination of rising unemployment, of right-wing politics, of increasing hopelessness in many levels of society, of growing racism, etc, should cause concern. It is better to work on the assumption that something akin to Nazism could happen again and be proved wrong, than to work on the assumption that such things are inconceivable and to be proved wrong.

The first era of globalization, the late nineteenth century, was a period of unbounded dynamism and hope. It went badly wrong. World War I was then seen as the war to end all wars (*la der des der*, as it was called in France),[17] and look what happened. Vigilance is called for.

---

[15] Tony Judt, 'The Social Question Redivivus', *Foreign Affairs* (September/October 1997).
[16] Having politicians of that ilk is a threat to democracy. They become an even greater threat to democracy when they are granted recognition and legitimacy by the establishment, which is what the former chairman and co-founder of Sony, Akio Morita, did in agreeing to co-author a book with Ishihara, *The Japan That Can Say 'No'* (1988).
[17] *La der des der* was slang for *la dernière des dernières*, 'the last of the last', meaning the last war.

Future Prospects of *Pax Americana*

Winston Churchill's famous remark that democracy is the worst form of government, with the exception of all the others, will have to apply, for now anyway, to the US as global hegemon. The *Financial Times* economics leader-writer, Martin Wolf, neatly encapsulated the current global situation by remarking[18] that 'the world has only one power, the United States, and it does not know where it is going'.

The United States is arguably the first world power in history that is not bent on conquest. Although the Vietnam War was clearly wrong strategically, geopolitically and morally, its origins lay initially more in naïvety and miscalculation than in sinister plots.[19] In the four decades or so following world war two, there were undoubted excesses and abuses of power by the United States. Since the end of the Reagan era, however, under both the Bush and Clinton administrations, the United States can be generally deemed to be a far more benign than malign power. The benefits from *Pax Americana* strongly outweigh the liabilities. Especially in respect to the Asia-Pacific region, where the greatest likelihood of a possible major confrontation could arise, the American presence is the only assurance (but not guarantee) for peace.

Martin Wolf's dictum nevertheless applies strongly in virtually every field. On the trade front, while it was the United States that conceived, nurtured and pushed through the Uruguay Round, no sooner was the WTO established than America became the institution's greatest threat. Whatever Bill Clinton's foibles may be in many matters, in him the United States has one of the most intellectually and politically committed free-trade Presidents it has ever had, certainly since Kennedy. And yet the refusal by Congress to grant the President fast-track authority sends a confused and disturbing signal to the global trading community. The construction of Globalization-II is fragile. If the major architect is going to start throwing rocks at it ...

In regard to the Middle East, and Iraq in particular, Gerald Segal believed that ultimately it will be American weapons such as Microsoft and Mickey Mouse, rather than the Marines, which will lead Saddam to surrender.[20] Perhaps, but it is not clear that this strategy is that well thought out in the Oval office. On Iraq, Bosnia, Somalia and the Middle East peace process, the Wolf dictum applies: the United States does not know where it is going.

There are many problems in the United States. For one thing, whereas the 'normal' pattern is that as societies become more sophisticated, they become more

---

[18] At the first Evian Group Conference (1995) on 'the international economic order in the post-Uruguay Round: agenda for Europe and Asia'.
[19] David Halberstam, *The Best and the Brightest* (1969).
[20] Gerald Segal, 'Not Bombs but *Baywatch*', *Newsweek* (9 March 1998).

secular, poll after poll shows that the overwhelming majority of Americans believe in God and attend church, synagogue or mosque. This, among other things, tends to lead Americans to see virtually everything through a moral or religious prism. This includes international affairs. Hence, as a number of critics have claimed, the United States does not engage in foreign policy, but rather tends to engage in foreign crusades. It will be recalled that the war to oust Iraq from Kuwait was presented as a war for democracy.

The proselytism in American policy is in turn a consequence of politics and public opinion. In most societies, the general public has no opinion and absolutely no interest in its country's foreign affairs. Analysis and debate on such topics is left to establishment elites. Exceptions may be when some jingoism can be practised, for example with Thatcher in Britain's war against the Argentine over the Falkland Islands (Malvinas).

In the United States, the American public has no knowledge of foreign affairs – indeed no knowledge of geography, history, and so on – and does not pay much attention to foreign news, but this does not prevent it from having views. These grassroots views become the matter of heated debate in Congress. When one takes into consideration the fact that roughly 75 per cent of the new members of Congress elected in 1994 did not even own passports, the fact that the United States does not know where it is going becomes less surprising. Thus at the end of the twentieth century we have an extraordinary situation whereby the nation which has the greatest power the world has ever seen is also one of the most parochial societies the world has ever seen. The sophistication in the analysis of world-class think-tanks such as the Brookings Institution contrasts with the prevalent ethos of American society which, as an American senior executive of Digital Corporation once told me while we were waiting for a plane at Nice airport, 'is a nation of Archie Bunkers'.[21]

Pax Romana was destroyed by the barbarians and *Pax Britannica* by the Germans and the Japanese. The United States has no current rival as world power and it is difficult to envisage any emerging over the next quarter of a century. The greatest threat to *Pax Americana* is the United States itself. The multilateralism that Washington contributed to build and then arduously fought for in successive GATT rounds, notably during the seven tortuous years of the Uruguay Round, is now being jeopardized by its increasing proclivity to resort to unilateralism. The global reach of American military power is increasingly threatened by the strong isolationist streak that is prominently re-emerging in the American body-politic.

The withdrawal of the United States from its commitment and obligations as *primus inter pares* of the multilateral trade and security system would result in a

---

[21] Archie Bunker is a character in a US television series of the 1980s modelled on the British character Alf Garnett from *Till Death Do Us Part* and who typifies the 'typical' Reagan-voting know-nothing American working-class white male.

vacuum. The vacuum would in most likelihood be filled not by a successor, but by anarchy.

The Japan that Should Say (and Do) Something Constructive

In other publications[22] I have indicated the role I believe Europe could, under the present circumstances, realistically assume as a means of providing support to *Pax Americana*. Although the European Union has made significant progress in recent years in presenting a more coherent, constructive and open trade policy, which has included occasionally restraining some of the US's more aggressive bouts of unilateralism, on the foreign policy and security front the situation remains very weak. A more integrated, stronger and outward-looking Europe will provide a more solid framework as a means of ensuring brighter prospects for this potentially very exciting era of globalization. Certainly a great deal more needs to be done to overcome European introversion and myopia for it to play a more positive role in the global multilateral system.

As this volume focuses on Japan, however, I shall conclude the chapter with some thoughts on its potential contribution.

No country has benefited more from *Pax Americana* than Japan. Transformed in the early 1950s from defeated enemy to pampered protégé, Japan was allowed, indeed encouraged, by the United States to develop its industry behind protectionist walls and to export to the American market, all the while being protected by the US nuclear umbrella without any reciprocal obligation. Perhaps unsurprisingly, a major result of this very special treatment has been the absence of a foreign policy in Japan and a proclivity to behave in a fashion referred to as *amaeru* in Japanese, that might be translated as the behaviour of a spoiled brat.[23]

Japan's contribution to the multilateral system and to the peace and prosperity of others besides itself can best be described as generally reluctant and reactive. When it does come, it is usually exclusively in the form of cash, sometimes abundantly so, but poor in ideas. Much was made of the fact that some $11 billion was contributed by Japan to efforts in the Gulf War, but the sum was not accompanied by any thoughtful contribution on how, for example, the conflict in the Middle East might be seen from an Asian perspective. The whole campaign by the Japanese Foreign Ministry in seeking to secure a permanent seat on the United Nations Security Council was based on the argument of the size of Japan's

---

[22] Jean-Pierre Lehmann, 'Reorganizing Western Cooperation: A Prescription for Collective *Pax Americana*', *Pacific Review*, 1994.
[23] Jean-Pierre Lehmann, 'Japanese Attitudes Towards Foreign Policy', in R Grant (ed), *The Process of Japanese Foreign Policy: Focus on Asia* (London: Royal Institute of International Affairs, 1997).

monetary contribution to the UN. No sense was provided of what Japan would actually do with its permanent seat. The overall impression one has is that Japan's vision of the world does not extend much beyond its own borders. Japan, as has been remarked, has given more piquant meaning to the concept of insularity.

The East Asian financial crisis that broke out in the summer of 1997 and continues to this day may ultimately prove to be a severe test of the global multilateral system and the peace and prosperity it has produced and should safeguard. Tokyo has come under considerable criticism from Americans, Asians and Europeans for having been such a passive, ineffective, indeed often negative actor. What is most striking again has been the paucity of ideas.

In a quite extraordinary display of bad-tempered tantrum at the criticism of Tokyo being voiced around the world, the official spokesperson of the Japanese Foreign Ministry, Mikie Kiyoi, wrote letters to the international press, including one to the *Financial Times* ('Europe's free-riders should help meet cost of bailing out Asia', 4 March 1998) and one to the *International Herald Tribune* ('Giving Japan Credit', 3 March 1998).

She concludes the letter to the *Herald Tribune* by writing: 'While Japan can claim credit for Asia's success story, it should not take the blame for its failure'. There can be little doubt anywhere in the world outside Japan that one of the most serious causes of global instability is Japan's inability to make genuine peace with its neighbours. Not only have the wounds of the past, therefore, not healed, but Japanese politicians and officials repeatedly engage in means to add additional salt. The butchery of millions, the rape, torture, vivisection, the usage of humans to experiment with bacteriological weapons, and so on, have not elicited recognition, let alone repentance, on the part of Japan. Callousness is perhaps the mildest term that can be used to describe Japanese attitudes towards their neighbours. It is unimaginable that the spokesperson of the German foreign ministry would write something along these lines in respect to Germany and Europe. That is the difference between Germany and Japan and also a major reason why Europe's peace is reasonably secure and Asia's is not.

As a letter in response to Ms Kiyoi's pointed out, Japan's failure to act in the face of the Asian crisis comes in a number of guises, including perhaps especially in its unwillingness to open its market to Asian exports.[24] The closed nature of the Japanese market is in turn a reflection of the country's domestic problems, in particular political and institutional rigidities.

At a more global level, a cause for disappointment with Japan is how poor its contribution (apart from money) has been to international institutions. Several examples can be given. Thus, although the Japanese control the management of the Asian Development Bank, its intellectual influence is generally considered

---

[24] Daniel J. Murphy, 'Japan putting up barriers when it should help its Asian neighbours', *Financial Times* (6 March 1998).

conspicuous by its absence. Those (few) senior positions held by Japanese have ranged from the highly problematic to, as in the case of the recent head of the WHO, the unmitigated disaster. Because the Japanese are poorly trained in foreign cultures and languages, their ability to communicate in multicultural settings is handicapped. Even then, however, Japan's best and brightest stay at home, with the exception of its women (for example Mrs Ogata), who would probably have difficulty getting a place in the sun in Japan. Japan is the world's second biggest economy, yet there are very, very few articulate Japanese voices to be heard in the halls of the WTO, the IMF, the World Bank, the OECD, UNCTAD, and so on.

While Japan's contribution to official international institutions has been extremely weak, the situation in regard to NGOs is even worse. Though Japan renounced the use of military might itself and relies on the United States to engage in conflict on its behalf, one might have expected more contribution on the humanitarian front. Not only, however, has Japan not brought about its own version of international humanitarian organizations (such as Oxfam or Médecins sans Frontières), but membership in Japanese committees of groups such as Amnesty International and Greenpeace is very slender. As a formidable economic power which has been able to bask in the unparalleled protection of the United States, Japan's contribution to the maintenance of the multilateral economic and security system should be much greater.

Conclusion

These are great times, full of the most fantastic opportunities. They are also very fragile times. This *fin de siècle* offers vistas that find no precedent apart from the immediately previous *fin de siècle*. Let us hope that the beginning of the twenty-first century will not bring the tragic disappointments that the beginning of the twentieth century brought. In fact, we need to do more than hope. We have to work very hard at it and remain vigilant.

Chapter Five

Multilateralism and International Security: The Global Level

François Heisbourg

Definitions

In dealing with the global level of multilateralism and international security, some definitions are in order. What will be attempted in this chapter is a combination of two approaches:

- An appreciation of the security impact of global multilateral institutions, which in practice means the United Nations and the organizations which belong to the UN family (the International Atomic Energy Agency, the International Monetary Fund) as well as those security treaties which are global in scope (such as the Nuclear Non-Proliferation Treaty or the Chemical Weapons Convention). The G7/G8 will also be mentioned in this context.
- When applicable, an assessment of the global security impact of organizations or treaties which are regional in scope. For instance, NATO's influence has not been confined to its direct area of military responsibility: as the main security institution in the key area of the Cold War confrontation, its achievements had a major, albeit indirect, impact on international security outside of Europe. In the post-Cold War era, its emerging out-of-area responsibilities and its eastward enlargement have potentially non-negligible global security implications.

In all cases, I will also attempt to focus my remarks on the manner in which multilateralism and international security pertain more specifically to East Asia in general and Japan in particular. This two-pronged approach is adopted not least in view of the generally predominant role of non-global organizations in shaping international security. My analysis will flow along broadly chronological lines: the Cold War legacy, post-Cold War paradoxes, directions of change.

The Cold War Legacy

The UN between Paralysis and Achievement

Even a cursory reading of the UN Charter[1] suffices to remind one of the great gap between the aspirations of 1945 and Cold War reality. The Charter's written words harken back to Wilsonian principles with teeth (notably Chapter VII) added on. Pride of place in the Security Council was given to the victors of 1945 at the expense of the 'enemy states'.[2] Very soon,[3] the spirit in which the UN operated was essentially shaped by the reality of the East–West confrontation.

Nowhere was this more visible than in the decision-making of the UN Security Council. Apart from a fluke such as the endorsement of military intervention in Korea in June 1950, made possible by the Soviet Union boycott of the Council, the UNSC was only exceptionally able to act decisively. This was exemplified by the Soviet Union's repeated use of the veto,[4] most spectacularly before decolonization and the 1965 reform of the Security Council made it possible for USSR to occasionally marshal a plurality on some issues – in which case the US wielded its own veto, notably on Middle Eastern affairs. The European powers used the veto much more sparingly, but occasionally felt compelled to do so when the US and the USSR exceptionally did not find themselves on opposite sides of an issue.

Not only did this block effective decision-making in most instances; it also made it impossible to fulfill the more far-reaching provisions of the UN Charter: in particular, Chapter VII provisions were hardly brought into force, with the happenchance exception of the Korean operations.

However, it would be a mistake to draw from this situation of decisional paralysis and unfulfilled ambitions the conclusion that the UN and the UN family of institutions played a purely marginal role in international security. If the US and the USSR were more often than not in opposing camps, there were three main areas in which a degree of convergence of security interests led them to at least tolerate substantial UN involvement and sometimes to jointly and actively promote the UN's international security role.

---

[1] See articles 43 to 46 of Chapter VII as illustrations.
[2] See article 53 of the UN Charter.
[3] For instance the Military Staff Committee ceased any substantive work in 1948. See Sydney Bailey, *The Procedures of UN Security Council* (Oxford: Clarendon Press, 1975).
[4] The boycott was related to the USSR's refusal to sanction the continued representation of China in the UNSC by the Nationalist Government.

The first, and possibly most important and durable area of common interest was the preservation of the nuclear monopoly and its positive spin-off, non-proliferation policy. As long as the nuclear monopoly was absolute (that is, American), there could naturally be no congruence of interests between the United States and Stalin's Soviet Union, hence the failure of the first attempt to provide the United Nations with a major role in this area: the far-reaching Baruch Plan was thus turned down by the Soviets in 1946. Once a nuclear duopoly was in place, co-operation became possible, exemplified by Eisenhower's Atoms for Peace speech in 1953. The creation of the International Atomic Energy Agency in 1957 was the first step in a continuous process of expanding the UN role in nuclear non-proliferation, with each advance being triggered by an event portending the runaway dissemination of nuclear weapons. Thus, the 1964 Chinese nuclear explosion provoked the drafting of the NPT; the 1974 Indian nuclear explosion prompted new activity by the IAEA;[5] the break-up of the Soviet Union and the Iraqi nuclear program led to the establishment of a tougher IAEA safeguards regime ('93 + 2'); and the creation of a UN Special Commission for implementing UNSC resolution 687 in Iraq.

Notwithstanding the reactive rather than proactive nature of the UN family's non-proliferation activity during the Cold War, this is one Cold War legacy which has been broadly successful: if three unrecognized nuclear states have emerged since the 1960s (India, Israel, Pakistan) in addition to the 'official five' of the NPT, this is a far different situation from that forecast by President Kennedy in March 1962: 'Personally, I am haunted by the feeling that by 1970, unless we are successful, there may be ten nuclear power instead of four, and by 1975, fifteen or twenty'.[6] The fact that more than 180 sovereign states have officially relinquished the nuclear option – of which only the merest handful can be considered as not fully complying with that pledge – is a global security effect of the first magnitude.

Furthermore, the impact on East Asian security is particularly important, given the combination of regional instability and industrial capability which would otherwise make this region a prime candidate for runaway proliferation. This indeed has been one of the fears inspiring the apparently successful multilateral attempt at curbing North Korea's nuclear ambitions (to which I will return).

The largely selfish motives of the superpowers thus laid the foundations for a set of policies which have outlasted the Cold War (whether they will survive the situation created by the recent Indian and Pakistani tests remains to be seen).

The second field of superpower co-operation within the UN system was linked to the growing recognition by the US and the USSR that regional crises had to be contained in order to defuse the risk of a direct and open military clash between the superpowers, with a nuclear war as its all-to-be feared corollary. While often fuelling regional conflicts, each of the superpowers grew increasingly cautious of the attendant risks of regional wars spinning out of control. Thus, the Security

---

[5] Notably the adoption of the London Guidelines and the Convening of the International Nuclear Fuel Cycle Evaluation (INFCE).
[6] Quoted in John Newhouse, *The Nuclear Age* (London: Michael Joseph, 1989), p. 193.

Council was used, notably in Middle Eastern contingencies, as a vehicle for dousing uncomfortably hot blazes, for example at the time of the Yom Kippur war.

This function of the UNSC is in keeping with the Charter. Paradoxically – and as, we shall see, this is only one in a set of recent paradoxes – the disappearance of the superpower confrontation has also eliminated one particular incentive to use the Security Council to set a limit to certain regional crises. Consequently, a number of conflicts (not least in Africa) have been receiving less active attention from the Security Council than would probably have been the case during the Cold War. In this respect, the post-Cold War UN, and notably the UNSC, may have been reasonably better at ending some of the unfinished business of the Cold War (Angola, El Salvador, Namibia and Mozambique come to mind) than at dealing with more recent purely *sui generis* crises (Liberia or the Great Lakes horrors in Africa, for instance).

Thirdly and finally, the superpowers on occasion found common ground when dealing with decolonization issues: democratic instincts and Communist aspirations could quite often be satisfied at the expense of what President Sukarno used to call the 'Oldefos' – the old declining forces of traditional imperialism. With the superpowers opposing (USSR) or refusing to align (USA) with the European imperial powers, certain conflicts of decolonization witnessed a substantial degree of UN activism. Dag Hammarskjold's role as UN Secretary General in the Congo crisis of 1960 was far from negligible – indeed, on a par with Secretary-General Kofi Annan's recent mission to Bagdad; and the UN deployment of Blue Helmets in ex-Belgian Congo to quell the Katanga secession (largely fostered by the erstwhile colonial power) in 1963 was in practice an enforcement operation, rather than a peacekeeping operation. Naturally, overt colonial empires have disappeared as a major feature of the geopolitical landscape and therefore this area has thus been made doubly redundant following the demise of the Soviet Empire.

In summary, superpower confrontation no doubt acted as a brake on the effectiveness of multilateral diplomacy, but it also provided it with a significant scope of action linked in turn to that confrontation. To the extent that the UN's record was determined by the Soviet–American conflict, a country such as Japan could only play a marginal role (beyond contributing a sizable share of the UN budget), even if one sets aside the *diminutio capitis* resulting from its initial 'enemy state' status.

NATO: The Global Impact of a Regional Security and Defence Organization

It is impossible to prove a counterfactual, and therefore one should refrain from presuming to describe what Europe and the world would have looked like in the absence of a successful NATO in Europe. However, what we do know is that there was no hot war on the territory of continental Europe from the creation of NATO in 1949 until the peaceful end of the Cold War four decades later, a situation presumably entrenched by the formal establishment in 1955 of a military bloc by the states of the Soviet Empire. Causality cannot be automatically derived from that correlation, but the correlation itself cannot be disproved or disregarded.

In East Asia, a different security system prevailed, even setting aside the China factor which had become clearly distinct by 1960–61, with a set of bilateral defence and security relations between the US and individual allied states – Taiwan, South Korea, Japan – were arrayed in a hub-and-spokes system, with minimal military co-operation between each of the spokes. A symmetrical set of arrangements eventually linked the USSR to 'brother states' – Mongolia, North Korea, North Viet Nam, China – during the 1950s. These arrays provided a degree of security of each of the partners, but they did not ensure the absence of open conflict whether in the Korean Peninsula, the Formosa Straits or Indochina. In South-East Asia, a multilateral organization, ostensibly along NATO lines, was set up within the framework of the Manila Treaty (1954). However, during its brief life,[7] SEATO never managed to emulate NATO's peace preservation achievement. Multilateral inter-allied co-operation between SEATO partners never developed much beyond an unsatisfactory and implicit remake of the hub-and-spokes system of North-East Asia: the US held quasi-exclusive sway over an Asian flock whose members hardly co-operated with each other. In a sense, SEATO at its best looked like a more volatile version of NATO's southern flank at its worst, with Athens and Ankara co-operating with Washington, much more than with each other. If nuclear deterrence presumably played a role in preventing large-scale[8] direct superpower confrontation in East Asia, it did not suffice in maintaining a form of peace along lines comparable to those which prevailed in continental Europe. If a hub-and-spokes system had prevailed in Western and Central Europe, would the Cold War have remained cold along what was the quintessential fault-line of the East–West confrontations? Whatever the hypothetic answer to this hypothetical question, NATO did function on the whole as a multilateral regional defence and security organization, and the truce did hold – an outcome of global, not only regional importance. The end of the Cold War naturally challenged NATO severely: in the absence of the Soviet-American confrontation, NATO's core

---

[7] Substantive SEATO meetings ceased in 1965. The Manila Treaty remains extant, and in theory still commits its signatories (the US, France, UK, Australia, New Zealand, Pakistan, Thailand, the Philippines).

[8] It is now public knowledge that Soviet and American airmen fought each other during the Korean War; see G.F. Krivosheev, *Soviet Casualties and Combat Losses in the Twentieth Century* (London: Greenhill Books, 1997) (translation of *Grif Sekretnosti Sniat*, Moscow, 1993), p. 281.

military business disappeared; more ominously, with the end of the Cold War an end was also brought to the war-preventing effects of the Alliance system in Europe.

The Paradoxes of the Post-Cold War Era

A certain reading of the functioning of multilateral institutions under Cold War conditions led many[9] to expect the following broad trends:

— Since the UN had been paralyzed by the East–West confrontation, the disappearance of that paradigm would lead to an unfettering of the shackles which had prevented the UNSC, amongst others, from realizing more of the potential contained in the Charter.
— Since NATO was created as a result of the perceived Soviet threat to the European democracies, the disappearance of these conditions would normally have implied some reduction of NATO's role as the pivotal regional security organization.

With nearly a decade's hindsight, we now know that neither of these two reasonable assumptions has been clearly fulfilled: the UN has only on occasion proven to be more decisive than during the Cold War; and NATO has remained the primordial European security organization, with prospective knock-on effects on global security which few would have forecast seven or eight years ago. A summary of paradoxes can thus be listed.

A first paradox and its cause has already been mentioned: to the extent that some regional conflicts no longer impinge on superpower interests and relationships, there is little pressure for the UNSC to act vigorously. The most spectacular example – because it is also the most gruesome, involving the most massive genocide of the post-Cold War era – concerns the slayings in Rwanda between April and June 1994. The genocide was remarkably documented in real time, yet nothing serious was done by the Security Council until most of the killing had already taken place. Nor has the subsequent record of the UN in the Great Lakes area been particularly impressive.

---

[9] At the time of the Gulf crisis of 1990–91 President Bush's statements on the New World Order posited a major role for the UNSC (under US leadership, naturally); in Minister Genscher's scheme of 'interlocking institutions', NATO was one among others, notably at the time of the signing of the CSCE's ambitious Paris Charter in November 1990.

A second and related paradox has to do with an *ab ovo* internal contradiction of the UN Charter which had always existed but which was thrown into sharp relief by the removal of the Cold War confrontation. The Security Council could no doubt act more vigorously than hitherto since US–Soviet opposition no longer inhibited its actions; but this only happened exceptionally (notably with the Gulf War and Somalia) because the prevention or resolution of most post-war crises implied some degree of intervention in the domestic affairs of sovereign states. Such interference is seen as anathema by most member-states of the UN and by many members — not least veto-bearing China — of the Security Council. Article 2 of the Charter (and notably § 7)[10] is thus invoked to refuse action in the name of the sovereign rights of states. During a brief period, attempts were made with some success to resolve the contradiction within the Charter in favor of an interventionist stance: *le droit d'ingérence* was considered by many to be implicit in UNSC Resolution 688 of April 1991, which paved the way for a non-Blue Helmet military operation, with robust rules of engagement, in the Kurdish part of Iraq. Similarly, resolution 794 contained language[11] which gave the UN a mandate of quasi-colonial scope in Somalia. However, this trend did not develop: the transition from Cold War to post-Cold War provided only the briefest of openings, which was curtailed by the mixed results of *droit d'ingérence* in Somalia and indeed in Bosnia, by the growing reticence of a less compliant Russia, by a more assertive China, and by a politically less willing and financially less able United States. At the same time, neither the Europeans nor the Japanese exerted an equivalent countervailing influence to these trends.

A third paradox is that a geostrategic earthquake as powerful as the dissolution of the Soviet Empire and the end of the Cold War did not provoke a corresponding shock-wave on the institutions of UN family. There was a widespread expectation, soon after the fall of the Berlin Wall, that the Security Council in particular would rapidly undergo a transformation going further than the reform of 1965.[12] Germany (as such, or, less likely, in the framework of the 'Europeanization' of the French and British seats), and Japan were widely expected to become permanent members: after all, World War II had formally ended, at least in Europe, with the '2 + 4' treaty of September 1990.

A connected paradox concerns the G7/G8. Since it became rapidly apparent that substantial UN Security Council reform was not going to occur soon, an alternative would have been the development, at least on an interim basis, of the political and security roles of the G7/G8, of which Japan and Germany are prominent and active members. This has hardly happened except on a limited

---

[10] 'Nothing contained in the Charter shall authorize the United Nations to intervene in matters which are essentially within the domestic juridiction of any state ...'

[11] In resolution 794, the UNSC authorized the use of 'all necessary means to establish ... a secure environment for humanitarian relief operations in Somalia'.

[12] Which expanded membership of the Council from eleven to fifteen members, with all new members being non-permanent and non-veto-bearing.

number of nuclear-related issues.[13] This can no doubt be explained by the reluctance of incumbent permanent members of the Security Council (fearing both the reduction of their powers there and the political downside of appearing to create a rich man's world government) as well as by the reticence of would-be permanent members refusing to give the appearance of settling for second best.

A fourth paradox relates to the multilateral handling of nuclear issues. With the Soviet–American nuclear stand-off no longer shaping much of the international strategic landscape, major strides could have been expected towards the fulfilment of (for instance) the Final Statement of the 1978 UN General Assembly Special Session on Disarmament.[14] Indeed, significant progress was made in curbing horizontal proliferation (exemplified by the successful NPT Review Conference of 1996 and the adoption of the '93 + 2' programme by the IAEA) and in reducing the American and ex-Soviet strategic nuclear arsenals.[15] However, these were extensions of previously established trends, not the somewhat more radical departures suggested *inter alia* by the Canberra Commission in 1997.[16] As in the case of UN institutions, there has been a lot more inertia built into the system here than could have been confidently forecast in the heady days of 1989–90. The triumph of the nuclear have-nots has remained limited.

The list of paradoxes extends to regional organizations with actual or potential global consequences. Here we have to embroider upon the Sherlock Holmes analogy of the 'dog that didn't bark': in effect, what we have is a kennel of dogs, one of which barked unexpectedly loudly, and three others which keep surprisingly quiet.

First, we have NATO, which has remained the pre-eminent European security organization. It is not as if there had been many serious expectations that NATO would disappear – the depth and the breadth of the transatlantic security and defence relationship always excluded an outcome similar to the sudden evaporation of the artefact known as the Warsaw Pact – but few would have bet in early 1992 that the Bosnian crisis would, four years later, lead to the belated

---

[13] For example, the agreement at the 1992 G7 Summit in London not to export civilian nuclear facilities and materials to states refusing the application of full-scope safeguards on all of their nuclear installations; the endorsement at the 1997 G8 Summit in Denver of Mox nuclear fuels as a means to eliminate surplus military-grade plutonium.

[14] See notably § 47 of the 'Program of Action' of the Final Document Special Session of the General Assembly on Disarmament 1978': 'the ultimate goal in this context is the complete elimination of nuclear weapons'.

[15] The number of operational strategic warheads (on START-limited delivery vehicles) dropped from c. 13,000 (US) and c. 10,800 (Soviet) in 1989 to c. 7,250 each in 1997.

[16] 'Report of the Canberra Commission on the Elimination of Nuclear Weapons', Commonwealth of Australia, August 1996.

triumph of NATO, under US leadership, as the single decisive peace-enforcer in Europe. After all, during the first three years of that crisis, NATO proved to be as marginal and feckless *vis-à-vis* events unfolding on Bosnian territory as all the other organizations which became involved in one way or another: the UN, the WEU, the EEC and the OSCE were not, then, in a class apart from NATO in terms of lack of decisiveness. The eleventh-hour intervention of NATO in mid-1995, however, broke the trend of international failure in Bosnia.

Two sets of related events were strongly accelerated in the wake of that success: the enlargement of NATO, and the redefinition of NATO's strategic concept. In the summer of 1996 the US President, followed willy-nilly by his European counterparts, transformed the hazy prospect of enlargement into an actual process, with a first set of three new members due to be admitted before the end of the decade (assuming successful parliamentary ratification, where relevant). This in turn has a short-term and a long-term impact on the security positioning of Russia, including in its relations with the East Asian states, not least China and Japan (see below, 'Directions of Change'). NATO's strategic concept, which was last revised in 1991, during the first stages of the new era, was reformulated in April 1999. Some influential American analysts[17] suggested a new transatlantic bargain, which in essence would entail a trade-off between unstinting US involvement in European security affairs and European support of American global commitments, including within the Middle East and East Asia. The new strategic concept eschewed such an ambitious revision of what NATO is about, but the debate, along with real-life differences (for example on Iraq) is not settled; it may influence the future degree, scope and nature of global American security and defence commitments. In any case, NATO's air campaign against Serbia in the spring of 1999 confirmed both the Atlantic Alliance's major role and the military and strategic preponderance of the United States *vis-à-vis* the European Allies.

The three dogs that did not bark include, firstly, the European Union's *Un*Common Foreign and Security Policy.[18] In 1990–91, there was lot of brave talk, not least in Paris, Bonn and Brussels about the European Community's inevitably expanding role in foreign and security policy. In anecdotal terms, this feeling was encapsulated at the time of the Yugoslav break-up in the spring of 1991 by the statement of the Luxembourgeois Presidency of the European Council that *l'heure de l'Europe a sonné*.[19] As subsequent events demonstrated, Europe's hour did not strike – if anything it tolled. This non-event was underlined by the impossibility of the Europeans putting under a European flag (that of the WEU) the otherwise successful purely European operation in Albania in the spring of 1997. It wasn't until late 1998 that a serious effort was made by Britain and France to establish a

---

[17] See David C. Gompert and S. Stephen Larrabee (eds), *America and Europe: A Partnership for a New Era* (Cambridge and New York: Cambridge University Press, 1997).

[18] On the shortcomings (and their causes) of CFSP see: 'La politique de sécurité de l'Europe à l'Horizon 2000', Groupe d'experts à haut niveau de la PESC, Bruxelles, 19 December 1994.

[19] Statement by Foreign Minister Jacques Poos.

European security and defence policy within the EU. This was endorsed by the EU partners in 1999/2000. This development is of some importance to East Asia, which has good reasons to supplement or complement its external security relationships with a European dimension (with ASEM as a potential vehicle). However, it will take time for Europe to develop its force protection capabilities – with a force of 60,000 soldiers planned for 2003 – let alone generate the political institutions capable of decisive crisis management.

Secondly, the great hopes invested by many European countries in the CSCE/OSCE similarly came nowhere near the lofty commitments of the Paris Charter of November 1990.[20]

In the Genscherian scheme of 'interlocking institutions', the CSCE was to have been one of the key components. Today's OSCE is not useless – it accomplishes good work, notably in monitoring elections – nor is it devoid of potential. Simply, it has not become what many thought it should, an outcome due in part to American reluctance towards the CSCE during the early post-Cold War years.

This is an absence which probably has implications for East Asia, even if the hypothesis is unverifiable: a Russia playing an important role as a European power in a strong OSCE would presumably have been a different partner than the comparatively weaker and less clearly European-focused Russia that we have instead.

Thirdly and last, but not least, the end of the Cold War did not lead to a substantial rise in East Asian security organizations commensurate with the growing political and economic importance of the region. No doubt APEC has become slightly more political and less exclusively economic. ASEAN actually manages on occasion to work on security issues. And the creation of the ASEAN Regional Forum and of ASEM has opened scope for new political and security debates. Yet there is nothing remotely comparable to existing Euro-American security institutions on the horizon, notwithstanding the numerous potential areas of conflict in East Asia: even OSCE is muscular in comparison to ASEAN or ARF. This non-development is the all the more glaring insofar as the region's intrinsic importance and sensitivity has risen in parallel with the quasi-removal of Europe as one of the major potential sources of global insecurity, a dubious privilege it held during the Cold War.

As will be emphasized further, this absence of effective multilateral security organizations in East Asia is a source of global, not simply regional concern.

---

[20] See Joint Declaration on CSCE signed in Paris on 19 November 1990.

Directions of Change

An examination of future prospects for multilateral diplomacy and international security will build on three essential postulates. Firstly, the reasons which have limited the growth of the UN's international security role since the end of the Cold War continue to prevail, even if some progress has been (and hopefully will continue to be) registered. Therefore, we will still be stuck with what I have called the post-Cold War paradoxes.

Secondly, East Asia will, even more so than in the recent past, continue to be a region whose security travails will have global repercussions, a characteristic which it shares with the Middle East – but not with Europe, which has become a zone of relative moderate military calm from a global standpoint: Bosnia as such is regionally important for Europe rather than for the rest of the world. Conversely, upheaval in Indonesia, or the playing out of power relations between China, Japan, the US and the two Koreas may have a strong extra-regional impact, not least because of their interaction with economic and financial turmoil (the same can be said, for similar reasons, about the Gulf).

Thirdly, however important some directly political and military issues may be, these can rarely be analysed (let alone dealt with) independently of upstream economic aggravating or accelerating factors – Indonesia being an illustration of this from the first months of 1997 onwards – or their downstream economic consequences (the same Indonesian illustration applies). In other words, economic multilateralism plays a major security role. The success or the failure of the IMF in Asia has a global security impact. Similarly the success or the failure of the euro will have more than regional consequences, and they will not be confined to the economic sphere.

These postulates having been posed, directions of change over the next decade or so could follow a number of not necessarily converging lines. Some of these lines may veer sharply in one direction or the other, as a function of strongly contrasting binary outcomes: for example, the euro will or will not happen; it will or will not succeed in a sustained fashion – given its nature, it is unlikely to half-happen.

The Implications of UN Reform

The UN Security Council may finally be enlarged, not least to include Japan (presumably as a permanent, veto-holding member). Even if this were to happen, there is no reason to expect that such an enlarged Security Council – *a fortiori* if the enlargement extends to a number of other Asian, African and Latin American countries – will be more decisive than the current one. A larger number of veto-bearers will not normally translate in terms of greater positive decision-making power. Paradoxically, the same would hold true if the veto were abolished: major powers such as the US or China (for instance) are presumably not going to allow their sovereignty to be limited by majority voting alone. Even that 'ever closer

Union'[21] in Europe has not been able to agree that such a form of decision-making should prevail for important diplomatic and external security issues. Therefore, the UN and the UNSC will at best resemble today's in terms of decisiveness. However, Japan's entry could have substantial security implications: globally, Japan – as the second-largest funder of the UN system – could become more engaged, if she wants to (which is a big 'if') as a major player in the international security arena. Additionally, and more or less inevitably Japan as a permanent UNSC member will have to balance much more visibly its power relations with the US, China, and Russia – for example on such issues as the implementation of UNSC resolution 687 by Iraq.

This will hardly be comfortable for the Gaimusho, but ultimately it is probably healthy that this type of engagement should play itself through the mediation of the UNSC on a host of issues rather than be confined, as it is today, to the East Asian cockpit. I expect it to be easier for Japan (and easier on Japan's partners) to exercise its power – and notably its bountiful 'soft power'[22] – at the global level, than to play the part of a major regional military power in East Asia: a non-Bismarckian power like Japan will not easily be accommodated by, nor readily adapt to, a still very Bismarckian — some would say Wilhelminian[23] — part of the world. That being said, a higher-profile Japan at the global level will not find it easy to reconcile the essential US–Japanese security relationship with the necessity to stand up and be counted in the UNSC on issues where it will not want to find itself at odds with other veto-bearing countries of Asia.

The Global Implications of Weak Regional Security Organizations in East Asia.

Korea remains divided, with North Korea and South Korea fielding massive military forces while each is going through the throes of very different, but deep, economic and social difficulties. Indonesia is plunged in the depths of an economic, social and political crisis which by February 1998 was on the verge of 'explosion'.[24] China's future as a *status quo* or non-*status quo* power remains undecided, with the threat of a massive, albeit possibly avoidable, domestic banking breakdown, the whole being spiced by the unresolved course of Beijing–

---

[21] See § 11 of preamble of Treaty of European Union ('Résolus à poursuivre le processus créant une union sans cesse plus étroite').
[22] Joseph S. Nye and William A. Owen, 'America's Information Edge', *Foreign Affairs*, 75:2 (March–April 1996).
[23] See Paul Wolfowitz, 'Bridging Centuries: fin de siècle all over again', *National Interest*, 47 (Spring 1997).
[24] 'Indonesia's coming explosion', leader title, *The Economist* (21 February 1998).

Taipei relations and the relationship with the Indian subcontinent. This may not be Europe in 1914 but it looks a good deal like Europe in the last decades of the nineteenth century. Any major breakdown of security in East Asia will relaunch an economic and financial crisis; this has, for the time being been brought under tentative control by the massive intervention of the IMF and by the widespread and heartfelt hope for major Japanese reflationary measures.

Given these and other[25] challenges, the 'golf course' diplomacy of ASEAN and ARF is not sufficient, even if it compares favorably with the long-standing dearth of broad-gauged multilateral dialogue in North East Asia. What can be done? Interestingly, one limited but truly multilateral effort appears to have met with some success in dealing with nuclear proliferation in the Korean Peninsula, in the form of KEDO (Korean peninsula Energy Development Organization) to which Japan, the US, Australia, the EU and others have contributed. Hopefully, this attempt will be able to fulfil its promise, despite the stinginess of the US Congress and the economic crisis in South Korea. But it does show that a multilateral approach can be made to work in North-East Asia. Kim Dae Jung's election in South Korea may provide a new opportunity to deal with the infinitely delicate issues of Korean division, and eventual reunification, in a multilateral framework. Japan would have a major part to play in this respect, not least because multilateralism takes the edge off bilateral approaches burdened by the unsavoury freight of history, and poisoned (amongst non-participants) by the feeling of being left out.

Possibly, one of the most globally important security implications of a regional approach would be the result of a non-security initiative, that is through the addition of a regional Asian economic initiative to supplement – and influence – the work of the IMF and the World Bank. Here again, Japan is absolutely key; and here also, multilateralism may work better politically than solely Japanese attempts at injecting money (as has been done during the recent East Asian crisis) here and there. Lasting peace in Western Europe was guaranteed militarily by NATO but it was politically rooted in the multilateral machinery (the European Payments Union, the OECE – ancestor of OECD – the Coal and Steel Community) established after World War II. Although this array was not a substitute for bilateral reconciliation between France and Germany, that process was facilitated by, and converged with, the establishment of multilateral mechanisms and habits. The (multilateral) treaty of Rome, creating the EEC, and the (bilateral) Elysée treaty sealing Franco-German reconciliation were the capstones of two mutually reinforcing processes.

Both the short term – preventing a relaunching of the Asian financial crisis – and the long term – facilitating the political and security insertion of Japan in a region in which World War II has not formally nor psychologically come to an end – militate strongly in favour of a multilateral regional economic initiative.

---

[25] The 'ASEAN way' has proven equally ineffective in the face of regional environmental challenges such as the so-called 'haze'.

Last, and hopefully not least, there is the as yet elusive prospect of a deeper Euro-Asian political security relationship. In contrast to what has been said about other institutions, with the creation of ASEM the organizational machinery has begun to be put in place before substantial non-economic grist has been brought to the diplomatic mills. Within a few years, that situation may change. We should know soon – certainly little later than 2002, when the euro (launched on 1 January 1999) will be operating under all its aspects – if the relevant states of the European Union have successfully abandoned national sovereignty in monetary affairs, one of the essential ingredients of state sovereignty since the emergence of nation-states. If that happens to be the case, it is possible that the euro-states will begin to share sovereignty in the political and security arenas. And even if that proves not to be the case, a successful euro will more or less inevitably become a reserve currency, and that in itself will force upon the Euro-states a greater global political role.

Therefore, the European–North-American–East Asian Triangle could begin to function in a less isocelian and more equilateral manner: that would create its own problems, not least in terms of handling the security relationships which Europe (via NATO) and several Asian states have with the US. It would probably no longer be possible to compartmentalize these two sets of relationships on separate tracks, as they are in practice seen, not least from a American perspective – an essential one since only the US will continue to have the capability of projecting force in both Europe and Asia. Under such conditions, the case for a grand bargain of the sort alluded to earlier could become compelling for Washington.

Similarly, and independently of what happens with the euro but at around the same time, NATO expansion – which is an issue due to be revisited by the Atlantic Partners in 2002 – will have to take into account its repercussions in Asia. A Russia which would have become strongly antagonist towards the US (because of missile defences, for example) and NATO would seek an anti-Western balancing relationship with China, a point strongly made by the historian John Lewis Gaddis.[26] That prospect would definitively not make life easy for Japan, which has nothing to gain from an anti-Western Russia–Chinese coalition. At the global level, an anti-Western Sino-Russian collusion would certainly be destabilizing; fortunately, it is still eminently avoidable, given the very serious differences of interest which currently limit the scope for a Moscow–Beijing convergence.[27] Conversely, a Russia which may have become, in the fullness of time, a member of

---

[26] See John Lewis Gaddis, 'History, Grand Strategy and NATO Enlargement', *Survival* (IISS/OUP, Spring 1998).
[27] On this score, 'the Limits of Sino-Russian Strategic Partnership' Jennifer Anderson, *Adelphi Paper* no. 215 (IISS/OUP, 1997).

NATO would probably be seen by Beijing as a different – possibly more malign? – entity than is currently the case; this would also apply in a way to Japan: with Russia in NATO, a Japan–Russia peace treaty would become highly desirable.

* * *

All of the above considerations, and more or less irrespective of specific outcomes (Japan in or out of the UNSC; the euro happening or not; Russia leaning West or East, and so on) point to a much less comfortable global security environment for Japan. Lack of comfort does not necessarily mean hardship or a reduced role: on the contrary, the discomfort flows directly from the contradiction between greater influence and political inertia.

Under post-Cold War conditions, given its geography (as part of the key East Asian region), and by virtue of its economic weight and its greater role in the UN, Japan's actions (or lack thereof) have greater direct or indirect international security consequences.

The Japanese political system proves extraordinarily resistant to playing a role commensurate with that weight. It would be a tragedy in the political (as in the economic) sphere, if that inertia were to prove insuperable.[28] International security requires a more active Japan, strongly engaged in multilateralism whether at the global or at the regional level.

---

[28] See 'Japanese Domestic Politics and Foreign Policy', Prof. G. Curtis, the IISS 39th Annual Conference, Singapore 11–14 September 1997 (unpublished paper).

PART III
REGIONAL MULTILATERAL ARRANGEMENTS

Chapter Six

The Eurasian Component of Pan-European Security and Co-operation: The Role of the OSCE in the Caucasus and Central Asia

Victor-Yves Ghebali

Once established in 1975 by the Helsinki Final Act, the Conference on Security and Co-operation in Europe (CSCE) operated until the end of the Cold War as a constellation of thirty-five participating states including all the European sovereign nations of that period (except Albania) plus the USA and Canada. Although two of its political actors were Eurasian powers (the USSR and Turkey), it performed as an Euro-Atlantic process concerned by developments taking place 'from the Atlantic to the Urals'. Thus, while the human rights commitments of the Helsinki Final Act were applicable on the territory of all the participating states, the CSCE follow-up evaluation meetings (Belgrade, 1977–78; Madrid, 1980–1983; Vienna, 1986–89) did not address violations in the Asian part of the USSR or issues related to the treatment of the Kurdish ethnic minority in Turkey. Moreover, the implementation of the 1975 Helsinki regime of military confidence-building measures (CBM), and subsequently of the 1986 Stockholm regime of confidence and security-building measures (CSBM), concerned the whole of continental Europe but only an insignificant portion of the Asian hinterland.[1]

---

[1] Under the Helsinki CBM regime, the CSCE participating states were committed to send prior notification of military exercises conducted on their territory with 25,000 (or more) ground troops. However, this regime allowed any participating state 'whose territory extends beyond Europe' to notify just its military activities taking place within *a 250-kilometer-wide area* from its frontier facing (or shared with) any other European participating state – an arrangement adopted at the request of the USSR which invoked the considerable extent of its European territory and also the fact that the territory of the two North American participating states was not covered. In accordance with a Turkish demand, the Helsinki regime excluded the obligation to provide any prior notification in cases where the 250-kilometre-wide area bordered or faced a non-CSCE participating state: that provision actually concerned Turkey's frontiers with Iran, Iraq and Syria as well as the USSR's frontiers with Iran. As to the CSBMs of the 1986 Stockholm regime, they were applicable in the whole of continental Europe and in an area of 250 kilometres on the Asian part of the USSR and Turkey. For more details, see Victor-Yves Ghebali, *Confidence-Building Measures Within the CSCE Process. Paragraph-by Paragraph*

After the collapse of communism, the CSCE underwent a structural and functional overhaul and was renamed – with retrospective effect – 'Organization for Security and Co-operation in Europe' (OSCE).[2] It also welcomed some twenty new political units, thus raising its constituency up to fifty-five participating states 'from Vancouver to Vladivostok'. An enlargement of such a magnitude essentially resulted from a decision under which all the former members of the USSR, including the Republics of Caucasus (Armenia, Azerbaijan, Georgia) and Central Asia Republics (Kazakhstan, Kirghyztan, Tajikistan, Turkmenistan, Uzbekistan), were considered eligible for regular membership.[3] Basically dictated by the necessity of binding all the USSR's successors states to the pan-European commitments on human rights and arms control previously subscribed to by Moscow, as well as by the concern of preserving the Muslim states from the contagion (or temptation) of religious fundamentalism, that decision transformed the OSCE into a plain Eurasian institution viewing the Caucasus and Central Asia as part and parcel of Greater Europe.

Within the OSCE, the new Eurasian actors do not form either a global diplomatic cluster or any sub-regional grouping or groupings: there is no tripartite Caucasus bloc because the Nagorno-Karabakh conflict has remained an unsettled conflict, and no Central Asian caucus because the political agendas of the concerned states are divergent.[4] However, as new participating states, they presented two common denominators. First, they brought with them a number of protracted armed conflicts (Nagorno-Karabakh, South Ossetia, Abkhazia, Tajikistan) whose management inevitably falls on the shoulders of a inexperienced OSCE. Second, falling short of any democratic tradition (due to a long-standing incorporation into authoritarian political structures), all of them revealed a structural inability to meet the basic OSCE human dimension standards. As a response, the OSCE developed, on the basis of its concept of comprehensive and co-operative security, some sort of Eurasian political strategy. This consists of conflict management and democratic stabilization. From a more global regional perspective, it also includes a special relationship with Japan and South Korea.

Analysis of the Helsinki and Stockholm Regimes (New York: United Nations, 1989; UN Publications Sales No. GV.E.89.0.5).

[2] As from 1 January 1995.

[3] See Journal No. 2 (28 January 1992) of the 6th Meeting of the CSCE Committee of Senior Officials.

[4] However, since a couple of years or so ago, four Republics of the former USSR including two of the Caucasus states have regularly been performing as an active diplomatic cluster known as GUAM: Georgia, Ukraine, Azerbaijan and Moldova. Their common denominator is that all of them are confronted with situations of actual (or potential, in the case of Ukraine) territorial secession involving the Russian Federation as a key political actor. In 1999, Uzbekistan joined the group, which is now known as GUUAM.

Conflict Management

While remaining a forum which debates politico-military security issues and formulates human dimension standards, the OSCE of the post-Cold War period were attributed operational capacities to address all phases of the conflict management cycle: early warning, preventive action, peacemaking and post-conflict rehabilitation. For those purposes, it mainly disposes of 'Long-Term Missions'[5] and (for ethnic conflict prevention) a High Commissioner on National Minorities. At present, the OSCE is involved in the management of some fifteen conflictual situations of varying degrees of intensity. Within this general picture, Eurasia accounts for not less than five conflicts necessitating peacemaking efforts in the Caucasus and post-conflict rehabilitation activities in Central Asia.[6]

Peacemaking Activities in the Caucasus

In this region, bottlenecked between the Black Sea and the Caspian Sea, the OSCE addresses the conflicts which have erupted within Azerbaijan (Nagorno-Karabakh), Georgia (South Ossetia and Abkhazia) and also the Russian Federation (Chechnya) with different techniques.[7] The Nagorno-Karabakh conflict is managed by the Minsk Group (a body attempting to hammer out a political comprehensive solution) and by a Personal Representative of the OSCE Chairman-in-Office whose tasks are to promote confidence-building measures and to conduct investigations about alleged violations of the ceasefire – not counting a Vienna-based *High-Level Planning Group* (HLPG) which prepares, since December 1994, contingency plans for the deployment of a pan-European peacekeeping force in Nagorno-Karabakh.[8]

---

[5] Some of those filed missions are however dubbed 'Assistance Group' (Chechnya), 'Presence' (Albania), 'Advisory and Monitoring Group' (Belarus), 'Verification Mission' or 'Task Force' (Kosovo).

[6] Outside the Caucasus and Central Asia, the OSCE is managing conflictual situations in the Balkans (Macedonia, Bosnia-Herzegovina, Croatia, Albania, Kosovo), Central and Eastern Europe (Moldova, Ukraine, Belarus) and the Baltic region (Estonia, Latvia). For a comprehensive analysis of the OSCE's conflict management activities see Victor-Yves Ghebali, *L'OSCE dans l'Europe Post-communiste, 1990–1996. Vers une Identité Paneuropéenne de Sécurité* (Brussels: Bruylant, 1996), pp. 181–430, 604–622.

[7] As a basically internal Russian matter, the Chechnya conflict remains beyond the scope of the present analysis.

[8] On March 1992, the Ministerial Council agreed on the principle of convening in Minsk, under the aegis of the OSCE, a conference designed to serve as an ongoing forum for the negotiation of a peaceful settlement of the Nagorno-Karabakh conflict. Contrary to standard OSCE practice, the conference was designed as a restricted body of eleven participants: the direct state parties (Armenia and Azerbaijan), the acting OSCE Troika (Czech and Slovak Republic, Germany and Sweden), the host country (Belarus) and a handful of interested countries (France, Italy, the Russian Federation, Turkey, the USA) – it being also understood that the Armenians and the Azeris of Nagorno-Karabakh

As to the South Ossetian and Abkhazian conflicts, they are managed by means of a single Long-Term Mission to Georgia operational since December 1992. Headquartered in Tbilisi and disposing since April 1997 of a branch office in Tskhinvali (South Ossetia), the Mission was initially created to facilitate negotiations on a peaceful settlement of the conflict in the breakaway region of South Ossetia; but in 1994, its mandate was extended to the other breakaway region, Abkhazia, and to Georgia as a whole: in addition to assisting in the definition of a new political status for South Ossetia and monitoring the tripartite military 'peacekeeping' forces deployed there under the auspices of the Commonwealth of Independent states (CIS), the Mission also supports support the peacemaking efforts of the United Nations in Abkhazia and contributes to the development of democratic institutions in the Republic of Georgia at large. All conflicts (including that of Nagorno-Karabakh which also constitutes a confrontation between Armenia and Azerbaijan) are fundamentally of an intra-state nature.[9] As such, they call for three main general remarks.

Firstly, the Caucasus conflicts raise a fundamental politico-legal issue (self-determination of peoples vs. territorial integrity of states) which entails a direct clash between two principles of the Helsinki Decalogue.[10] In fact, all conflicts generated political secession formally justified by the wishes of the concerned populations to create a new independent sovereign state (the Abkhaz), to integrate an existing kin nation-state (the Armenians populating the enclave of Nagorno-

---

could occasionally be invited as 'interested parties'. Owing to lack of agreement among the parties to the conflict, the Minsk Conference was never convened. However, its members have been meeting for the same purpose (but without Armenia and Azerbaijan) as the Minsk Group. In August 1995, the OSCE Chairman-in-Office decided to appoint a Personal Representative based in Tbilisi (Georgia) with branch offices in Baku (Azerbaijan), Yerevan (Armenia) and Stepanakert (Nagorno-Karabakh).

[9] Azerbaijan views the Nagorno-Karabakh issue as an inter-state conflict resulting from a direct assault of the Republic of Armenia against its territorial integrity. However, Armenia denies having any territorial claim and sustains that there is only an intra-state conflict. The Armenians of Nagorno-Karabakh argue that the territory 'has never, legally or otherwise, belonged to a sovereign independent Azerbaijan. Its inclusion in 1921 in the structure of the Azerbaijani SSR was unlawfully ordered by a political party (not even a government) of a third country, that is, the Caucasian Bureau of the Russian Communist Party. During the USSR's existence, Nagorno-Karabakh was part of a multi-layered colonial system and was subjected to Soviet Azerbaijan, not on a contractual basis, but by an administrative reference to the Soviet Constitution' (*Nagorno Karabakh. A White Paper* [Yerevan: Armenian Center for National and International Studies, 1997], p. 8). The Armenian government points out that when Azerbaijan declared independence from the USSR in 1991, 'it re-established its 1919–1920 independence, thus nullifying those legal acts of the Soviet era that affixed Azerbaijan's authority over Karabakh' (Address of the Armenian Minister of Foreign Affairs to the OSCE Permanent Council: PC.DEL/429/98, 8 October 1998).

[10] 'Territorial Integrity of States' and 'Equal Rights and Self-Determination of Peoples' respectively represent Principles IV and VIII of the Helsinki Decalogue.

Karabakh) or, as in the case of the South Ossetians, to join their ethnic kindred living in a non-autonomous political entity: the Republic of North Ossetia-Alania, a sub-part of the Russian Federation. The position held by the OSCE *vis-à-vis* that doctrinal issue in the specific context of the Caucasus conflicts is crystal clear: territorial integrity prevails over the self-determination of peoples insofar as the external dimension of the latter (implying independence) is concerned.

The OSCE cared to reaffirm the territorial integrity of Georgia in many official pronouncements, including the December 1996 Lisbon Summit Declaration.[11] However, it has failed to do so as regards to Azerbaijan because of the persistent outright opposition of Armenia.[12] When the Lisbon Summit considered the principles recommended by the co-chairmen of the Minsk process for the settlement of the Nagorno-Karabakh conflict (territorial integrity of Armenia and Azerbaijan; the legal status of Nagorno-Karabakh defined in an agreement based on self-determination conferring 'the highest degree of self-rule' within Azerbaijan; guaranteed security for the whole population of Nagorno-Karabakh) all participating states expressed their support – except Armenia which opposed any kind of language hinting that Nagorno-Karabakh belonged to Azerbaijan. Given the circumstances, the OSCE Chairman-in-Office took the unprecedented initiative of issuing a special statement (attached to the Lisbon Summit Declaration) recapping on the three above-mentioned principles and regretting 'that one participating state could not accept this'.[13]

Obviously concerned by a possible snowball effect in Europe and elsewhere, the OSCE has clearly excluded independence for ethnic minority populations claiming a right to self-determination. At the same time, in an effort to reconcile the principles of the territorial integrity of states and the self-determination of peoples, it has recognized for those ethnic minorities some sort of right to a wide form of self-rule including guarantees for full human rights protection and preservation of their collective identity. OSCE peacemaking efforts in the Caucasus have thus been suggesting solutions based on full respect for the

---

[11] 'We [the participating states] reaffirm our utmost support for the sovereignty and territorial integrity of Georgia within its internationally recognised borders' (paragraph 20 of the 1996 Lisbon Summit Declaration). For other statements see the 1993 Rome Ministerial Council Decisions (paragraph I.2.1), the 1994 Budapest Decisions (first paragraph of Chapter I) and Decision No. 1 of the 1998 Oslo Ministerial Council.

[12] When the OSCE framed the mandate of the Minsk process, it did not make any reference whatsoever to the principle of territorial integrity of states. Motivated by the desirability of giving *carte blanche* to the OSCE mediators, that omission was also due to lack of experience in the field of conflict management – Nagorno-Karabakh being the first conflict submitted to the full management of the OSCE.

[13] S(96) JOURNAL No. 2 of 3 December 1996, Appendix 1. Armenia reacted by means of a statement stressing its conviction 'that a solution of the problem can be found on the basis of international law and the principles laid down in the Helsinki Final Act, above all on the basis of the principle of self-determination' (ibid., Appendix 2).

territorial integrity of the states of the region while providing for the largest possible autonomy status to the breakaway territories. A compromise of that kind is certainly not too high a price to put an end to destabilizing regional conflicts. The trouble is that it also condones, more or less implicitly, territorial ethnic homogeneity – usually achieved through ethnic cleansing.

Secondly, conflict management activities in the Caucasus are conducted with poor co-ordination between the OSCE and the United Nations. Given the development of armed conflicts in Greater Europe (and the encouragement given by the United Nations' Agenda for Peace to regional bodies to contribute to the global burden of collective security), the Helsinki Follow-up Meeting proclaimed the OSCE, in July 1992, a 'regional agreement' under Chapter VIII of the Charter.[14] Subsequently, the UN and the OSCE signed a framework agreement dedicated to 'ensuring co-ordination and complementarity in planning and carrying out activities, to avoiding duplication and, where necessary, to assisting one another'.[15] Since then, a growing interface has developed, particularly in the field of conflict prevention and crisis management in several regions. In the Caucasus, its record has remained uneven.

In Nagorno-Karabakh, a sound division of labour apparently prevails: conflict management activities here are performed, both at the negotiating and operational level, by a leading organization (the OSCE) which invites the United Nations Secretariat to be represented in the meetings of the Minsk Group and regularly briefs the Security Council on the progress achieved by the latter.[16] The most significant part played by the United Nations is to provide political support to the OSCE by formally endorsing the settlement proposals tabled by the Minsk Group. It did so in 1993 through Security Council resolutions 822 (30 April), 853 (29 July), 874 (14 October) and 884 (12 November). However, the division of labour presented one flaw which must not be underestimated: the Security Council resolutions clearly affirmed that Nagorno-Karabakh was part of Azerbaijan. Although no political meaning could be attributed to it,[17] that discrepancy between the United Nations and the OSCE has been undermining the credibility of the

---

[14] Helsinki Decisions 1992: paragraph 2 of Chapter IV; see also paragraph 25 of the 1992 Helsinki Summit Document. The *Agenda for Peace* (UN document: A/47/277 – S/24111 of 17 June 1992) referred to the role of regional organizations in its paragraph 154.

[15] CSCE Communication No. 166 and UN Document A/48/185 of 1 June 1993. The 1993 Framework Agreement for Co-operation and Co-ordination was followed by specific agreements concerning Macedonia, Bosnia-Herzegovina, and so on. The OSCE participates in the work of the General Assembly as an observer since the adoption by the latter, on 22 October 1993, of Resolution 48/5.

[16] The OSCE has also drawn upon the United Nations in its planning for a pan-European peacekeeping operation in Nagorno-Karabakh.

[17] This just had to do with the fact that the resolutions of the Security Council are not taken by consensus, but through a majority vote.

Minsk Group and encouraging the parties to the conflict to 'shop around' between the two organizations.

The division of labour in Georgia is of a more 'schizophrenic' type since the peacemaking responsibilities of the OSCE are strictly limited to South Ossetia and those of the United Nations to Abkhazia. Likewise, the Russian-led 'peacekeeping' forces in South Ossetia and Abkahzia are respectively observed in total separation by the OSCE and the United Nations. Such a dichotomy only exists because Georgia requested the United Nations to handle the Abkhaz conflict in Autumn 1992, that is to say before the OSCE's decision to establish a Long-Term Mission in Tbilisi.[18] Although the UN receives regular information on the OSCE activities in South Ossetia and the OSCE participates as an observer in the political negotiations conducted by the United Nations for the settlement of the Abkhaz conflict, that sort of arrangement allows a more formal than substantial co-ordination. It must also be noted that the United Nations has refused to follow up the suggestion, made in 1992 by the OSCE, to designate a single joint representative for Georgia as a whole. Ultimately, in 1996, it permitted the OSCE to appoint an officer to the UN Human Rights Office in Sukhumi, thus accepting some field co-ordination in human dimension activities. In a place where two breakaway regions challenge the territorial integrity of the same single state and where three international organizations are active through (two) distinct field missions and (three) peacekeeping operations, all this certainly does not reflect an integrated approach.

Thirdly, all peacemaking efforts undertaken in the Caucasus have so far failed to yield results. Since 1992, the OSCE has been in a more or less complete deadlock over Nagorno-Karabakh, South Ossetia and Abkhazia. The main reasons for the lack of breakthrough or meaningful progress have to do with the problem of ethno-nationalism (which permeates all conflicts), the limits of the OSCE's conflict management capacities and, more particularly, the ambiguous political role played by Russia in the region.

In all of the Caucasus conflicts, ethno-nationalism represents a parameter of overwhelming weight. Each of them opposes populations which differ in terms of religion and/or language. The Nagorno-Karabakh conflict confronts Christian Armenians (who speak an Indo-European language) with Muslim Turkish-speaking Azeris. South Ossetians and Georgians are both basically Christians, but the latter speak a Kartvelian (South Caucasian) language and the former an Iranian

---

[18] In Abkhazia, the role performed by the United Nations is two-fold: the sponsorship of a Geneva-based peacemaking process under the leadership of a Personal Representative of the Secretary-General, and the conduct of a peacekeeping operation: UNOMIG (United Nations Observer Mission in Georgia). UNOMIG was established by Security Council resolution 858 of 24 August 1993. Its mandate includes, besides the monitoring and verifying of the effectiveness of the ceasefire, the observation of the CIS (Russian-led) 'Collective Peacekeeping Forces'.

(Indo-European) one; in any case, the Georgians do not consider the South Ossetians as a true indigenous ethnie of Georgia.[19] By contrast, Abkhaz and Georgians who spoke related languages (respectively north-western and southern branches of the family of the Caucasian languages) constitute founding ethnies of the Georgian nation;[20] however, they remain basically separated by Islam which predominates in Abkhazia because the latter was dominated by the Turks for a longer period than the former. Nagorno-Karabakh Armenians, South Ossetians and Abkhaz offer clear cases of 'concentrated' (as opposed to 'scattered') ethnic minorities. In 1989, the year of the ultimate census conducted in the USSR, the first two groups represented the overwhelming majority of the population in their respective regions (Armenians: 73.4 per cent; South Ossetians: 70 per cent), while the Abkhaz represented only 17.8 per cent (against 47 per cent of Georgians) in Abkhazia.[21] Whatever the percentage, all those groups were small in number: 93,267 Abkhaz, 70,000 South Ossetians and 137,2000 Nagorno-Karabakh Armenians. Yet, each of them has considered itself not as an ethnic minority but as a people entitled to the right of self-determination.

Admittedly, ethnic differences by themselves do not suffice to automatically generate ethnic conflicts. In most cases, those conflicts erupt either when abuses against a minority group reach an intolerable level or when ethnicity is instrumentalized for a variety of purposes by political leaders. Nagorno-Karabakh illustrates the first case and Georgia the second. In Nagorno-Karabakh, the enmity between the two ethnies had a long-standing history: the Azeris considered the Armenians of Nagorno-Karabakh as intruders whose presence was the outcome of the secular Czarist policy of Christians resettlement in the Russian Empire; for their own part, the Armenians of Nagorno-Karabakh (who argued that their territory has belonged to Armenia since the most ancient historical times) accused the Azeris of a series of pogroms interpreted as a prolongation of the genocide carried out against them by the Turks in 1915. Georgia offered a quite different situation, characterized by endemic ethnic tensions and not deeply-rooted hatred.[22] Just before the collapse of Communism, Georgia's population included some 30

---

[19] The Ossetians are the offspring of the Iranian Alans who mixed with the Caucasian populations in the early Middle Ages. Traditionally, the Georgians reject the concept of South Ossetia; instead, they refer to the Samachablo territory located in the Shida Kartli region (*Human Rights and Democratization in the Newly Independent States of the Soviet Union* [Washington: Commission on Security and Co-operation in Europe, 1993], p. 155).

[20] Georgia grew out of the unification, in the eleventh century, of three kingdoms: Abkhazia, Kartli and Kakhetia.

[21] Initially forming the majority population (90 per cent), the Abkhaz undertook a mass exodus from Abkhazia to Turkey and Greece following the Russian–Turkish war of 1877–78.

[22] For instance, since 1978, the Abkhaz have been over-represented at parliamentary level: they detained 28 seats against 26 for the Georgians and 11 for the other ethnies.

per cent of ethnic minorities mainly concentrated in the Autonomous Republics of Adzharia and Abkhazia as well as in the Autonomous Region (Oblast) of South Ossetia. The Soviet power incorporated those ethnic territorial entities within Georgia in order to neutralize and better control Georgian as well as non-Georgian nationalism.[23] When Georgia proclaimed independence (in 1991), it proceeded to eliminate the consequences of fifty years of unwanted cultural Russification. Initiated by a charismatic ultra-nationalist President (Zviad Gamsakhurdia), the promotion of Georgian national identity regrettably unfolded at the expense of non-Georgian ethnic groups since it began with a new law establishing the supremacy of the Georgian language. The provocative and uncompromising posture of the Georgian leadership, who refused to enter into a constructive dialogue with ethnic minority groups while accusing them of collusion with Moscow, exacerbated ethno-nationalistic claims hitherto more or less acute in the two regions. Following armed hostilities accompanied by ethnic cleansing operations, South Ossetia and Abkahzia proclaimed independence on 19 January 1992 and 23 July 1992 respectively.[24] In both cases, two factors contributed to the success of secession: military support from Russian- (formerly Soviet-)stationed troops and an ongoing civil war in Georgia.

Conflicts due to ethno-nationalism are more complex than any other type of intra-state conflict. Involving non-state actors (warlords, irregular military troops) who do not feel bound to respect the basic rules of international humanitarian law, they easily lead to ethnic cleansing and even genocidal situations. They pose insuperable obstacles for effective diplomatic mediation because their protagonists are generally driven by emotional feelings more than by rational goals, and because a global compromise would obviously give the secessionists less than what they already had: *de facto* independence. A purely co-operative institution such as the OSCE remains basically unfit to cope with such conflicts whose ending

---

[23] The most typical example being that of the Ossetian people, who were distributed between Northern Ossetia (Russian Federation) and Southern Ossetia (Georgia) and, in consequence, obliged to use either the Cyrillic or the Georgian alphabet.

[24] The South Ossetians seceded not in view of forming a new state but just to join their kindred in the 600,000-populated North Ossetia-Alania (Russian Federation), that is, they considered Russification preferable to 'Georgianisation'. Actually, the North Ossetians (who are Muslims contrary to most of South Ossetians) have not been quite enthusiastic about reunification mainly because their Republic includes the Prigorodny region, a territory claimed by Ingushetia as having initially belonged to the Chechnya-Ingushetia Autonomous Republic (unlawfully abolished in 1994 and re-established in 1957). Given that a reunification with South Ossetia (involving modification of administrative borders within the Russian Federation) would politically strengthen the Ingush claims, the North Ossetians have preferred not to challenge the territorial integrity of Georgia. It should also be noted that North Ossetia-Alania has signed the ceasefire agreement of June 1992 and contributes to the quadripartite body which monitors it.

is conceivable either with a military victory by one of the warring parties or with a coercive intervention by a coalition of willing states – but not by means of standard mediation techniques.[25]

Belonging to what Moscow calls the 'Near Abroad', the Caucasus represents a zone in which Russia have traditionally had and still has today (mainly in relation to the issue of Caspian oil resources), considerable political, geostrategic and economic interests.[26] It is Moscow (and not the OSCE or the UN) that has brokered ceasefires in South Ossetia (June 1992), Abkahzia (September 1992, July 1993, May 1994) and Nagorno-Karabakh (May 1994). Russian troops are present in South Ossetia and Abkahzia under the guise of CIS military 'peacekeeping' forces, an unnatural situation which has compelled the OSCE and the United Nations to monitor their activities there.[27] The pan-European peacekeeping force that the OSCE intended to deploy in Nagorno-Karabakh was never set up because Moscow asked for the lion's share in regard to its composition and command. Anyhow, Russia can hardly claim to possess the basic quality expected from a mediator: impartiality. Despite being one of the co-chairmen of the Minsk process,[28] it has never hesitated to conduct separate negotiations with the two parties to the Nagorno-Karabakh conflict, thus duplicating or circumventing the peacemaking efforts of the OSCE. In addition, Moscow has been favouring Yerevan in terms of financial and military support, most presumably because the territory of Armenia (which separates Azerbaijan from Turkey) presents the advantage of breaking the geopolitical continuity between Ankara and the Turkish-speaking Republics of Central Asia.

Similar remarks can be applied to the Georgian case. In South Ossetia, the Moscow-dominated quadripartite Joint Control Commission (Russia, Georgia and the two Ossetias) which monitors the ceasefire, plays a peacemaking role

---

[25] However, due to the generally successful operations of the High Commissioner on National Minorities, the OSCE has a positive record in the prevention of ethnic conflicts.

[26] Especially in relation with the extraordinary vast reserves of gas and oil presumed to exist in both the Caucasus (Azerbaijan) and Central Asia (Kazakhstan and Turkmenistan).

[27] In Abkhazia, the CIS Collective Peacekeeping Forces continue to operate notwithstanding that their mandate expired on 30 June 1998 (paragraph 21 of UN document S/1999/60, 20 January 1999). The Georgian side has long been arguing that the presence of the CIS Forces could no loner be acceptable 'unless the decisions of the CIS summit meeting of 28 March 1997 on the expansion of the security zone and the repatriation of the refugees and internally displaced persons were implemented' (paragraph 8 of UN document S/1997/558, 18 July 1997 and UN Press Release SC/6708 of 30 July 1999).

[28] Russia became one of the co-chairmen of the Minsk Group at the end of 1994, following a formal decision made by the Budapest Summit. Since 1997, the Minsk Group is also co-chaired by France and the USA (the presence of the latter having been requested by the Azeris to counterbalance France's alleged pro-Armenian bias).

duplicating to some extent that of the OSCE. In Abkhazia, Russia carries on direct negotiations with the parties in addition to its official participation in the UN-sponsored Geneva process as 'facilitator'.[29] Besides, it cannot be denied that military assistance provided for by Russia in 1992–93 significantly contributed to the success of secession in both South Ossetia and Abkhazia, and that the brokering of ceasefire agreements there was made conditional on a number of major political and military concessions from the Georgian government. Although Moscow has formally recognized the territorial integrity of all the Caucasus countries, its policy aims at containing violence below escalation level but also maintaining enough tensions to justify Russia's mediation efforts and politico-military presence.

The conflicts in Nagorno-Karabakh, South Ossetia and Abkhazia have taken a heavy toll in human lives, producing hundreds of thousands of refugees and displaced persons. They continue to stand in the way of economic development and regional co-operation in the Caucasus. Does that mean that the peacemaking efforts of the OSCE (and of the United nations) have had no positive effects whatsoever in the region? While obviously unable to impose terms of settlement as regards South Ossetia, Abkhazia or Nagorno-Karabakh, the OSCE has nevertheless demonstrated its relevance through the performance of functions related to confidence-building and support to democratic processes. From this perspective, its record concerning South Ossetia appears as not purely negative. First, the OSCE Long-Term Mission facilitated and fostered an ongoing dialogue between political representatives of both sides, including between the President of Georgia (George Shevardnadze) and the leader of South Ossetia (Ludvig Chibirov).[30] Second, it is

---

[29] Since November 1997, the Geneva process has operated on the basis of a Co-ordinating Council including the two parties, the Russian Federation as facilitator, the OSCE and the so-called Group of Friends of the Secretary-General for Georgia. In addition, there are three working groups respectively focusing on the following issues: security problems; refugees and internally displaced persons; and economic and social problems (Talking points of the Special Representative of the UN Secretary-General at the 167th Meeting of the OSCE Permanent Council on 7 May 1998: OSCE document PC.DEL/179/98).

[30] On 14 June 1994, a Georgian–South Ossetian declaration countersigned by the OSCE provided for a pragmatic co-operation in fighting organized crime, restoring rail and road communications, economic reconstruction, housing and refugees (Secretary-General's *Annual Report 1994 on OSCE Activities*: DOC. 1071/94, p. 5). On 16 May 1996, the two parties (together with Russia and North Ossetia-Alania) signed in Moscow a 'Memorandum on Measures to Ensure Security and Reinforce Mutual Confidence' (REF.SEC/219/96 of 14 April 1996). In August of the same year, a Georgian–South Ossetian summit was held in Vladikavkaz (*Annual Report 1996 on OSCE Activities*: DOC.SEC/3/96, pp. 4–5); subsequent summit meetings took place in November 1997 and June 1998 respectively in Java and Borjoni/Georgia (*Annual Report 1998 on OSCE Activities:* SEC.DOC/2/98, p. 8). In October 1996, the OSCE Long-Term Mission obtained the consent of the authorities of South Ossetia to open a branch office in

actively promoting the development of a democratic civic society in Georgia by carrying out regular visits to detention sites and attending trials of political prisoners, contributing to human rights education in primary and secondary schools, organizing the training of journalists and, along with the ODIHR, monitoring the advance of legal reforms in the country, and so on.[31] All those efforts have generated a notable evolution of minds in Tbilisi. The government and most of the political parties of Georgia now admit that the Georgian side has a part of responsibility for the events which pushed South Ossetia onto the path of secession. More significantly, they agree to offer South Ossetia an autonomy status not limited to cultural autonomy. Unfortunately, there has been no matching reaction in South Ossetia. Convinced that time works in favour of *de facto* independence, the South Ossetian leadership has been playing the game of negotiation without making concessions on matters of substance. Its strategy aims at gaining time while not alienating the OSCE, in order to get some humanitarian and economic assistance.

In Abkhazia, where the United Nations operates as the leading agency, the role of the OSCE is only that of a political observer to the Geneva peacemaking process, and of a subsidiary human rights field monitor.[32] As such, its imprint on the Abkhaz problem is negligible, all the more so given that the latter has been worsening.[33] So far, there has been no progress on the two most basic issues of constitutional status and the return of refugees and internally displaced persons: to

---

Tskhinvali and there organized a round table between journalists of both sides (*Annual Report 1996 on OSCE Activities*: DOC.SEC/3/96, p. 5). On 17 April 1997, a new Memorandum on the non-use of violence and the return of refugees was signed (*OSCE Long-Term Field Activity. Compendium of Reports prepared by the Research Staff of the OSCE Parliamentary Assembly*: PA.GAL/16/98, 16 July 1998, p. 28). More lately, the first ever meeting between the heads of executive branches of government took place in Tskhinvali in order to start up negotiations on an 'Intermediary Document' formulating principles of a comprehensive settlement (PC.FR/1/99 of 28 January 1999).

[31] *OSCE Long-Term Field Activity*, op. cit., p. 28. The steady progress made towards democracy was rewarded in 1999 by the admission of Georgia to the Council of Europe.

[32] Before seconding one of its officials to the Human Rights Office established in December 1996 by the United Nations in Sukhumi, the OSCE contribution mainly consisted of visits to Abkhaz prisoners in Georgia and Georgian prisoners in Abkhazia (*Annual Report 1996 on OSCE Activities*: DOC.SEC/3/96, p. 5).

[33] In May 1998, serious military incidents erupted in the Gali district, a region in the west of Georgia inhabited by Georgians but partly controlled by the Abkhaz. As a consequence of the Abkhaz gaining full control of the region, 50,000 people were again forcibly ousted from their homes. At the end of the same year, the OSCE Oslo Ministerial Council agreed on the principle of 'exploring [with the United Nations] the utility of the establishment of an OSCE office in the region of Gali' (MC(7).DEC/1 of 3 December 1998). There has been no positive reaction from Tskhinvali whose leaders do not forget that the OSCE, through the Budapest 1994 and Lisbon 1996 Summits Declarations, formally accused Abkahzia of ethnic cleansing.

Georgia's offer concerning the transformation of Abkhazia into a subject of a Georgian Federation, the Abkhaz leader (Vladislav Ardzinba) responded that it could only accept a loose confederation between two sovereign states – on the ground that re-subjugation to Georgian sovereignty would initiate a process of irreversible assimilation. Likewise, the repatriation of some 300,000 existing refugees and displaced persons (a precondition posed by Georgia) is resisted by the Abkhaz who, representing only a small fraction of Abkhazia's population, prefer cementing the ethno-demographic changes brought about by the 1993 civil war.[34] Although facing a less than supportive attitude from Moscow, the Abkhaz leadership has not softened its uncompromising position.[35] At present, the deadlock is practically total.[36]

In Nagorno-Karabakh, all the successive Minsk Group proposals for a comprehensive settlement have been rejected by the parties: the 1993 'Adjusted Timetable of Urgent Steps to Implement UN Security Council Resolutions', the 1996 'Framework for a Package Deal', the 1997 'two-staged-approach' and, most recently, the 1998 concept of a 'Common state'.[37] Armenia rejects the self-rule option (including the 'Common State' concept) on the ground that the Armenians

---

[34] The latest decision to hold in Abkahzia presidential elections in the autumn of 1999 (following the parliamentary elections of November–December 1996 and the local elections of March 1998) has to be assessed against that specific background. The illegality of past and scheduled elections has been denounced by the United Nations, the OSCE and the European Union.

[35] Lest it create a legal precedent applicable to Chechnya (and also given the prospects of a international decision on the channelling of Caspian oil via Russian pipelines crossing Georgia), Russia has become much less supportive to the Abkhaz cause.

[36] The only visible results of the Geneva peace process are related to the 1998 and 1999 declarations on bilateral confidence-building measures adopted in Athens (paragraph 10 of UN document S/1998/1012, 29 October 1998) and Istanbul (OSCE document: SEC.DEL/214/99 of 10 June 1999).

[37] The 1993 'Adjusted Timetable' envisaged a step-by-step approach providing for the withdrawal of Armenian troops from occupied Azeri territories, the establishment of a permanent ceasefire under OSCE monitoring, the lifting of the blockade imposed by Azerbaijan to Armenia and the formal convening of the Minsk Conference (UN Document S/26732 of 15 November 1993). The 1996 'Framework' suggested the evacuation of occupied territories, Armenia's unhindered access to Nagorno-Karabakh and the attribution of a wide status of self-rule to Nagorno-Karabakh within Azerbaijan accompanied by security guarantees (UN Document S/1996/259 of 10 April 1996); the principles underlying the 'Framework' were reaffirmed in Appendix 1 to the December 1996 Lisbon Summit Declaration which all the participating states except Armenia endorsed (see footnote 13). The 1997 two-staged approach offered demilitarization of the line of contact and the return of refugees on the one hand and autonomy status for Nagorno-Karabakh on the other hand. In 1998, the Co-Chairs of the Minsk Group informed the CIO about 'a new approach to resolving the Nagorno-Karabakh's status under their consideration that seeks to apply creatively the concept of a common state' (SEC.INF/363/98 of 12 October 1998).

of Nagorno-Karabakh are entitled to self-determination – and that anyhow human rights and security guarantees for ethnic minorities could never be effective within in a state like Azerbaijan which has no such thing as civil society.[38] As to Azerbaijan, it rules any settlement formula which does not reconfirm its territorial integrity.[39] The real positive aspect of OSCE's painstaking efforts concerns the so-called 'crisis-monitoring' function performed since 1995 by the Personal Representative of the Chairman-in-Office for Nagorno-Karabakh; entailing verification about allegations of ceasefire violations, it represents a limited but relevant means of conflict recurrence prevention.

Post-conflict Rehabilitation in Central Asia (Tajikistan)

Unlike the conflicts in the Caucasus, the inter-state conflict which erupted in May 1992 in Tajikistan had no real ethnic connotation. It was a civil war waged along regional, clanic and ideological cleavages.[40] As such, it opposed the Khujand and Kulyab regional groups and clans (who have been monopolizing power all through the Soviet era) to those of Garm and Pamir over political and economic power-sharing. Taking advantage of Russia's military support, the neo-Communist secular-oriented Khujand–Kulyab coalition defeated, in few months, the amalgam of democratic, nationalist and Islamic forces formed by the Garmis and the Pamiris. The defeated groups (all of them indiscriminately dubbed 'Islamic fundamentalists' by the government) took refuge in northern Afghanistan. Reorganized near the border, they initiated as from April 1993, with the backing of the host state, military operations of harassment against the Tajik and Russian (national or CIS) forces. The civil war, which formally ended in mid-1997, provoked over 60,000 casualties. It also produced 60,000 refugees (who fled to Afghanistan) and more than 600,000 internally displaced persons – not counting the migration of a large number of Russian and Kirgyz to Russia or Central Asia. In Tajikistan, the OSCE did play a much more significant conflict management role than in the Caucasus. The main reason for that has to be accounted for the positive support eventually given by Moscow to the peacemaking process and the

---

[38] Statement of the Armenian Delegation at the 61st Permanent Council Meeting (REF.PC/179/96 of 7 March 1996).

[39] On the 'Common State' concept, Azerbaijan argues that such a concept, 'having no precedent in international practice, contradicts the very OSCE principles' (OSCE document PC.DEL/76/99, 25 February 1999). What complicates the matter in the Nagorno-Karabakh conflict is that some 20 per cent of the territory of Azerbaijan (in addition to Nagorno-Karabakh itself) has been captured by the Armenians.

[40] Tajikistan, the only Iranian-speaking country of (otherwise Turkish-speaking) Central Asia, became independent with a number of serious handicaps. The poorest and the least industrialized Republic of the USSR, it represented an artificial conglomerate of regions with no real ethnic or historic relevance. As a result, Tajikistan was never able to develop a strong national identity.

sound functional division of labour achieved between the respective OSCE and United Nations activities in the country.

Firstly, the positive role of the Russian Federation. Apart from just being a territory of the 'Near Abroad', Tajikistan shares a 1,387 kilometre-long border with the Islamic Republic of Afghanistan. This particular fact enabled Russia to meddle into Central Asia more deeply than in the Caucasus. It supplied the regime with political and economic assistance which turned Tajikistan into a kind of protectorate. Under the umbrella of CIS-sponsored Collective Peacekeeping Forces, Russian troops were deployed for the official purpose of helping the Tajik neo-Communist regime to cope with internal and external military threats. As a direct participant to the peacemaking efforts sponsored by the UN since 1994, Russia did not encourage the Tajik regime to accept power-sharing with the United Tajik Opposition (UTO) until it realized that there could be no military solution to the conflict and that a political compromise would promote regional security without eliminating or reducing its influence in Tajikistan. Concerns raised by the military success of the Taliban forces in Afghanistan accelerated Moscow's evolution. Finally, under serious pressure exerted by Russia (and Iran as regards the UTO), the warring parties signed in the Russian capital, on 27 June 1997, a United Nations-sponsored 'General Agreement on Establishing Peace and National Accord in Tajikistan' (General Agreement).[41]

Secondly, the sound division of labour between the OSCE and the United Nations. When the conflict erupted, the Tajik government turned to the United Nations and not the OSCE. In response, the United Nations initiated a political peace process ('Inter-Tajik Talks') co-ordinated by a Special Envoy of the Secretary-General.[42] It also tasked a United Nations Mission of Observers in Tajikistan (UNMOT) to monitor the respect of a temporary ceasefire agreement and to liaise with the CIS military forces and the Russian Border Guards present in

---

[41] The General Agreement (UN document A/52/219 – S/1997/510, Annex I) was the ultimate element of a complex series of previous accords: the Protocol of 17 August 1995 on the Basic Principles for the Establishment of Peace and National Concord in Tajikistan (S/1995/720, Annex); the Protocol of 23 December 1996 on the Basic Functions and Powers of the Commission for National Reconciliation (S/1996/1070, Annex II); the Protocol of 13 January 1997 on Refugees (S/1997/55, Annex); the Statutes and Additional Protocol adopted on 21 February 1997 in relation to the Commission for National Reconciliation (S/1997/ 169, Annex I and II); the Protocol of 8 March 1997 on Military Issues (S/1997/209, Annex II), the Protocol of 18 May 1997 on Political Issues (S/1997/ 385, Annex) and the Protocol of 28 May 1997 on the Guarantees of the Implementation of the General Agreement (S/1997/410. Annex).

[42] The Inter-Tajik Talks successively took place, from 1994 to 1997, in Almaty, Ashgabat, Bishkek, Islamabad, Kabul, Mashad (Iran), Moscow, Tehran and Khudesh (Afghanistan).

the country.⁴³ Preoccupied by the human rights situation prevailing in Tajikistan, the OSCE decided to establish there a Long-Term Mission. Operational since February 1994, the Mission was charged with promoting democracy-building and respect for human rights in the whole country, and also to encourage national political reconciliation in support of the United Nations peacemaking efforts. The Mission's work basically related to the human dimension was widened in 1995 when, following a request made by the UNHCR to take over the latter's mandate to provide protection to returning refugees and displaced persons, the Mission opened three branch offices in southern Tajikistan (Kurgan Teppa, Sharituz and Dusti).⁴⁴ By addressing a host of practical issues concerning, for instance, ownership or occupation of homes and land, correct treatment of prisoners and army draftees, equal distribution of humanitarian aid by the local authorities, those offices 'achieved a functional combination of work on individual protection human cases and general activities which promote human rights principles and conflict resolution'.⁴⁵

The sound division of labour established during the peacemaking process between the OSCE and the United Nations moved toward close co-operation and co-ordination in the phase of post-conflict rehabilitation. Indeed, for fundamental practical purposes (return of refugees, demobilization of the UTO fighters and their integration to governmental structures, reform of police, security and armed forces, and so on) the 1997 peace accords established two main bodies: a Commission for National Reconciliation (CNR) and a Contact Group of Guarantor States and Organizations. Headed by a representative of the UTO, the first organization had to carry its activities in conjunction of both the United Nations and the OSCE. Consisting of the accredited Ambassadors of the guarantor states in Dushanbe (Afghanistan, Iran, Kazakhstan, Kirghyztan, Pakistan, Russia, Turkmenistan and Uzbekistan) and of representatives from the United Nations, the OSCE and the Organization of the Islamic Conference, the second body was mandated to monitor the implementation of the peace agreements and to provide to the parties expertise, consultancy services and good offices.⁴⁶ A great deal still remains to be achieved in

---

⁴³ UNMOT was established by the UN Security Council Resolution 968 of 16 December 1994.

⁴⁴ In 1998, the Mission was authorized to open two further field offices in the Khujand and Garm regions.

⁴⁵ OSCE Mission to Tajikistan. Review of Field Office Activities: SEC.FR/103/98 of 24 March 1998.

⁴⁶ Following serious Tajik–Uzbek tensions, Uzbekistan has not been represented in the Contact Group since November 1998 (paragraph 14 of UN document S/1999/514 of 6 May 1999). On 3 November 1998, a force under the command of a former Tajik army colonel launched (allegedly from Uzbekistan) a successful offensive against the province of Khujand. The situation was re-restabilized within a month by the regular troops of Tajikistan with the help of the UTO (paragraph 14 of UN document S/1999/124 of 8 February 1999). Although Uzbekistan denied having assisted the rebels

order to translate all formal agreements into concrete action. As a guarantor organization, the OSCE closely participates in that process in a wide range of areas related to the human dimension. It supports the CNR and co-operates with the United Nations on matters concerning constitutional reform, democratization and, especially, elections.

Democratic Stabilization

Contrary to other international organizations where new members are admitted on the basis of prior requirements, the OSCE accepts those states pledging to meet its normative standards after formal admission. As a result, the granting of membership to all of the successor states of the USSR (other than Russia) automatically confronted the OSCE, as from January 1992, with a hitherto unknown situation – purely passive participation or just absenteeism from a large number of states unaware of the exact nature of their international commitments and possessing scarce experience in the field of multilateral diplomacy. The repeated absence of numerous countries from deliberations constituted a real problem for an organization operating by consensus: it hampered serious discussion of issues important to the concerned states themselves and, from a more general perspective, weakened the political weight of actual decisions. In order to meet the challenge, the OSCE adopted, in July 1992, an American-inspired Programme of Co-ordinated Support for Recently Admitted Participating states (RAPS). Co-ordinated by the Warsaw-based Office for Democratic Institutions and Human Rights (ODIHR), the Programme was above all 'pedagogical' in purpose. It aimed at helping the RAPS to participate more fully in OSCE institutions and activities and to better implement their commitments by means of on-site seminars as well as 'diplomatic, academic, legal and administrative expertise and advice on all [OSCE] matters'.[47] In 1995, a Voluntary Contributions Fund was set up to cover the cost of travel to seminars, short-term internships and other projects for fostering the integration of the RAPS in the pan-European process.[48] In principle,

---

in any way, that incident caused a deterioration in the already strained relations between the two countries. It is to be recalled that the Soviet power initially created Tajikistan in 1924 as an Autonomous Region of Uzbekistan, before transforming it into a larger Autonomous Republic of Uzbekistan (1925) eventually upgrade to the rank of Republic of the USSR (1929). Tajikistan still resents as an injustice the fact that Samarkand and Bukhara (traditional centres of Iranian culture largely populated by Tajiks) remain under the rule of Uzbekistan as established by the Soviet power. Uzbekistan has similar feelings about the Tajik region of Khujand whose population is basically Uzbek. According to the Soviet census of 1989, there were 934,000 Uzbeks in Tajikistan and 1.7 million Tajiks in Uzbekistan representing 23.5 per cent of its total population.

[47] Helsinki Document 1992: Chapter XI.
[48] PC.DEC/23 of 2 March 1995.

the Programme for Co-ordinated Support concerned those participating states which have been admitted to the OSCE since 1991, that is to say the emerging democracies in Eastern and Central Europe and all the Republics of the former USSR. However, practically it focused on the Central Asian states and, much later, the Caucasus states. In both cases, the issues pertaining to the human dimension (human rights, democracy and the rule of law) constituted its core substance.

Central Asia

The activities of the OSCE in Central Asia are basically conducted through regional field offices with the standing support of ODIHR – and occasionally of the High Commissioner on National Minorities and the Representative on Freedom of the Media.[49] In 1995, the OSCE established at Tashkent, Uzbekistan, a Central Asia Liaison Office (CALO) in order to link the five states of the region more closely with the OSCE and to monitor their domestic evolution beginning with the implementation of their human dimension commitments.[50] Operational since June 1995, CALO organized seminars on all aspects of OSCE commitments and co-operated with the ODIHR on a number of practical projects. In the Lisbon Summit Declaration of 1996, the governments committed the OSCE to fostering its overall efforts in the region.[51] However, the OSCE waited until 1998 to create additional Centres in Astana (Kazakhstan), Ashgabat (Turkmenistan) and Bishkek (Kirgyztan) – but not in Tajikistan where a Long-Term Mission had been operating since February 1994. As CALO (which now focuses on developments taking place in Uzbekistan), each of the new structures is staffed by a team of three experts seconded by OSCE-participating states and respectively responsible for political and security matters, economic and environmental issues, and human dimension questions. Through the opening in early 1999 of those Centres the OSCE can claim it has achieved full presence in the region.[52]

While CALO and the Centres essentially serve as political antennae, the ODIHR provides tailored-made operational services. In October 1997, the

---

[49] The High Commissioner has performed some limited activities in Kazakhstan (CSCE Communication No. 26 of 10 June 1994 and REF.HC/14/96 of 11 December 1996) and Kirgyztan (CSCE Communication No. 27 of 13 June 1994, REF.HC/7/95 of 7 August 1995 and SEC.INF/131/99 of 30 March 1999). The Representative on Freedom of the Media visited Central Asia in 1999 and submitted a detailed report to the Permanent Council (FOM.GAL/10/99 of 12 May 1999).
[50] PC.DEC.28 of 16 March 1995.
[51] Paragraph 23 of the 1996 Lisbon Summit Declaration.
[52] Basic decisions establishing the Centres: PC.DEC/243, 244 and 245 of 23 July 1998. The Bishkek, Astana and Ashgabat Centres addressed their first report respectively on 26 January 1999 (SEC.FR/38/99), 1 February 1999 (SEC.FR/55/99) and 5 February 1999 (SEC.FR/78/99). CALO's 1999 programme in Uzbekistan: SEC.FR/228/99 of 18 March 1999.

government of Uzbekistan signed with the OSCE a Memorandum of Understanding for the implementation of concrete projects to be performed under the guidance of ODIHR.[53] Kirgyztan and Kazakhstan followed suit in the end of 1998.[54] The projects in question concerned three main rubrics. First, election assistance in the form of the production and broadcast of TV programmes to promote voter education (Kazakhstan), assistance in the implementation of a democratic election appeals procedure (Kazakhstan and Kirgyztan), training non-governmental election observers (Kirgyztan) and training for political parties to enhance participation in the electoral process (Uzbekistan). Second, consolidation of civil society by means of the development of dialogue on human rights issues between governmental officials and representatives of civil society (Kazakhstan, Kirgyztan and Uzbekistan) or training to increase the participation of women in political life (Kazakhstan and Kirgyztan). Third, support to democratic institutions including legislative reform assistance in Kazakhstan and Kirgyztan, establishment of an Ombudsman Office in Kazakhstan (or co-operation with the Ombudsman of Uzbekistan), services to the Kirgyz Commission on Human Rights, education in human rights standards to Uzbek senior official Border Guards and, more particularly, development of a population registration system compatible with international standards in view of the replacement of the Soviet propiska system.[55]

In December 1998, the Oslo Ministerial Council agreed in principle to strengthen the co-ordinated approach of the OSCE to Central Asia and requested the Chairman in Office to prepare a report to that end.[56] The Personal Representative appointed by the Chairman-in-Office to help on the matter tabled a set of recommendations. These envisage the establishment of an open-ended round table on the politico-military aspects of security in Central Asia; the OSCE monitoring on economic developments related to the democratization processes; the holding (at least twice a year) in the region of a regular meeting between the OSCE institutions and presences under the direction of the Chairman-in-Office, and, finally, the development of a flexible 'OSCE Calendar of Yearly Events' including a yearly visit by the Chairman-in-Office, regular or extraordinary meetings of the Permanent Council specifically devoted to Central Asia, meetings in the region at Troika, ministerial or summit level and 'a regular (e.g. yearly or biannual) event in Central Asia devoted to fostering regional co-operation organized by key international organizations active in this area'.[57]

---

[53] ODIHR.INF/11/97 of 15 October 1997.
[54] ODIHR.GAL/65/98 of 10 December 1998. Turkmenistan is expected to follow.
[55] For details on actual implementation see ODIHR.GAL/21/99 of 2 June 1999 and ODIHR.GAL/22/99 of 3 June 1999.
[56] MC(7).DEC/7 of 3 December 1998.
[57] Appointed to prepare the Chairman in Office's report, Ambassador Wilhelm Höynck (a former Secretary-general of the OSCE) visited the five Central Asian states in June 1999 for the purpose of collecting their views on the enhancement of OSCE activities in the

The interest expressed by the OSCE *vis-à-vis* Central Asia since 1992 is not unilateral. Having acquired a fair understanding of the OSCE values, commitments and working methods, the concerned states established permanent delegations in Vienna and demonstrated attachment to their pan-European membership. However, two main factors are posing limits to the political role of the OSCE in the region: the uncoordinated political agendas of the five Central Asian Republics and the divergence over priorities between these Republics as a whole and the OSCE.

The Central Asian states certainly face common challenges inherited from the Soviet period and which have worsened since independence: economic and environmental problems, ethnic tensions and indirect effects of the Afghan civil war. The first category of challenges concerns redistribution of scarce water resources, energy management, the Aral sea disaster ('a liquid Chernobyl' to quote local ecologists) and trans-border nuclear pollution. The economic problems have a potential to develop confrontation among the Republics.[58] As to the environmental problems, they represent a threat to the health of populations and also have a negative impact on the development of the economies and democratic institutions. Taken globally, both of them are putting at risk the security and stability of the region. Overt or potential ethnic tensions constitute another set of problems. Ethnic minorities account for some 27 per cent in Turkmenistan, 30 per cent in Uzbekistan, 35 per cent in Tajikistan, 48 per cent in Kirgyztan and even 57 per cent in Kazakhstan.[59] There are 10 million ethnic Russians (in a total population of 55 million) in Central Asia; they represent about 2.5 per cent in Tajikistan, 8 per cent in Turkmenistan, 20 per cent in Kirgyztan and 36 per cent in Kazakhstan or, from another perspective, 40 per cent of the 25 million ethnic Russians living outside the Federation of Russia. Finally, the persistence of the civil war in Afghanistan (a country outside the OSCE area) is seen as a great concern because of its spill-over effects: terrorism, religious extremism, drug trafficking, arms proliferation.

Not all of the Central Asian states are affected by the same threats nor do common threats affect all states in the same way. Although aware of belonging to a common geographical region (and holding in this capacity annual summits of Heads of States), they are marked by ancient differences which have increased since independence. Except on the issue of denuclearization of Central Asia, the

---

region. Text of Höynck's Report: CIO.GAL/58/99 of 14 July 1999. The idea of a Representative for a Central Asia was tabled as early as 23 October 1998 by the European Union (PC.DEL/470/98. 1998).

[58] During the Soviet era, water was allocated on the assumption that the region formed a single economic unit. Although the requirements have changed, the same regime still prevails. The political problem of reallocation is all the more complicated in that disastrous Soviet management has provoked a net decrease in the water supply.

[59] Despite Russia's insistence, only Turkmenistan has accepted (by means of a bilateral treaty concluded in 1993), a regime of dual citizenship.

foreign political agendas of the five Republics are not convergent. Kazakhstan's pet project – the Conference on Interaction and Confidence-Building Measures in Asia (CICA) – aiming at establishing a 'security model' in Asia has not been unanimously appreciated.[60] Turkmenistan adopted a regime of permanent neutrality approved by the United Nations General Assembly.[61] As previously mentioned, Tajikistan has become a *de facto* Russian protectorate and remains seriously at odds with Uzbekistan.[62] By contrast, Kazakhstan, Kirgyztan and Uzbekistan have created a common economic zone and are developing an overall political co-operation.[63]

The Central Asian Republics currently argue that the success of economic transition, the resolution of ecological difficulties and the termination of the Afghan civil are more crucial than democratization to achieving the goal of lasting security and stability. The OSCE position is quite the opposite. Having been unable to avoid the drift towards authoritarianism taken by all the concerned states as from 1995,[64] the OSCE is today determined to do its outmost in order to reverse the trend.

Caucasus

Integrated efforts towards the democratic stabilization of the Caucasus have been undertaken by the OSCE since 1999, much more recently than in Central Asia. Following up an assessment of their specific needs by a team mission of international agencies conducted by ODIHR, in November 1998 Armenia, Azerbaijan and Georgia signed with the OSCE an individual Memorandum of Understanding for the implementation of concrete projects in the human dimension field. Designed to be performed by the ODIHR alone or in co-operation with other

---

[60] Designed by Kazakhstan mainly to avoid a security *tête-à-tête* with Moscow, the CICA project includes Turkey and Central Asia (except Turkmenistan) as well as a number of countries from outside the OSCE area: Afghanistan, Iran, Mongolia, Israel and Palestine. On the CICA project, see OSCE Documents INF/283/95 of 29 December 1995, INF/41/96 of 1 March 1996 and REF.PC/408/96 of 26 June 1996.
[61] Resolution 50/ 80 A adopted by the United Nations General Assembly on 12 December 1995.
[62] See footnote 46.
[63] UN document A/51/779 of 21 January 1997.
[64] In Kazakhstan, Uzbekistan and Turkmenistan, the term of the President of the Republic was extended by means of simple referendum approved (as in the Soviet era) by over 90 per cent of voters. In Kirgyztan, the President of the Republic managed to obtain considerable extra-constitutional powers. It must not be forgotten that unlike the other Soviet Republics, the Central Asian Republics followed the path of independence reluctantly, without being driven by true nationalist feelings.

international organizations and local human rights NGOs, those projects dealt with election assistance and human rights promotion.[65]

Projects related to election assistance provided for a review of the existing legislation and the training of official personnel in all three countries. That task appeared particularly relevant in the case of Armenia and Azerbaijan, where the presidential elections of 1998 did not respect OSCE standards: the signature of the MOU allowed the OSCE to help in implementing the various recommendations made at the time by ODIHR for the improvement of the conduct of elections. The projects pertaining to human rights were more diverse. They included the production and/or broadcasting of radio and/or TV programmes to raise the awareness of the general public in all three countries, technical assistance to the Georgian Public Defender Office, the development in Azerbaijan of a national law enforcement focal point in connection with ODIHR's training programme on 'Techniques to combat organized crime', 'Civic Diplomacy' involving human contacts between Georgians, Abkhazians and South Ossetians through consultations on issues of common concern and, last but not least, programmes related to 'Registration of Permanent Residents'. Under this last, the OSCE is required to help all the three countries to overcome the *propiska* system of residence permits inherited from the Soviet rule which restricted the citizens' rights to move freely and to choose their place of residence within the country.[66] All projects are at an early stage of positive implementation with, however, a notable exception in the case of Armenia: according to an official report, the Armenian Election Code has been approved on February 1999 by the National Assembly 'without being submitted to ODIHR despite formal steps undertaken by ODIHR'.[67]

For the time being, and notwithstanding the contribution made by the High Commissioner on National Minorities to help Georgia to cope with the Meskhetians issue, the OSCE strategy for the democratization of the Caucasus

---

[65] *Report on the Joint Assessment Mission of International Organisations to Azerbaijan, Georgia and Armenia*: ODIHR.GAL/13/98 of 3 April 1998 (the Mission was composed of representatives from the Council of Europe, the UNHCR, the Commission of the European Union, the Danish Refugee Council and the Soros Foundation). Text of the three Memoranda: ODIHR.GAL/64/98 of 7 December 1998. For details on actual implementation see ODIHR.GAL/21/99 of 2 June 1999 and ODIHR.GAL/22/99 of 3 June 1999.

[66] While Georgia abolished the *propiska* system (by enacting a 1996 law on the procedure for registration and identification of Georgian citizens and aliens residing in the country), Armenia only lifted certain restrictions associated with it. In Azerbaijan, the most recent legislation on citizenship does not quite conform with internationally recognized standards.

[67] ODIHR: *Semi-Annual Report. Spring 1999*. Warsaw, OSCE/ODIHR, 1999, p. 24. For the implementation calendars of projects related to the three countries, see ODHIR.GAL/21/99 of 2 June 1999.

rests exclusively on ODIHR's shoulders.[68] The Permanent Council's decision to establish an OSCE Office in Yerevan and also in Baku seems to indicate that the time is becoming ripe for on-site permanent OSCE structures in the region.[69]

Partnership with Japan and the Republic of South Korea

Japan and South Korea have been associated to the OSCE since 1992 and 1994 respectively. At the end of 1995, both states were granted, by the OSCE Permanent Council, the same formal status – that of 'Partner for Co-operation'.[70] In practice, however, the extent and modalities of their partnership remain dissimilar: while Japan's contribution to OSCE meetings stems from a permanent decision, Korea is invited only on a case-by-case basis.

Japan

The issue of Japan's association to the OSCE was initially raised by Italy in the context of the first meeting of the Ministerial Council convened in Berlin in June 1991. Arguing that Japan was not only an adjacent state to the CSCE but actually 'a major player in the world political and economic scene, and its impact on the very nature of European stability is evident and destined to grow', the Italian Foreign Minister consequently suggested that the OSCE 'should look for new and special forms of associating Japan ... commensurate with its importance – if necessary going beyond present procedural arrangements'.[71] Considered as premature by many participating states, the Italian proposal was not approved. However, upon the continued insistence of Italy, the Ministerial Council inserted in its Summary of Conclusions a last-minute paragraph acknowledging that the OSCE 'must remain open to dialogue and co-operation with the rest of the world' and requesting the Committee of Senior Officials 'to explore the idea and to report to a

---

[68] The Meskhetians (or Meskhetian Turks) had been living along the Georgian–Turkish border before being collectively deported to Central Asia in 1944. Two meetings sponsored by the High Commissioner (HCNM.GAL/8/98 of 16 September 1998 and HCNM.GAL/1/99 of 18 March 1999) addressed the issue which came into focus after the Council of Europe's decision to include the return of the Meskhetians over a period of twelve years as a precondition of Georgia membership.

[69] The Yerevan Office will basically promote 'the implementation of OSCE principles and commitments as well as the co-operation of the Republic of Armenia within the OSCE framework, in all OSCE dimensions, including the human, political, economic and environmental aspects of security and stability' (PC.DEC/314 of 22 July 1999).

[70] PC.DEC/94 of 5 December 1995. In 1999 Thailand was also granted the same status.

[71] Non-Paper entitled 'Contribution by Italy to the First Council Meeting', 18 June 1991.

future meeting of the Council'.[72] At the next OSCE Ministerial Council meeting (Prague, January 1992), the Italian Foreign Minister reopened the issue with more success, since the Council decided to request the forthcoming Helsinki Follow-up Meeting 'to recommend practical ways to establish a flexible dialogue between the [OSCE] interested non-participating states or groups of states, for example through contacts between the said states and the Chairman-in-Office of the Council or of the Committee of Senior Officials'.[73] The Helsinki Follow-up Meeting (March–July 1992) examined different formulas concerning the status to be specifically attributed to Japan tabled by the USA (associate member), Finland (special observer) and the European Union (special guest).[74] From want of consensus all of them were rejected. However, the Follow-up Meeting adopted a set of provisions concerning 'Relations with non-participating states' which expressly referred to Japan. The Helsinki Decisions of July 1992 announced that Japan would be invited on a regular basis to attend OSCE meetings including 'those of the Summits, the Ministerial meetings, the Committee of Senior Officials meetings and of other appropriate [OSCE] bodies which consider specific topics of expanded consultation and co-operation'. It also stated that Japan's representatives may contribute to such meetings, without participating in the preparation and adoption of decisions, on subjects in which Tokyo has a direct interest and/or wishes to co-operate actively.[75] Japan was singled out and given preferential status for three main official reasons: its genuine interest *vis-à-vis* the OSCE, its sharing of OSCE's basic values and its active 'engagement in European co-operation relevant organizations' – a phrase actually referring to OECD.[76]

Initiated in the autumn of 1992, Japan's working relations with the OSCE developed in a most remarkable rapid and positive way. Tokyo's role did not remain limited to passive representation at pan-European meetings. It included direct contributions to certain OSCE operational activities related to conflict prevention or management. Thus, in 1992–93, Japan seconded experts and furnished telecommunications equipment to the OSCE's Long-Term Missions in the Federal Republic of Yugoslavia (Kosovo, Sanjak and Voivodina), Macedonia and Bosnia-Herzegovina. It also provided a significant number of observers for the purpose of monitoring elections in Bosnia-Herzegovina (1996, 1998) and Eastern Slavonia.[77] In addition, since 1995, Japan has been contributing to the

---

[72] Summary of Conclusions of the Berlin Meeting of the Council (19–20 June 1991): paragraph 19.
[73] Prague Document on Further Development of CSCE Institutions and Structures (31 January 1992): paragraph 45.
[74] Alexis Heraclides: *Helsinki-II and its Aftermath. The Making of the CSCE as an International Organization* (London: Pinter, 1993), pp. 114–117.
[75] Helsinki Decisions (July 1992): paragraphs 10 and 11 of Chapter IV.
[76] Ibid., paragraph 9.
[77] OSCE: SEC.GAL/40/98 of 26 June 1998 and PC.DEL/299/98 of 2 July 1998.

administrative cost of the OSCE at a rate of about 300,000 Austrian schillings a year.[78] The reasons for that outstanding development are twofold. First, since the collapse of Communism, the decisions made by OSCE in the field of military security have a direct bearing on Japan's interests, because the territory of the Caucasus states and that of the Central Asian states are part of the zone of application of the Vienna regime on CSBMs as well as of all pan-European arms control decisions.[79] Second, while being a financial contributor to the economic reconstruction of Central and Eastern Europe, Japan remains the only member of the G8 not belonging to the OSCE: association to the latter represents for it the natural political counterpart of the economic co-operation between Japan, Europe and the USA.

Republic of South Korea

The involvement of Korea within the OSCE has taken place at a later period than that of Japan and on a different basis. It was only on April 1994 that the Seoul Government officially requested 'to take part in [OSCE] meetings and contribute to the cause of the [OSCE]'.[80] On June 1994, the Committee of Senior Officials reacted favourably by authorizing it to participate as an *ad hoc* observer to the forthcoming Budapest Review Conference and Budapest Summit; it also decided that Korea would get access to the official documentation of the Organization and be invited on an *ad hoc* basis to those pan-European meetings for which it might have special interest.[81] While being aware that the OSCE experience was not fully transferable to other regions of the world, the government of Seoul nevertheless justified its application by arguing that the OSCE could offer useful references or guidelines for the promotion of security and stability in the divided Korean peninsula. It also stressed that its association and Japan's could encourage the establishment of a fruitful co-operative relationship between the OSCE and the nascent ASEAN Regional Forum (ARF).[82] As Japan (but on a smaller scale) Korea contributed to the monitoring of the 1996 elections in Bosnia-Herzegovina by means of experts and financial support.[83] Seeking 'a more stabilized and continued relationship', it requested the 'institutionalization' of the partnership status by

---

[78] OSCE: REF.SC/33/96 of 22 March 1996, REF.PC/139/97 of 7 March 1997 and REF.PC/463/97 of 2 June 1997.
[79] For a comprehensive analysis of the Vienna regime on CSBMs see Victor-Yves Ghebali, *L'OSCE dans l'Europe post-communiste, 1990–1996*, op. cit., pp. 181ff.
[80] OSCE: DOC.91 of 21 April 1994.
[81] Journal No. 3 (15 June 1994) of the 27th Meeting of the Committee of Senior Officials (Decision 5 h and Annex 5). See also paragraph 18 of the Budapest Summit Declaration (1994).
[82] REF.RM/91/96 of 4 November 1996.
[83] REF.PC/260/96 of 18 April 1996 and REF.RM/91/96 of 4 November 1996.

means of a formula which would permit its attendance at major OSCE meetings and bodies on a permanent basis.[84] Although supported by the European Union during the 1996 Vienna Review Meeting, the Korean claim did not receive a positive response.[85] The Vienna Meeting did not go beyond welcoming the interest displayed by Seoul for pan-European activities and expressing the readiness of the OSCE to co-operate with Korea and other states in fields of common interest – a statement which the Declaration adopted soon after by the Lisbon Summit merely reconfirmed.[86] Today (1999), the two Asian Partners for Co-operation do certainly not enjoy an equal status nor play the same kind of role at the OSCE. Given their differing national goals in regard to pan-European affairs, Japan and the Republic of South Korea have so far also been unable to present any common front within the OSCE.

In the drafting process of a 'Charter for European Security' the issue of 'adjacent areas' (those geopolitical areas represented by the OSCE Far Eastern and Mediterranean partners for co-operation) has re-emerged. Two main ideas were envisaged in this perspective: the first one is that strengthened co-operation with Japan and Korea could be related to joint activities undertaken within OSCE field missions in Central Asia; the second idea raises the possibility of closer contacts with the ASEAN Regional Forum, which is considered as OSCE's closest counterpart in the region.[87] Neither of them was finally retained.[88]

Conclusion

From 1992, when the Republics of the Caucasus and Central Asia were granted membership (together with all the other components of the former USSR), the OSCE steadily began to extend its sphere of activities beyond the traditionally-defined geographic borders of Europe. It devotes today a considerable part of its energy to promoting peace and stability in Eurasia, by means of several on-site missions or offices as well as standing or *ad hoc* activities on behalf of ODIHR, the High Commissioner on Nation Minorities or the Representative on Freedom of the

---

[84] REF.RM/91/96 and REF.RM/92/96 of 4 November 1996.
[85] REF.RM/278//96 of 19 November 1996.
[86] RM(96) JOURNAL No. 15 (22 November 1996), Annex 4 and paragraph 24 of the Lisbon Document 1996.
[87] PC.SMC/127/98 of 5 November 1998.
[88] Ibid. On the Charter issue, see Victor-Yves Ghebali, 'The OSCE Exercise for a Security Model: Towards a Document Charter on European Security', *The International Security Review* (RUSI) (1999), pp. 116–131, and also the author's forthcoming article in *OSCE Yearbook 2000*.

Media. The Chairman-in-Office also pays annual highly-symbolic political visits.[89] Eurasia is not (as the Mediterranean) an 'adjacent area' to Greater Europe but part and parcel of it. Likewise, the eight new Eurasian participating states no longer constitute an anomaly within the OSCE: their integration into the pan-European system is now practically completed. The impact of the OSCE in the Caucasus has, admittedly, been much limited for two basic reasons. First, the projection of democratic stability through the integrated approach designed by the OSCE is just at its very beginning. Second, the political settlement of the Nagorno-Karabakh, South Ossetian and Abkhaz conflicts remains more elusive than ever – all the more regrettably in that comprehensive political settlements would boost the democratization process in each of the three countries. Beyond the inherent complexity of the conflicts in question, the difficulties encountered by the OSCE have also to be attributed to Russia's role as a partial (or in any event not disinterested) mediator. In Central Asia, the record of the OSCE is also small, but more promising.

---

[89] There are now OSCE presences in all Caucasus and Central Asian countries except Azerbaijan. The Chairman-in-Office's annual visits to Caucaus and Central Asia were inaugurated in 1993 (report on first visit: OSCE Communication No. 159 of 25 May 1993).

Chapter Seven

The Regional Level: A European Perspective

Fred Tanner

With the disappearance of the Soviet Union as a negative external integrator, the regional security institutions in Europe face today a crisis of collective solidarity and discipline. The absence of an unitary and overwhelming threat has led to the erosion of the broad strategic consensus that has united the Western states during the Cold War. The planned extension of NATO and the EU sustains this erosion, because it increases the diversity of interest and stakes among the member-states.

This chapter claims that the increasing diversity of interests, combined with parochialism is likely to increase the propensity for replacing collective responses by unilateralism, *ad hoc* arrangements and a competitive use of institutions as instruments for national policies. This, in turn, could put into question the future utility of the current system of collective and co-operative security in Europe.

This essay will examine to what extent the multilateral institutions in Europe are able to satisfy the security needs of its member states. It will address the question of how multilateral arrangements can enhance or constrain national and international efforts to promote stability, good governance and peaceful settlements of conflicts in 'greater' Europe and its adjacent areas.

Diminishing Congruency of Alliance Interests

The overall territorial threat to all members of the Western alliance is – at least for the time being – a thing of the past. The understanding of security has become a more complex issue, which is due to a large extent to sub-regional risks and threats, that are emerging in the periphery of Europe or in adjacent regions. After 1990, intensive state formations took place in Eastern Europe, the Caucasus, Central Asia and the Balkans. In fact, today there are more states in Europe than ever before.

Potential for political instability exists all around the EU and NATO perimeters. Conflicts, or a high potential for conflicts, exist in the Caucasus, Central Asia, the Balkans and the Mediterranean region, including North Africa and the Middle East. Developments in all of these surrounding regions are relevant to European security. But, in contrast to the Cold War threats, today's security threats are not treated equally as high on the agenda of the Alliance members.

Many Allies have special national interests in some of the peripheries of the European continent and they find themselves competing for similar institutional support.

For instance, Germany and the new NATO Allies are primarily concerned with the Ukraine, the Caucasus and Russia, whereas Italy looks towards the Balkan and the Central Mediterranean region. Spain looks towards developments in the Western Maghreb region, and Greece and Turkey towards South-Eastern Europe, the Eastern Mediterranean and Central Asia. The congruence of security interest and the perception of political stakes are no longer in line with the Alliance membership. As a consequence, Allies are continuously finding themselves in disagreement as to how and if European security institutions should cope with risks and threats stemming from outside the institutional security web.

Two recent conflicts in Europe – the wars in Yugoslavia and chaos in Albania – have put the conflict management capabilities of security institutions to a test. In both cases, these security institutions in Europe (NATO, WEU, EU and OSEC) failed to provide the necessary support to national efforts to prevent or contain these conflicts. Instead, other organizations had to intervene at very high political and military risk. In the case of Yugoslavia, UNPROFOR had to pursue a 'mission impossible' and, in turn, predictably failed. In the case of Albania, Allies with high stakes in the region were forced into a futile forum-hopping affair before their 'one-off' coalition of the willing members to launch operation Alba. Possibly due to the inadequacy of these institutional responses to conflicts at Europe's threshold, the lessons learned on the political crisis response, forced interoperability and soft security building could improve the effectiveness of future European conflict prevention and co-operation.

Wars in Yugoslavia

The Yugoslav crisis showed the limits of both NATO and the WEU. NATO first had to undergo a political and doctrinal metamorphosis before it could play any role in the Balkans. Only with the Dayton Peace Agreement was NATO finally entering the realm of peace restoration activities.

The WEU, in turn, did not only encounter political constraints from some of its members; it was militarily simply unable to project any preventive or deterring power in the Balkans. With the outbreak of hostilities in Yugoslavia in 1991, the WEU Council considered four options for WEU intervention: logistics support, escort and protection, peacekeeping forces to monitor and to enforce a cease-fire, and peacekeeping and deterrent forces requiring about 20,000 combat troops and 10,000 support staff. The Council members were unable to come up with a consensus on any of these four options. Some WEU members preferred to refer the mission to the UN. With the tragic fate of UNPROFOR unravelling, the WEU decided instead to support only embargo enforcement operations in the Adriatic and on the Danube. Finally, carving out its own niche in the peacebuilding process, the WEU sent a police operation to Mostar in mid-1994.

The responses of all European institutions including NATO to the Yugoslav quagmire have been partial, timid and reactive rather than preventive. But the failure of institutions is a failure of states to act collectively towards the same objective. Thus, Europe's failure to prevent a war in Yugoslavia or in Bosnia was not a failure of the EU, the WEU or NATO. It was a failure of all the member-states, which were unable to come to a consensus with a common approach to the unravelling crisis.

Lessons learned from these operations in former Yugoslavia have resulted in the improvement of the WEU operational capabilities and 'the interoperability of the forces of members states' engaged in Non-Article V operations.[1] Also, new forces for crisis management have been created with Euromarfor. But, as the case of Albania shows, the lack of persuasion and different policy priorities make the use of alliance assets for crisis management purposes very difficult.

Operation Alba

With the rapid deterioration of the crisis in Albania in early March 1997, the OSCE Representative Vranitzky asked the OSCE Council to send a stabilization force of approximately 4,000 troops and policemen. Upon US pressure, who were concerned about further entanglement of NATO in the Balkans, the NATO Council decided not to contemplate this type of military operation. The WEU Council was also unwilling to take up the OSCE proposal.

Italy and Greece, the states bordering and directly affected by the Albanian crisis tried to prepare the political ground for an intervention through the EU. An informal CFSP ministerial meeting decided to send a high-level mission on the ground to examine ways in which the EU could help re-establish security in the country, particularly by sending civilian and military advisors. The mission recommended the involvement of the EU as a lead agency for the purpose of providing humanitarian emergency aid and the re-establishment of a police force. It also proposed the involvement of the OSCE and the Council of Europe for advancing the democratization process, human rights and elections. Finally, for providing security to these missions, the dispatch of a Multi-National Protection Force (MNPF) was recommended.

Italy, on the grounds of these recommendations attempted to use the WEU as the institution for planning and running the military operation. The operation would have been a Petersberg-type mission with WEU members acting under the authority of the WEU for humanitarian and rescue tasks, and the tasks of combat

---

[1] Assembly of the Western European Union, Report, Document 1583, 25 November 1997, part 2, p. 1.

forces in crisis management and peacemaking.[2] But, the solidarity of the WEU Allies was not strong enough to trigger an institutional support. The UK, but also Germany, opposed the request of Southern European members that a Special Session of the WEU Council should be convened for the purpose of confiding the WEU with the authority for the military operation.

The lack of collective discipline forced Italy to pursue the crisis management unilaterally and to seek a UN Security Council authority for a 'coalition of the willing' operation. Italy managed to get this authority within one day and then staged the operation outside any institutional framework. Together with its *ad hoc* partners, Italy had engaged in the mission planning and force deployment from scratch. Even the political co-ordination of the troop's contributing states had to be done through an *ad hoc* Political Steering Committee 'resembling WEU or CFSP'. After the successful end of the operation the WEU acknowledged that it had missed an opportunity for the organization to successfully contribute to an out-of-area mission.

This case of operation Alba shows the limited use of European security institutions if there is no congruency of member-states interest. The Southern European states were not able to use any of the numerous military forces that were available to the WEU. The WEU institutional support and some of the Forces Answerable to the WEU (FAWEU) could have been used for this operation. But, the use of the European corps with the presence of a strong German contingent would have been vetoed by Bonn, and even the Euromarfor, set up precisely for Alba-type operations, was blocked by Portugal.

Responses to Threats and Risks from the European Periphery

Many European states have today, in contrast to the Cold War period a high stake in sub-regional developments that lie outside the perimeter of NATO, the EU and the WEU. Can and should Europe play a role beyond its borders? The cases of the former Yugoslavia and Albania have painfully shown that no European institutions were able to respond to an unravelling crisis right on the doorsteps of Western European institutions.

There are two analytical perspectives to provide answers to this question. From a neo-liberal point of view, Europe has an interest in assuring a peaceful transition of these countries towards good governance and the liberal economic market. Europe can only be safe if its adjacent areas are included in a zone of democratic peace.[3] Under these premises, Europe would have to be prepared to pursue a policy

---

[2] Part II of the Petersberg Declaration of 19 June 1992.
[3] The Barcelona Document, for instance, that posits in its first chapter the objective of creating a zone of peace in the Euro-Mediterranean area.

of liberal internationalism in those areas that are threatened by authoritarian rule, or worse by threats or acts of ethnic cleansing or genocide. Western security-building in its periphery would include the promotion of liberal norms, which could happen through either co-operative sub-regional arrangements or the more muscled implementation of liberal peace agreements. Roland Paris argues that the prominent involvement of European institutions in peace-building in the Balkans, for instance, represents a form of liberal interventionism, as the reconstruction of a war-torn society would be in accordance with a mirror image of a Western pluralistic democracy.[4]

But liberal interventionism could also happen in the form of an outright military operation against an autocratic ruler whose actions blatantly violate the norms and values of a Kantian civil community. The NATO preparations for deterring Serbia's Milosevic in Kosovo must be understood on such grounds. NATO has never been able to communicate this criteria according to which its war planning was made against the Serbian armed forces.

From a neo-realist point of view Europe has today vital stakes with regard to great powers in the area such as Russia and Turkey, both of whom are playing a key role in the sub-regional alignments at the periphery of the European security perimeters. The neo-realist perspective would prescribe European states to assure a secure access to oil and gas reserves. In this context, a special emphasis should be put on the Central Asian region, or – according to Brzezinkski – the 'Eurasian Balkans', that are exposed to the ambitions of Russia, Turkey, Iran and China.[5] Central Asia and the Caspian Sea are unstable regions with a power vacuum, disputed borders, ethnic strife, but with large deposits of oil and gas. According to *The Economist*, the rectangle of land that 'stretches north-east from Arabia to where Kazakhstan meets China' holds up to three-quarters of the world's total reserves of oil and a third of its reserves of natural gas.[6]

How do current institutions and policy makers see out-of-area risks and threats and how do they respond to them? The institutional responses to the out-of-area threats are very diverse and primarily address risks and threats of a non-military nature. For instance, a recent report of the North Atlantic Assembly has identified the following risk factors coming from beyond the southern periphery of the Alliance. The first and foremost risk is the 'immigration explosion', that results either from an increase in the rate of illegal immigration or as a 'consequence of a huge influx of refugees trying to escape from a crisis'.[7] Second and third on the list are risks of terrorism and the proliferation of weapons of mass destruction. The report does not list any direct military threat potentialities from the south to the NATO territory.

---

[4] Roland Paris, 'Peacebuilding and the Limits of Liberal Internationalism', *International Security*, 22:2 (Fall 1997).
[5] Zbigniew Brzezinski, 'A Geostrategy for Eurasia', *Foreign Affairs* 76:5 (September/October 1997), 50–64.
[6] *The Economist* (3 January 1998), 18.
[7] North Atlantic Assembly, NATO's role in the Mediterranean, Draft General Report, 25 August 1997, p. 1.

In a slightly different approach, Alyson Bailes has identified three main types of security challenges to Europe:[8]

> 1. Conflicts in the region immediately adjoining the 'greater Europe' such as North Africa, the Middle East and South-West Asia.
> 2. Other generic security threats such as: the actual use or sharpened threat of the use of weapons of mass destruction, anywhere in the world; a resurgence of terrorist activities against European (or broader Western) populations, using either traditional or WMD techniques; terrorism in new dimensions, notably 'cyber-terrorism'; and accidents from inadequate storage or disposal of military wastes.
> 3. Threats in non-military dimension such as: disturbances in the supply of energy or other basic commodities for the European economy, disturbances in the financial system (including insurance), natural disasters, economic damage through climate/environmental change, short or long-term flows of illegal and/or unassimilable immigration to the European area.

The response of European institutions towards the risk from outside the defence perimeters varies to a great extent. Stabilization is sought by the extension of the Alliance perimeters paralleled by liberal outreach programmes. Finally, the defence planning and crisis management contingencies are increasingly geared towards out-of-area operations. The following three sections will examine how effectivly these various responses are implemented and to what extent they are indeed increasing stability in the periphery of the Alliance area.

Extension of Defence Perimeters

The eastward extensions by NATO and the EU are an attempt to knit together the various societies subscribing to liberal democracies. It represents an extension of a value consensus that deserves to be collectively defended. But can European states extend and deepen their security arrangements without simultaneously threatening others?

The neo-realists expect from the NATO expansion a balancing effect by Russia and other states sooner or later.[9] This does not necessarily exclude more cooperation between NATO states and Russia on matters such as arms control and joint conflict management.

US voices were calling for simultaneous enlargement of the EU and NATO or for an EU enlargement first. The basic official claim is that an EU membership

---

[8] Alyson J.K. Bailes, *Challenges for European Security*, Paper presented at the Geneva Center for Security Policy, 15 June 1998 (attribution with permission of author).
[9] For an analytical perspective that explains balancing on the grounds of military capabilities and ideology, see Stephen M. Walt, *The Origins of Alliances* (Ithaca: Cornell University Press, 1987).

would assure the connection between Europe's security and its economy. The more discreet and more serious argument is the American fear that a NATO expansion could spoil US–Russian accommodation over co-operative build-down of weapons of mass destruction on Russian soil.[10] Given the way the enlargement debate has taken its course, it is safe to predict that the NATO extension will become a serious test of US–European burden sharing. This has been highlighted by the threat from French President Chirac that France would not pay for the American goal of NATO enlargement, because the French-supported candidates Romania and Slovenia were not retained.[11]

A number of analysts argue that the deepening of the EU through a monetary union may hinder the consolidation of the liberal order that is emerging in Eastern and Central Europe. As Timothy Gordon Ash puts it: 'Liberal order, not unity, is the right strategic goal for European policy in our time.'[12] Europe may be split up into an inner and outer wall; a new artificial division of Europe may emerge. In this sense, the move towards a European monetary union represents a high risk for the efforts of a Continental consolidation.[13] Furthermore, the Amsterdam Summit of 1997 brought common border management policies to the core competencies of the EU.

The historian John Lewis Gaddis raises a similar critique, but from a different angle. He argues that the widening of the EU should precede NATO extension, as the main challenges today in Europe are economic and not military. According to Gaddis, the EU's 'single-minded push to achieve a single currency among its existing members' leaves it by default to NATO to try to 'reintegrate and stabilize Europe as a whole'.[14]

The Building of Security around Europe

Given the risks and threats that are directly affecting Europe's security agendas, the Western institutions have attempted to project influence into areas outside their collective defence boundaries. In addition to the membership extensions of NATO, the EU and the WEU, these institutions have launched a number of co-operative programmes with the purpose of creating a zone that becomes safe for democracy. These are partnerships with hard and soft security programmes in the framework of

---

[10] Howard Baker Jr., Sam Nunn, Brent Scowcroft and Alton Frye, 'Enlarge the European Union Before NATO', *IHT* (6 February 1998).
[11] Stanley R. Sloan, 'The US Role in the World: Indispensable Leader or Hegemony?', CRS Report for Congress, 10 December 1997, p. 4.
[12] Timothy Garton Ash, 'Europe's Endangered Liberal Order', *Foreign Affairs* 77:2 (March/April 1998), 52.
[13] For a rather alarmist view of about the consequences of the introduction of the Euro, see Martin Feldstein, 'EMU and International Conflict', *Foreign Affairs* (November/December 1997), 60–73.
[14] John Lewis Gaddis, 'History, Grand Strategy and NATO Enlargement', *Survival*, 40:1 (Spring 1998), 147.

PfP, EACC and the special arrangements with Russia and the Ukraine. Non-military programmes and dialogue programmes have been launched by all security institutions with regard to the Mediterranean. NATO and the WEU have their dialogue programmes, the EU has the Euro-Med Process, and the OSCE the Mediterranean Dimension.

The most ambitious programme is Partnership for Peace (PfP) which is regional in scope but bilateral in practise. The non-committal nature of PfP with the possibility of creating a special 'à la carte' programme, has allowed over forty countries from Western and Eastern Europe, the Baltic states, Central Asia and the Balkans to work with NATO. The PfP arrangements are placed in the soft security network of the Euro-Atlantic Partnership Council. The Council's mandate is to promote the enhancement of the PfP programmes and to co-ordinate the co-operation of the partners in the following areas: political consultations about security-related issues, functional discussions on defence and defence-related activities, and peace support and disaster relief.

NATO also maintains a dialogue with a number of Southern Mediterranean states. NATO's 1997 Summit in Madrid decided to widen the scope and enhance the ongoing Mediterranean Dialogue, and to establish a new committee, the Mediterranean Co-operation Group, to further that end. The outreach remains rather weak, however, as it is on a bilateral basis only and with no operational dimension.

The WEU promotes a less ambitious outreach programme than NATO and concentrates on consultations and co-operation along the lines of the Petersberg Declaration, namely humanitarian and rescue tasks and peace support. Associate Partners come from Central Europe and the Baltic. Some of them are involved in the WEU police training operation in Albania (MAPE) through the Associate Partnership. The WEU also maintains a rather weak dialogue with a select number of states from the Mediterranean region.

The EU sustains its outreach through the Accession Partnership, association agreements and multilateral partnerships. The Barcelona Process, for instance, has an objective to address the root causes of conflict and migration from the South towards Europe. It has three areas of co-operation: security, economic and cultural. The security co-operation is paralysed as some Arab states have established an explicit link between the Middle East Peace Process and the Euro-Med Partnerships. In this context, it is unlikely to create any co-operative crisis management functions for the Mediterranean in the foreseeable future.

The South-East European region and the Mediterranean have not been included in the expansion plans of the EU and NATO.[15] It is possible, however, to expand

---

[15] Malta was not included in the expansion track, after the newly elected Maltese Government froze its application to the EU in late 1996. The inclusion of Cyprus hinges on a settlement of Turkish–EU relations.

the security space in Europe to the Balkans and to Central Asia with WEU Associate Partner status, NATO's Partnership for Peace, the Euro-Atlantic Partnership Council and the OSCE Stability Pact. Operational association has already been achieved with the inclusion of military contingents from countries such as Morocco or Egypt into the integrated command of IFOR or SFOR.

Instruments for Crisis Management and Peace-building

The extension of the Alliance frameworks and the structuring of outreach programmes towards the periphery of Europe may help to foster a culture of co-operation and it may support states in their difficult transitions towards good governance and liberalism. But how can the European institutions react to a threat or a risk that rapidly needs to be taken care of in a Non-Article V situation? Can European institutions project power into adjacent areas, such as the Balkans, the Mediterranean or Central Asia for the purpose of peacemaking, peace enforcement or peace-building? And to what extent are the force requirements of such missions compatible with NATO's classic mandate of collective defence?

As the examples of Yugoslavia and Albania have shown, Alliance crisis management is based on common interest rather than on collective security. For this purpose, the Alliance will not be able to maintain its utility if it can only provide crisis management instruments for contingencies that do not require collective consent, nor would it exclusively draw from collective Alliance assets.

The Europeans do not have the military capability or the organizational unity to project power beyond their borders. According to a WEU study, European-only assets without American troops and logistical support would be able to project no more than 10,000 troops beyond the alliance boundaries.[16] This shortcoming of power projection is a reason why some European states have insisted on developingwithin NATO a European Security and Defence Identity that would facilitate the use of collective NATO defence assets for a WEU-led operation.

The WEU is the military arm of the EU and it can be used for operations in which the US does not wish to be involved. But with the acceptance of a European Security and Defence Identity by NATO, the WEU can use NATO collective assets and capabilities for such operations. The implementation of such operations may be facilitated by the concept of Combined Joint Task Forces (CJTFs). In fact, the CJTF concept was accepted by the Europeans as a trade-off for not pushing the WEU into an operational military organization.

A European command with CJTF could provide the Europeans with greater freedom to undertake Non-Article V. operations. This would still be better than a 'coalition of the willing'. The move towards a European Command structure has the benefits of bringing France back into the military planning of NATO: France joined the Alliance's Military Committee in December 1995.

---

[16] Assembly of the WEU, 'Europe's Role in the Prevention and Management of Crises in the Balkans', 5 November 1997, Document 1589, p. 2.

Given the need for a reorientation of NATO and the WEU towards the south, some analysts proposed to provide the defence organization with the creation of a northern and a southern orientation within the Western security community.[17]

The northern outlook is to assure continuity with the classic Article V mission of deterring any kind of aggression against NATO territory. As to the south, NATO has to prepare for the projection of power and military intervention. This new orientation towards the South requires consultative mechanisms, an adjustment of the force posture and command structure. The consultative process, that should be in close co-operation with the EU and the WEU would have to lead to the decision whether a NATO or the WEU or some kind of combination under the Combined Joint Task Force arrangement.

The trend of creating more flexibility of military response towards sub-regional challenges has also been reflected by the creation of new forces that are geared primarily for crisis management in out-of-area operations. Eurofor (European Rapid Operational Force) and Euromarfor have been set up by Southern European member-states for that purpose. Eurofor and Euromarfor are military forces that can be used primarily by Southern European states, but these forces can also be made available to NATO and WEU for Non-Article V missions. The main mission objectives of these forces are to support humanitarian missions, emergency evacuations of national citizens, peace support missions, and peace enforcement missions.

In the aftermath of operation Alba, the Southern states accelerated the creation of other crisis management instruments. In late 1997, Italy and Spain decided to establish the Spanish–Italian Amphibious Force (SIAF), which could serve the national security interest of these two nations but that could also be employed in the framework of WEU as well as of NATO.

Multilateralism vs. Renationalization of Defence

What if the various adjustments and reforms of European institutions and NATO are not sufficient to meet the emerging requirements of out-of-area missions? In light of the fading Alliance-wide threats, the question needs to be addressed: to what extent can the existence of multilateral regimes prevent the renationalization of defence policies of European states? Are NATO, the EU and the intensive web of institutional arrangements in Europe sufficient enough to guarantee that states are not falling back to basic self-help behaviour?

---

[17] See, for instance, Hans Binnendijk, 'Next, NATO Needs to Give Itself a Southern Strategy', *IHT* (17 March 1998), 8.

Recent scholarly work about 'structural liberalism' argues that 'binding security practises' prevail over traditional balancing.[18] European states are profoundly integrated in a web of liberal institutions and regimes and the warning of some realist scholars about the revival of German nationalism and aggression seems to lack much credibility.[19] The common defence culture of NATO that has marked Europe's history for the last fifty years can certainly not be discounted in regard to overcoming nationalism or neutralism.

Furthermore, the growth of integrated command structures and multilateral forces in Europe would raise the level for re-nationalization of defence. Germany, for instance, has extensively worked towards integrating its economic and military power in European and trans-Atlantic multilateral regimes. Its economic, and potentially military, clout increasingly contributes to influence and shape the use of these instruments and regimes. Frankfurt will become the capital of the euro, and German commanders increasingly assume leadership posts within NATO command and NATO led-operations, such as IFOR or SFOR.

The incentive of European states to defect from multilateral security institutions is not very high, as the 'collective identity of democratic states' does not favour an approach of individual *sauve qui peut*.[20] By and large, the Europeans are good multilateral citizens as long as their national identity can be retained in the security arrangements. This means that states are prevented from going national in today's European security constellation, while they refuse to submit their security policy to a supranational security framework and integrated armed forces. In fact, institutions such as NATO or the WEU are precisely criticized because they are subject to national vetoes and therefore can only act through collective discipline. States continue to be the main actors in international security, or as Zelikov puts it, 'only governments can legally authorize their citizens to kill people and destroy property, and only governments are politically and morally accountable for such choices'.[21]

With the end of the Cold War, defence budgets have decreased and European states are encountering serious problems in maintaining and modernizing their armed forces. This combined with the increased integration of Command structures and of forces, this means European nations find themselves unable to mount major unilateral military campaigns outside their homelands. Finally, the process of multinationalization of defence steadily continues after the end of the Cold War.[22]

---

[18] Daniel Deudney and G. John Ikenberry, 'Structured Liberalism: The Nature and Sources of Post Western Political Order', *Ciao* (May 1996), 2.

[19] John Mearsheimer, 'Back to the Future', *International Security* (Summer 1990).

[20] For the argument of collective identity acting as a constraint to renationalization see Peter J. Katzenstein, 'Introduction', in Peter J. Katzenstein (ed.), *The Culture of National Security* (New York: Columbia University Press, 1996), pp. 1–32.

[21] Philip Zelikow, 'The Masque of Institutions', *Survival*, 38:1 (Spring 1996), 8.

[22] Multinational forces answerable to the WEU are today: the European Corps (French, German, and Belgium units), the Multinational Division (Belgian, Dutch and German units), the UK/Netherlands amphibious force, Eurofor and Euromafor (Italian, French, Spanish and Portuguese units).

Conclusion

The broadening horizon of European security poses a serious challenge to security institutions in Europe. This study has shown with several recent cases that European and trans-Atlantic security institutions cannot fail, but their members can fail to 'give life to the principles, norms, rules and procedures enshrined in these organizations'.[23] The crisis of collective discipline is accentuated by the extension of both NATO and the EU. More diversity, parochialism and different outlooks of the Alliance members towards geographically diverse sub-regions will complicate consensual decision-making in both security policy and crisis management. The danger consists in a compartmentalization of security concerns and the development of sub-regional response mechanisms at the cost of Alliance-wide security and conflict management instruments.

The spectre of the massive flows of refugees and the presence of morally unacceptable practises such as ethnic cleansing, but also power vacuums and the anticipated rivalry over the rich resources in Central Asia, will compel the European security community to shape the conditions beyond the current boundaries of the security arrangements.

Soft security programmes such as PfP, the peace-building efforts in Bosnia or the Barcelona Partnerships indicate that the European outreach efforts will be based on liberal internationalism, rather than on neo-Wilsonianism. In these efforts, the OSCE plays an increasingly important role as it has shown in the peace-building phase of Bosnia or the norm-building in Central Asia and the Caucasus.

When it comes to crisis management or peace enforcement, the EU can neither speak with one voice nor can it engage in out-of-area peace enforcement activities. Only NATO currently has the capability of sustaining a large-scale military campaign outside the NATO perimeters. But structurally and organizationally, Europe is very close to engaging in WEU-led operations with NATO assets and logistics. What is lacking is a coherent relationship between NATO and the EU. In the meantime, the propensity for unilateralism and one-off coalitions is not likely to diminish. Challenges such as peace support, humanitarian aid, mass refugee management, disaster relief, peacemaking and peace-building will continue to test the effectiveness of European crisis management instruments and the power of persuasion of individual member states.

---

[23] Ernst B. Haas, 'Regime decay: conflict management and international organizations, 1945–1981', *International Organization*, 37:2 (Spring 1983), 190.

Chapter Eight

Multilateralism and International Political Economy – the Regional Level: An American Perspective

David Sylvan

In recent years, much has been made of the disjunction between deepening economic interdependence in Asia and the relatively low degree of policy sco-ordination and political integration among Asian countries.[1] This discussion has been sparked by reflection among both policy-makers and scholars as to the differences between European and Asian experiences; it has been given added impetus in recent years with the widening of ASEAN, the APEC Summits and, since 1997, the regional financial crisis in East Asia.

My intention in this chapter is to argue that concern over the disjunction between economic and political trends is misplaced. I do so by laying out a framework within which we can start to think systematically about regions, both generally and with particular application to Japan and East Asia. Using this

---

[1] Peter Drysdale and Ross Garnaut, 'The Pacific: An Application of a General Theory of Economic Integration', in C. Fred Bergsten and Marcus Noland (eds), *Pacific Dynamism and the International Economic System* (Washington: Institute for International Economics, 1993); Richard Higgott, Richard Leaver, and John Ravenhill (eds), *Pacific Economic Relations in the 1990s* (Boulder: Lynn Rienner, 1993); Jeffrey A. Frankel and Miles Kahler (eds), *Regionalism and Rivalry: Japan and the United States in Pacific Asia* (Chicago: University of Chicago Press, 1993); Vinod K. Aggarwal, 'Comparing Regional Co-operation Efforts in the Asia-Pacific and North America', in Andrew Mack and John Ravenhill (eds), *Pacific Co-operation: Building Economic and Security Regimes in the Asia-Pacific Region* (St Leonards, Australia: Allen and Unwin, 1994); Miles A. Kahler, 'Institution-Building in the Pacific', in ibid.; Richard Higgott and Richard Stubbs, 'Competing Conceptions of Economic Regionalism: APEC versus EAEC in the Asia Pacific', *Review of International Political Economy*, 2 (1995), 516–535; Yoichi Funabashi, *Asia Pacific Fusion: Japan's Role in APEC* (Washington: Institute for International Economics, 1995); Stephan Haggard, 'Regionalism in Asia and the Americas', in Edward D. Mansfield and Helen V. Milner (eds), *The Political Economy of Regionalism* (New York: Columbia University Press, 1993); and M. Bernard and J. Ravenhill, 'Beyond Product Cycles and Flying Geese: Regionalization, Hierarchy, and the Industrialization of East Asia', *World Politics*, 47 (January 1995).

framework, I shall argue that the geographical boundaries of economic regions are in the process of shifting at an ever more rapid pace, and that the disparity between economic and political trends, far from being a troublesome anomaly, represents instead the likely future of the world-economy.

World-Economies

The standard way of thinking about regions is that they are in some sense defined with respect to one or more geographical features. Thus, we may speak of Asia, East Asia, North-East Asia, Korea and the Ongjin Peninsula, to cite but a small number of the regions to which a given place may be said to belong. This geographical view is certainly correct up to a point, but it misses two essential facts. First, although there are any number of geographic features which could serve to define a region, only some of them fill this function at any given point in time. Second, the regions which we do tend to speak about share something more than the particular geographical feature which may supply their name: perhaps the people who live there speak the same language, or have the same religion, or adhere to the same political groupings. From this perspective, there is no such thing as a region defined in purely geographical terms; instead, there are as many ways of defining regions as there are human activities in which we are interested.[2]

One vitally important set of activities revolves around the production and distribution of goods. This set of activities is an economy, although, as Karl Polanyi pointed out long ago, the activities need not necessarily involve either production for profit or distribution by market means.[3] The distinctive feature of economies, as opposed to isolated acts of production and distribution, is that the activities form an internally ordered set: that is, the production of goods in one

---

[2] The arguments above, and the general approach I am taking in this paper, can roughly be placed in the tradition of economic geography. See Paul Vidal de la Blache, 'Tableau de la géographie de la France', in E. Lavisse, *Histoire de la France depuis les origines jusqu'à la Révolution*, vol. 1, pt. 1 (Paris: Hachette, 1903); Walter Christaller, *Die zentralen Orte in Süddeutschland: Eine ökonomisch-geographische Untersuchung über die Gesetzmässigkeit der Verbreitung und Entwicklung der Siedlungen mit städtischen Funktionen* (Jena: Fischer, 1933); August Lösch, *The Economics of Location* (1940; English translation, New Haven: Yale University Press, 1954); Derment S. Whittlesey, 'The Regional Concept and the Regional Method', in P. James and C. Jones (eds), *American Geography: Inventory and Prospect* (Syracuse: Syracuse University Press, 1954); George K. Zipf, *Human Behavior and the Principle of Least Effort: An Introduction to Human Ecology* (Cambridge, Mass.: Addison-Wesley); and Walter Isard, *Location and Space-Economy: A General Theory Relating to Industrial Location, Market Areas, Trade, and Urban Structure* (Cambridge, Mass.: MIT Press, 1956). Cf. François Perroux, 'Economic Space: Theory and Applications', *Quarterly Journal of Economics*, 64 (1950), 89– 104.

[3] Karl Polanyi, *The Great Transformation: The Political and Economic Origins of Our Time* (New York: Rinehart, 1944), ch. 5; see also idem, 'The Economy as Instituted Process', in K. Polanyi, C. Arensberg, and H. Pearson (eds), *Trade and Market in the Early Empires: Economies in History and Theory* (New York: Free Press, 1957).

place is dependent on the distribution of goods produced in another place. What we can say is that at any given time, there are at least two kinds of such sets.

The first is local. If, quite arbitrarily, we say that 'local' means that distribution to the end-user is no more than a day's journey from the producer, then we can say that throughout most of human history, the vast majority of people have been engaged in producing food and other goods for local consumption. As Paul Krugman has pointed out, even today, in the post-industrial era, many, if not the majority, of our daily economic interactions are local; arguably, as services occupy an ever greater proportion of economic output, the 'locality' of economic life will increase.[4] This is one useful corrective to the standard newspaper accounts of 'globalization' as an irresistible force destroying all that is local.

The other kind of set is what, following the great historian Fernand Braudel, we can call a 'world-economy'.[5] This concept, it is important to understand, does not necessarily mean the physical world; rather, it refers to the physical limits within which different economic activities will regularly and intensely be carried out in an interlocking way. For example, what we might nowadays call the Mediterranean Basin was for many centuries a world-economy. Goods – food items, handicrafts, building materials, and so forth – produced in one area of the Mediterranean were regularly transported to other areas where they were consumed. Such consumption usually took a market form, although in other world-economies, markets were less common than other forms of exchange, such as reciprocal gift-giving. What is important, and what made the activities into a genuine world-economy, is that the production of certain goods occurred largely for purposes of their eventual transport and consumption elsewhere in that world. By contrast, although goods were certainly carried from time to time between worlds (as in the transport of silk from China to the Roman Empire), the vast majority of the production of such goods was not carried out with that type of transport in mind.

Regions in a World-Economy

World-economies have three characteristics worthy of discussion. First, they tend to have particular boundary qualities. Braudel discusses, but in the end rejects, the possibility that world-economies are usually sixty days from one 'end' to the other, that is, that it takes no more than sixty days for goods to be transported from one area in the economy to another. None the less, even if we cannot come up with a single number, there is no doubt that when distances are too long, regular interactions are simply not possible.

---

[4] Paul Krugman, 'The Localization of the World Economy', in *Pop Internationalism* (Cambridge, Mass.: MIT Press, 1996).
[5] Fernand Braudel, *The Mediterranean and the Mediterranean World in the Age of Philip II*, 2nd rev. edn. (1966; English translation, New York: Harper and Row, 1972), part 2, section 1, subsection 1; *idem, Civilization and Capitalism, 15th – 18th Century* (1979; English translation, New York: Harper and Row, 1984), Vol. 3, Ch. 1.

Second, world-economies tend to have internal ordering principles. Braudel claims that world-economies have a 'core', often, though not always, a city in which production and distribution techniques are most refined (and in which, under capitalism, value-added is higher than elsewhere). This implies that world-economies also have a peripheral zone, as well as an intermediate set of areas. One cannot infer from this that the core governs or rules the rest of the world-economy; still, the core exercises an important attractive force, serving as a technical model to be emulated. In this sense, we can understand better why cities lacking overwhelming military force at their disposal, such as Venice or, later, Amsterdam, were able to play such an important economic role that they attracted some of the most renowned artists of the age.

Third, world-economies need not coincide with political units. Certainly, it has been the case that particular world-economies – the Mediterranean in the time of the Roman Empire; the Chinese world-economy – covered more or less the same area as the zone of influence of a particular empire, but this has not always been the case. To cite only a few of the many examples: the world-economy of the Indian Ocean was for many centuries one in which numerous kingdoms were involved; so too was the Mayan world-economy; and, most recently, the modern world-economy (see below) has boundaries that include numerous states. Arguably, one of the major sources of political conflict throughout the centuries has been the periodic attempt by powerful political units to take over different areas of the world-economy in which they are involved.[6]

With these points in mind, we can now return to the issue of regions. For various reasons, certain goods tend to be produced in areas which are relatively limited in size.[7] Although such clustering cannot really be called a division of labour (particularly as regards agricultural products and certain handicrafts), it none the less tends to be reinforced by exchange processes, so that a given world-economy will be characterized by regular transportation between areas of concentrated production. Such areas obviously are regions, as we have used the term above. For the political and economic elites of a particular region in a world-economy, it matters enormously whether their region is in the core, the periphery, or the intermediate zones of that world-economy. Since, until recently, the geographical boundaries of regions would change only very slowly, with devastating consequences when a particular product (for example, silver, or beaver furs) became scarce, the impetus for political conflict over the ownership, or at least the control, of regions was considerable.

It should be pointed out that regions of a world-economy, as I am using the term, are areas of integrated production of certain types of goods. As such, they are characterized by interlocking dependencies of labour supply and embodied

---

[6] Cf. Immanuel Wallerstein, *The Modern World-System*, 3 vols (New York: Academic Press, 1974–89); Andre Gunder Frank, *World Accumulation, 1492–1789* (New York: Monthly Review Press, 1978).

[7] For the argument about firms in a capitalist economy, see Harold Hotelling, 'Stability of Competition', *Economic Journal* 39 (1929): 41–57.

technology, as well as of raw materials, intermediate products and finished goods. To be sure, one can ascertain the existence of regions by looking at trade statistics, but such data are at best partial indicators of regional boundaries. The real question is whether production is carried out on an integrated basis. A good clue to answering the question is to look at the structures of political rule in the different areas of the potential region. Given the need for ensuring a regular labour supply in the different parts of the region, the political structures of those parts must be compatible (for example, liberal regimes with liberal; corporatist with corporatist). This assuredly does not mean that we should expect formal political integration or policy co-ordination (though they are not ruled out); instead, we are talking about isomorphism between 'domestic' political arrangements.

From Multiple World-Economies to a Single World-Economy

One of the most important historical events of the last few millennia is the way in which, one after another, different world-economies have been incorporated into a single, all-encompassing world-economy. The process was led by European states which, by fits and starts, either established dense networks of trade with regions belonging to other world-economies or simply annexed such regions into burgeoning empires. Thus, the Mediterranean world-economy of 1500 had, within a century, become a European world-economy, with the Baltic region, the North Sea, the Valley of Mexico and the Andean highlands of South America incorporated into it. A century later, Russia had begun to be incorporated, as had portions of West Africa and, to a lesser extent, portions of the Hudson and St. Lawrence river basins, India and various South-East Asian archipelagoes. By 1800, the Ottoman Empire had started to be absorbed; by 1900, the European world-economy included almost the entire physical globe. Thus, for the first time ever, the last few centuries have seen the disappearance of all but one world-economy.

Three things about this world-economy are worth noting. First, it has for a long time reached around the entire globe, even if in certain areas, that reach only extended to certain ports or particular littoral strips. As far back as the seventeenth century, Andean silver was making its way both to China and the Levant, while African slaves were being shipped to the Caribbean, Ceylonese spices to Amsterdam and Great Lakes furs to London. Those trading links, moreover, were interlocked, so that when new products came on line, they had a knock-on effect in many other regions – including those not yet incorporated into the European world-economy. For example, as the fur trade and the slave trade both exhausted sources of supply close to the Atlantic, pressures to keep supplying these products led to wars many hundreds of miles inland.[8] In short, there is nothing new about globalization: it is as old as the single world-economy.

---

[8] Eric R. Wolf, *Europe and the People Without History* (Berkeley: University of California Press, 1982), Chs 6–7.

Second, that world-economy has for a long time involved highly complicated sets of exchanges in which multiple actors have participated, directly and indirectly. To be sure, states have tried unceasingly to monopolize trade and channel it bilaterally, but such attempts have never succeeded for very long. Quite the contrary: the various 'triangular' trade routes so well-known to historians of the seventeenth and eighteenth centuries turn out to be rather simplified paradigms of typical exchange relationships in the world-economy. The Indian Ocean trade is a perfect case in point. First Portugal, then the Netherlands tried to force its products (spice, pepper, silks and so forth) into rigid channels between Asia and Western Europe; invariably, however, such attempts were succeeded by an ever more complicated set of intra-Indian Ocean exchanges involving multiple sources of supply, finance, and transportation. By the middle of the seventeenth century, Bengal silk was being sold by the Dutch in Japan and Javanese sugar by the English in Persia.[9] Just as there is nothing new about globalization, so too there is nothing new about multilateralism.

Third, the single world-economy has since its inception been beset by financial crises. Periodically, large trading institutions or investors have gone bankrupt, with numerous casualties (some private, some public) following in their wake. One thinks of the Dutch 'tulip mania' crisis of the 1630s, of the so-called Mississippi and South Sea Bubbles of 1719 (which ruined investors in Geneva, the Netherlands, Hamburg and northern Italy, as well as in France and England), of the various panics of the nineteenth century, of the Great Depression and, most recently, the East Asian crises that began in 1997. Along with these busts, of course, have also come booms; and although one might take with a grain of salt Schumpeter's famous notion of entrepreneurial capitalism as involving 'creative destruction', it is clear that as the world-economy expands in extent and financial resources, the shifts of investors into and out of certain regions can accentuate shifts in regional definitions. I will come back to this point below; for now, let me simply observe that regions rise and decline much faster in the single world-economy than in its predecessors.

Japan as a Region of a World-Economy

Prior to the inception of the single world-economy, Japan was a region of what we could call the Chinese world-economy. The adjective 'Chinese' is in this case something of a misnomer, as the world-economy extended well beyond Chinese borders and included areas – notably Japan – which were not ruled by China. Yet

---

[9] *The New Cambridge Modern History*, Vol. 4 (Cambridge: Cambridge University Press, 1970), Ch. 21; Vol. 5 (Cambridge: Cambridge University Press, 1961), Ch. 17. See also K.N. Chaudhuri, *Trade and Civilisation in the Indian Ocean: An Economic History from the Rise of Islam to 1750* (Cambridge: Cambridge University Press, 1985); idem, *Asia Before Europe: Economy and Civilisation of the Indian Ocean from the Rise of Islam to 1750* (Cambridge: Cambridge University Press, 1990).

the adjective 'Chinese' is worth keeping: because of the immense productive weight of China in that world-economy; because so many of the exchanges passed through China; and, most importantly, because the institutionalization of trade was structured along a Chinese tributary pattern.[10] This does not, of course, mean that profit or other motives were absent from trade (at least for some of the parties); but it does mean that, in principle, trade was to be channeled as a form of political tribute, with 'gifts' given in exchange.

Prior to the Ming dynasty (1368–1644), the Japanese had traded extensively with China (during the Southern Sung, for instance, not less than forty to fifty ships made the journey annually); this was continued even under the tense post-invasion period of the Yüan dynasty. The Ming, however, sought to channel trade into tributary forms, not only with Japan but throughout East Asia and into the Indian Ocean. Chinese subjects were also barred from going abroad, which reinforced the Ming tendency to make trade tributary. By the early fifteenth century, the Japanese had begun to follow this form, Ashikaga Yoshimitsu referring to himself as the 'King of Japan' and thereby being permitted to trade with the Chinese. Over the next century and a half, nineteen trade missions were sent to China. During this same time, considerable trade took place between Japan and Korea (both, in Chinese eyes, of equal status), with many more trade missions than between Japan and China. Although the Koreans imposed various controls on these missions, the trade none the less continued until the late sixteenth century, when Toyotomi Hideyoshi twice invaded Korea. In addition, both Japan and Korea traded actively with the Ryukyu Islands. As the Ryukyus were tributary to China and as they also were engaged in extensive trading relations with South-East Asia, Japan and Korea became engaged in indirect trade with these areas via the intermediary of the Ryukyus.

Several aspects of Japan's regional role in this world-economy are worth noting. First, and quite importantly, Japan was by then becoming a single economic entity. Only because of this unity, and the political unification that went along with it, could Japan have entered into tributary trade. We thus have a 'country' as a region. Second, although foreign trade represented only a small part of what we might anachronistically call the gross national product (this was true of all world-economies in this era), it none the less was of considerable political and economic importance. Profits from trade paid for the construction of villas and

---

[10] The discussion in this and the following paragraphs is based on *The Cambridge History of Japan*, Vol. 3 (Cambridge: Cambridge University Press, 1990), Ch. 9 (Kawazoe Shoji: 'Japan and East Asia'); ibid., Vol. 4 (Cambridge: Cambridge University Press, 1991), Chs 2 (Asao Naohiro, 'The Sixteenth-Century Unification'), Chs 6–7 (Jurgis Elisonas, 'The Inseparable Trinity: Japan's Relations with China and Korea'; 'Christianity and the Daimyo'); and John King Fairbank (ed.), *The Chinese World Order: Traditional China's Foreign Relations* (Cambridge, Mass.: Harvard University Press, 1968), chs by Mark Mancall ('The Ch'ing Tribute System: An Interpretive Essay'), Hae-jong Chun ('Sino-Korean Tributary Relations in the Ch'ing Period'), Robert K. Sakai ('The Ryukyu [Liu-Ch'iu] Islands as a Fief of Satsuma'), and John E. Wills, Jr. ('Ch'ing Relations with the Dutch, 1662–1690').

temples; the country's elite was clothed with foreign cloth, woven with foreign thread; and economic transactions in an increasingly monetized economy took place with foreign coins. Third, although tributary trade was certainly only a portion of Japan's total foreign exchanges (unofficial trade and piracy were quite significant), it served as the paradigm for the latter in terms of both products obtained and the political rule of those who obtained them.

In the sixteenth century, however, the regional role of Japan in this world-economy began to dwindle. With the arrival of the Portuguese (who, via their introduction of firearms and the activities of their Catholic missionaries had a major effect on internal Japanese politics) and, later, the Dutch, some of Japan's trade was diverted from the Chinese world-economy (although the Portuguese also served as a Chinese–Japanese trade conduit). Disputes between the Hosokawa and Ouchi houses led to an eventual abolition of trade with the Ming; later, the Tokugawa shoguns were unwilling to pay tribute, first to the Ming, then to the Qing, so that trade with China became relatively minor, passing mostly through the Ryukyus (which had been conquered by the Shimazu house in 1609) and, informally, through Chinese merchants in Nagasaki. The Koreans increasingly imposed controls on Japanese trade missions; when trade resumed after Hideyoshi's two invasions (thwarted, it should be said, with the aid of a Ming army that crossed the Yalu and, on behalf of its Korean tributary kingdom, defeated the invaders), it was restricted in principle to a single port of entry (Pusan), where traders were lodged in a walled compound (just as the Japanese were to deal with the Dutch in Nagasaki). By 1635, when the shogunate restricted foreign ships and foreign trade to Nagasaki and prohibited overseas Japanese from returning home, Japan's regional role in the Chinese world-economy was for the most part insignificant. The Chinese world-economy continued, but because of foreign wars and internal decrees, the Japanese region in that world-economy became, in quantitative terms, a shadow of its former self. Arguably, as this process continued, Japanese production ceased, except for a handful of products (themselves relatively unimportant for most Japanese elites, and even merchants), to occur largely for purposes of eventual transport and exchange with the Chinese world-economy; in this sense, Japan ceased to be a region of the latter. We thus have a long, slow curve: it took the better part of a century for Japanese trade with China to beome tributary in form and for Japan thus to become a region of the Chinese world-economy; this status then continued for another 150 years or so; and finally, it took almost another century for Japan gradually to deliquesce out of that world-economy. Hence, even in a tributary political economy in which, since it makes no sense to speak of an 'economy' as separate from political life, one might expect political upheavals to translate immediately into changes in production, it none the less took a long time for world-economy regions to be created or dissolved.

Japan in a Region of the Single World-Economy

During the nineteenth century, the Chinese world-economy ceased to exist. As it was absorbed into the single world-economy, so too were its peripheral regions. This absorption took place by commercial and military means (for example, the Opium Wars), the latter usually serving to help bring about the former. Thus, when Japan was 'opened' by Commodore Perry's gunships, the question that arose was how it would fit into the single world-economy. What region of that world-economy would it belong to, and in what zone (core, periphery, intermediate area) would that region be?

The answer came within several decades. By 1910, the Japanese had either occupied or annexed many of the areas with which they had traded in preceding centuries; the most important were Korea and portions of China (Taiwan, Manchuria).[11] These areas played an important role in Japan's industrialization drive which required vast inputs of foreign technology. That technology came from Europe and North America; to pay for it, Japanese exports had to rise. Food and raw materials from the formal and informal colonies played a vital role in making possible such increased exports (by feeding Japan's labour force and providing inputs to its machines). Thus, as Japan moved into the world-economy (foreign transactions went from 6 per cent of economic activity in the mid-1880s to 28 per cent by World War I), its shift from peripheral to intermediate status was enabled by the development of its own periphery, ever more tightly linked to Japan itself.

During and after World War I, Japanese industrialization continued. This growth required not only raw materials, but industrial products of various sorts: steel, chemicals, and so forth. While much of the infrastructure to produce these products was developed in Japan, Manchuria, Korea and (following the onset of war in the 1930s) North China also saw Japanese investment in heavy industry. The combination of Japanese investment in, imports from and exports to these areas meant that Japan was more and more a component part (albeit the controlling one) of a North-East Asian region in the world-economy (Taiwan was a part of this region, even though it is not geographically in the 'North-East' of Asia). As we would expect, the structure of political rule throughout this region was, to put it mildly, compatible with that of Japan itself. However, in spite of the hopes of some

---

[11] The discussion in this and the following paragraphs is drawn from *The Cambridge History of Japan*, Vol. 6 (Cambridge: Cambridge University Press, 1988), Ch. 5 (Mark R. Peattie, 'The Japanese Colonial Empire, 1895–1945'), Ch. 6 (Ikuhiko Hata, 'Continental Expansion, 1905–1941'), Ch. 8 (E. Sydney Crawcour, 'Industrialization and Technological Change, 1885–1920'), and Ch. 9 (Takafusa Nakamura, 'Depression, Recovery, and War, 1920–1945'); and from various chapters in the following three edited books: Ramon H. Myers and Mark R. Peattie (eds), *The Japanese Colonial Empire, 1895–1945* (Princeton: Princeton University Press, 1984); Peter Duus, Ramon H. Myers, and Mark R. Peattie (eds), *The Japanese Informal Empire in China, 1895–1937* (Princeton: Princeton University Press, 1989); and *idem* (eds), *The Japanese Wartime Empire, 1931–1945* (Princeton: Princeton University Press, 1996).

Japanese leaders for building North-East Asia into the centre of a separate world-economy, the region continued throughout the 1930s to be part of the single world-economy and, as we know, the attempt at creating the Greater East Asian Coprosperity Sphere ended in military defeat. Comparing the North-East Asian region of the single world-economy to the earlier Japanese region of the Chinese world-economy, the former arose far more quickly than the latter and flourished for a much shorter period of time. One might thus expect its dissolution to have occurred with equal celerity; and this is exactly what occurred.

Post-War Planning and Economic Regions

The end of World War II led to the rapid disappearance of the North-East Asian region of the world-economy. Ironically, this occurred in spite of, and not because of, United States policy. Originally, American officials had intended to break up Japan's economic and political hold over North-East Asia. However, the combination of the emerging Cold War with the Soviet Union and the economic devastation of Germany and Japan (endangering the economic world order outlined at Bretton Woods) triggered an intensive, fifteen-week policy rethink in Washington.[12] What resulted (the 'creation', to use the word with which Acheson titled his memoirs) was a combined political and economic strategy symbolized by the Truman Doctrine and the Marshall Plan. Germany and Japan, as well as areas in their regions of the world-economy, were to be built up economically, protected militarily, and normalized politically. The European Union and NATO are two institutional traces of this strategy.

For Japan, the strategy meant that the North-East Asia was intended to continue as a region of the world-economy. In January 1947, Marshall sent a note to Acheson asking him to 'Please have plan drafted of policy to organize a definite government of So. Korea and connect up its economy with that of Japan'. In May 1948, the CIA was singing the same song: 'As in the past, Japan for normal economic functioning on an industrial basis, must have access to the North-East Asiatic areas – notably North China, Manchuria, and Korea – now under direct, indirect, or potential control of the USSR'. Similarly, Kennan told State Department officials in 1949 that 'The day will come, and possibly sooner than we

---

[12] The discussion in this and the following paragraphs is drawn from numerous primary and secondary sources. Among the latter, I have relied especially on Bruce Cumings, 'The Origins and Development of the North-East Asian Political Economy: Industrial Sectors, Product Cycles, and Political Consequences', *International Organization*, 38:1 (1984), 1–40; idem, *The Origins of the Korean War*, Vol. 2 (Princeton: Princeton University Press, 1990), Chs 1–2; Melvyn P. Leffler, *A Preponderance of Power: National Security, the Truman Administration, and the Cold War* (Stanford: Stanford University Press, 1992), Chs 4–5; and John Gerard Ruggie, 'Multilateralism: The Anatomy of an Institution', in idem (ed.), *Multilateralism Matters: The Theory and Praxis of an Institutional Form* (New York: Columbia University Press, 1993).

think, when realism will call upon us not to oppose the re-entry of Japanese influence and activity into Korea and Manchuria'.

This goal was not achieved. Both North Korea and Manchuria remained completely outside the reach of Japanese firms for many decades. To be sure, in South Korea (especially after normalization with Japan in 1965) and, to a lesser degree, Taiwan, Japanese banks and industrial firms were present in loans, direct investment and in the supply of certain capital goods. None the less, as the difference in the structure of political rule between Taiwan and South Korea on the one hand, and Japan on the other suggests, the tight integration of Taiwan and Korea to Japan that characterized the heyday of the pre-war North-East Asian region no longer existed: in spite of the significant Japanese presence in these countries, they ceased to form a single productive unit.[13]

There are several reasons for this change. One is due to the effects of the Korean War: an elephantine American presence in both Taiwan and Korea, which by definition ate into the Japanese role. This resulted in exports oriented toward US markets, access to US capital, above all in the form of military and economic aid, and, most importantly, development of both import- and export-substituting policies eliminating possibilities which Japanese firms might otherwise have had. A second reason is the end of European colonial empires, which opened up to Japan any number of export markets in South-East Asia which had previously been

---

[13] On the points in this and the following paragraph, see Miyohei Shinohara, *Industrial Growth, Trade, and Dynamic Patterns in the Japanese Economy* (Tokyo: University of Tokyo Press, 1982); Makoto Itoh, *The World EconomicCrisis and Japanese Capitalism* (New York: St Martin's Press, 1990); Walter Hatch and Kozi Yamamura, *Asia in Japan's Embrace: Building a Regional Production Alliance* (Cambridge: Cambridge University Press, 1996); A.D. Morgan, 'Export Competition and Import Substitution: The Industrial Countries 1963 to 1971', in R.A. Batchelor et al. (eds), *Industrialization and the Basis for Trade* (Oxford: Oxford University Press, 1980); T. Uchino, *Japan's Postwar Economy* (Tokyo: University of Tokyo Press, 1983); Alice Amsden, *Asia's Next Giant* (Oxford: Oxford University Press, 1989); R. Wade, *Governing the Market: Economic Theory and the Role of Government in East Asian Industrialization* (Princeton: Princeton University Press, 1990); and various of the chapters in James A. Roumasset and Susan Barr (eds), *The Economics of Cooperation: East Asian Development and the Case for Pro-Market Intervention* (Boulder: Westview Press, 1992), in K. Kojima, ed., *Structural Adjustment in Asian-Pacific Trade*, Papers and Proceedings of the Fifth Pacific Trade and Development Conference, Vol. 2, The Japan Economic Research Center, Tokyo, July 1973, in Kozi Yamamura (ed.), *Policy and Trade Issues of the Japanese Economy* (Seattle: University of Washington Press, 1982), in Hugh Patrick and Henry Rosovsky (eds), *Asia's New Giant* (Washington, DC: Brookings, 1976), especially by Krause and Sekiguchi: 'Japan and the World Economy', and in Paul Krugman (ed.), *Trade with Japan: Has the Door Opened Wider?* (Chicago: University of Chicago Press, 1991), especially by Park and Park: 'Changing Japanese Trade Patterns with the East Asian NICs'. Many of these works insist on the formal similarities between the state-directed industrialization-and-export policies of Japan, South Korea and Taiwan, but underplay the economic significance of the political differences between Japan and the other two states (for example, the difficulties that a non-elected government has in protecting investments from a hated former colonial power).

closed to it. Third, the rules of the Bretton Woods regime – nondiscriminatory trade, convertible currencies, and forth – permitted the Japanese to interact far more extensively with the world-economy than was previously the case. For example, the exports that helped finance Japan's ascent to core status in the world-economy could not have occurred in the sustained way that they did had it not been for the Bretton Woods rules. All three of these reasons mean that if Japan is part of a region of the single world-economy, that region spans a much broader geographical area than North-East Asia. Although many commentators have played with the idea that the Greater East Asian Coprosperity Sphere has been re-created, I consider this just as inaccurate as the claim that Japan is still part of a North-East Asian region. Rather, one can say that Japan is either once more a region of its own; or, what now amounts to the same thing, that it is part of such a large region that the term has little meaning. The contrast with Europe – still alive (if not well) as a discrete region of the world-economy – is striking.

The American Syndrome

Beyond these reasons for the disappearance of the North-East Asian region, there is a fourth one which, in my view, is the most important of all. We can call it the American syndrome. The geographer Donald Meinig has pointed out how the settlement of North America and the development of the United States involved a continual process of regional creation and agglomeration.[14] The combination of a thinly populated terrain (in which massacres and resettlements of indigenous groups played a vital role), cheap land, a supportive federal government, extensive immigration and an ideology of Messianic liberalism, entire economic regions were brought into existence within a few years. As these regions interacted, they lost their identity and coalesced into larger regions, with the process repeating itself again and again. In this way, it was possible for a large country – the United States – to form *ab initio* and develop a strong sense of national identity in an astonishingly brief period of time.

There are, of course, many particularities in United States history, and I do not wish to suggest that US growth patterns serve as a model for within-country development in an explanatory, much less a normative, sense. Internationally, however, things are different, and it is well known that the Bretton Woods rules carry with them a strong 'made in America' flavour.[15] Given that Bretton Woods was in effect the codification of the American sense of political economy, it is all the more surprising that Washington policy-makers thought they would be able to re-create the North-East Asian region in the way that it had earlier existed.

---

[14] D.W. Meinig, *The Shaping of America: A Geographical Perspective on 500 Years of History*, 3 vols. (New Haven: Yale University Press, 1986–1998).

[15] The *locus classicus* here is Richard N. Gardner, *Sterling–Dollar Diplomacy* (New York: McGraw-Hill, 1969).

For to an increasing degree, the American syndrome has become international. The last few decades have seen an increasing fluidity and short-lived quality to the regions of the world-economy. As firms develop in size and resources, they are able, far faster than before, to set up entire new industries in areas whose economies had until then been quite different. For the most part, this is not primarily a matter of improved technology, communications or transportation, to cite some of the standard factors put forward in analysing the world-economy. Rather, with larger markets available than in the past, and with greater pools of capital available than ever before, it is possible to create and amalgamate new regions on a scale that hitherto has been unseen. The result is that, to an increasing degree, regions of the world-economy are temporary, provisional, and sure to be superseded. In addition, given the definition of regions of a world-economy as areas of integrated production of particular goods, regions today are becoming larger and geographically non-contiguous. Thus, if we focus on a complex of high-technology and heavy industries involving Japan, we can see that the geographical boundaries of this complex are rapidly expanding, though in a non-smooth, 'leapfrogging' fashion. In this sense, the rapid rise and fall of the North-East Asian region of the single world-economy represents, depending on one's point of view, either one of the last times that economic regions could have been created (with re-creation, even by a powerful state, being a failure); or else a harbinger of a future in which regions are so ephemeral as to be anachronistic.

Under these circumstances, the surprise is not that the North-East Asian region was not re-created but that the European region was. There are various reasons for this disparity, not least of which, in my view, is the greater compatibility of structures of political rule in the latter than the former. What seems clear, though, is that Europe is the anomaly, not Japan. To assume that because policy co-ordination and political integration went together with increasing economic interdependence in Europe, they should do so in Asia is to turn things upside down.[16] Regions of the world-economy are shifting boundaries so rapidly in Asia and elsewhere that there simply is no stable 'it' around which to coalesce politically. To make this effort now is at best a waste of diplomats' time and energy.

---

[16] Cf. Takashi Inoguchi, 'Missions, Mechanisms and Modalities of Fledgling Cooperative Regimes in the Pacific', in Armand Clesse et al. (eds), *The Vitality of Japan: Sources of National Strength and Weakness* (Houndmills: Macmillan, 1997).

PART IV
JAPAN AND MULTILATERALISM

Chapter Nine

Japan and Multilateralism: The Regional Level

Tsutomu Kikuchi

The purpose of this chapter is to analyse the perceptions and policies of Japan toward regional economic arrangements in the Asia-Pacific region in general and toward APEC (Asia Pacific Regional Co-operation Forum) in particular.

Asia-Pacific regionalism has been characterized by 'regionalism by declaration' rather than treaty. A lack of specificity in agreements is characteristic of the preference of many Asian economies for an informal and flexible approach to regional co-operation, in contrast with the Western preference for formal institutions established by contractual agreements.[1] In fact, as was shown in the ASEAN, building mutual trust and co-operation among Asian countries has required a long period of confidence-building to overcome a long history of mutual suspicion and inter-state conflicts. Some experts, conscious of this experience and of the sensitivities of Asian countries, have argued that attempts to institutionalize APEC are premature and may be counter-productive to the long-term promotion of co-operation.[2]

Japan has been sympathetic to these Asian concerns. The Japanese policy community has been sensitive to the possibly counter-productive consequences of pushing too hard and too fast toward contractual agreements within a regional co-operative framework such as APEC.

Various characteristics of APEC which has been developed so far have been consistent with Japanese basic interests. In fact, Japan has been successful in penetrating and expanding its economic presence in the APEC region through varied means taken in the APEC process. However, it remains to be seen whether APEC can develop as an effective regional co-operative institution in the coming years, given the current economic uncertainties in Asia and the current set of norms and principles of APEC.

---

[1] John Ravenhill, 'Economic Interdependence in East Asia: Its Growth and Effects on the Australian–U.S. Relationship', in Roger Bell (ed.), *Negotiating the Pacific Century* (New South Wales: Allen and Unwin, 1996), pp. 182–183.

[2] Ross Garnaut, 'Options for Asia-Pacific Trade Liberalization (A Pacific Free Trade Area?)', in Chia Siow Yue (ed.), *APEC: Challenges and Opportunities* (Singapore: Institute of South-East Asian Studies, 1994), pp. 94–112.

Japan, Regionalism and the Principle of Non-Discrimination

In the postwar era, Japan has been actively involved in regional co-operative activities with the rest of Asia, especially with the countries of South-East Asia. The Ministerial Conference for Economic Development of South-East Asia, the Asian Development Bank (ADB) and the Asia and Pacific Council (ASPAC) were a few among the key mechanisms for Japan's engagement in regional co-operative activities which Japan had developed since the 1960s.[3] Japan also took the leadership role in launching various ideas of regional co-operation such as the Pan-Pacific community idea advocated by the Japanese Prime Minister Masayoshi Ohira late 1970s.[4]

In spite of its eagerness in establishing regional co-operative institutions, Japan has been constantly reluctant to participating in discriminatory regional economic arrangements which might have had a negative impact on global free-trading arrangements.[5] It has been a firm belief held among Japanese political, business and academic communities that Japan as a global trading nation had to place the highest priority on maintaining a stable development of international regimes such as GATT. A free and open trading system supported by GATT has been indispensable for Japan's economic welfare. This belief was further enhanced by Japan's unhappy experience of having been discriminated against even since obtaining full membership of GATT.[6]

Thus, Japan has always taken a negative attitude to any regional integration scheme involving external discrimination. In fact, in participating in a series of multilateral negotiations under the GATT auspices, Japan had to fight against potential and actual threats to the non-discrimination principle of the GATT system.[7] Therefore, although some of the academics and former senior government

---

[3] For a most comprehensive analysis, see Susumu Yamakage, *Asean: sinboru kara shisutemu he [ASEAN: From Symbol to System]* (Tokyo: University of Tokyo Press, 1990).

[4] Tsutomu Kikuchi, *Eipekku: Ajia-Taiheiyo Sin-Chitujyo no Mosaku [APEC: In Search of a New Order in the Asia-Pacific]* (Tokyo: Japan Institute of International Affairs, 1995).

[5] Today more than 100 regional economic integration schemes are registered in the GATT/WTO. Japan is one of the few countries which does not belong to any of them.

[6] Japan entered GATT in 1955 after serious efforts to participate in the global economy. But more that thirty nations had applied Article 35 of GATT to Japan when Japan entered GATT. Japan had not been given the unconditional Most-Favoured Nation treatment. It was 1976 when the last nation which applied Article 35 lifted that restriction.

[7] For example, in the Tokyo Round negotiations, Japan had to wage battle against the move – mainly by the Europeans – to introduce the selective safeguard system into GATT. In the Uruguay Round negotiations, one of the major objectives of Japan was to contain the US unilateral measures such as Article 301 of the Trade Act of 1974 and

officials such as Professor Kiyoshi Kojima and Dr. Saburo Okita proposed to form such regional arrangements as a Pacific Free Trade Area (PAFTA) and the Organization of Pacific Trade and Development (PAFTAD) in the 1960s and 1970s in order to counterbalance the formation and consolidation of the European integration, to contain American protectionism, and to provide a collective leadership to maintain the global liberal economic order, these reflected their strong commitment to globalism (global application of the non-discrimination principle) manifested in the GATT system. Any regional economic integration scheme involving external discrimination has never been considered as a governmental policy by the successive Japanese administrations.[8]

Japanese trade and investment liberalization has been pursued at the two levels. One has been at the GATT level, and the other basically through bilateral relations with the United States under the strong pressure from Washington.[9] In this context, it should be noted that Japan's commitment to the non-discrimination principle has been reflected by the provision of the benefits of liberalization measures to all countries, not restricted to the United States, in a non-discriminating way so that the GATT principle of non-discrimination has been firmly maintained.[10]

With the fluctuation of the global economic system caused by the huge imbalance facing the world economy, the frequent resort to the unilateral measures by the United States, and the dramatic increase of FDI by Japanese enterprises in the Asian economies especially since the mid-1980s, Japan began to pay more attention to the possible regional arrangements of the Asia-Pacific as an instrument to enhance the global system, to moderate pressures from Washington, and to enhance the industrial infrastructure of the Asian countries. This also reflected Japan's growing awareness that Japan had to be prepared to meet the challenge of the world's continuing drive toward globalization and Japan's need to move to higher value-added production to cope with global mega-competition by creating a region-wide production network in Asia.

In spite of its deep-seated reluctance to engage in discriminatory regional arrangements, there are now emerging some common perception in Japan which

---

what is called Super 301. Another objective was to check newly emerging regional economic integration schemes with external discrimination such as CUSFTA and NAFTA. Both seem to Japanese eyes a violation of the universal non-discrimination principle of GATT.

[8] Tsutomu Kikuchi, *op. cit.*, Chapters 2 and 3.

[9] Japan's investment liberalization began in the early 1960s when Japan joined OECD, separately from Japan's response to the pressure from Washington.

[10] Japan's continued strong support for the MFN principle and its consistently critical attitude toward discriminatory trade principle has been appreciated by the GATT itself. See, Yoko Sazanami, 'GATT and Regional Arrangements can Live Together', *The Global Trend toward Regional Integration* (Tokyo: Foreign Press Center, 1993), p. 7.

regional arrangements will serve more as instruments to supplement to and enhance global free trading mechanisms.[11]

Tiding Over an Emerging Crisis of the Global Economic Order

Responding to the Global Imbalance: Japan and the Birth of APEC

There have been different views on to whom credit should be given for the birth of APEC in 1989. Certainly some of the Japanese Ministry of International Trade and Industry (MITI) officials claim that the credit should be given to the MITI, not the Australian Prime Minister Bob Hawke. Apart from the matter of who took the initiative in launching the APEC idea, let us briefly discuss the background to the Japanese proposal to set up a ministerial forum dealing with Asia-Pacific economic co-operation.[12]

There were three major reasons for this initiative: an emerging feeling of crisis about the future of global trading systems, pressure from Washington, and Japanese private sectors' interest in Asia. This also reflected Japan's pressing need to construct a region-wide comprehensive strategy for the future, based on which Japan had to construct regional production networks in Asia to strengthen comparative advantages of Japanese enterprises in an era of global competition.

The MITI took the lead. What they were most concerned about was, firstly, the huge imbalance facing the world economy which was caused by, among other things, the huge US trade deficit and its rising accumulated debt, the accumulated debt issues in the developing countries, and the rising trade surpluses being enjoyed by Japan, Germany and some Asian economies. Although there were many efforts to sustain the international economy such as the enhancement of policy co-ordination among the developed countries through the Summit, G5/G7, the strengthening of the free trading system by launching the GATT Uruguay Round of multilateral trade negotiations in 1986 and the regional endeavours to revitalize economies through the strengthening of regional trade arrangements such as the EU, these imbalances would endanger the smooth developments of the world economy as a whole. Without adequately rectifying the imbalances, the international financial system would become unstable and protectionism would

---

[11] See, for example, Hiroaki Fukami, 'An Evolution of the Movement toward Regional Integration', *The Global Trend Toward Regional Integration* (Tokyo: Foreign Press Center, 1993), p. 38.

[12] For an inside story of Japan's involvement in the preparatory process to establish APEC, see Noboru Hatakeyama, 'Tsusho Kosho: Kokueki wo meguru Dorama [Trade Negotiations: A Drama over National Interest]', *Nihon Keizai Shinbun [Japan Economic Journal]* (1996).

emerge. The world economy might be thrown into confusion. The 'Black Monday' incident in October 1987 indicated the warning of the market that the imbalance would not be sustainable.[13] Japan's response to Asia-Pacific co-operation was reconsidered in this context.

Secondly, the Japanese government faced continued pressure from the US to rectify the huge trade imbalance. This demanded that Japan not only to open its market further for foreign products, but also to look for other ways to rectify the US trade deficit; that is, to enhance the function of Asian economies as 'absorbers' (strengthening the capacities of Asian economies to import US goods), thereby diffusing the pressures from the US.

Given the political sensitivities which trade imbalance created in US domestic politics, the huge trade imbalance had to be rectified as soon as possible. Otherwise, the US might take more aggressive unilateral and protectionist measures to rectify the imbalance, which would have a grave negative impact on the future of the international trading system.[14] Together with the increasing resort of the US to unilateral measures, the conclusion of the Canada–US Free Trade Agreement in 1989 was seen as showing the US's inward-looking moves, thereby diluting the basic foundation of the GATT.

Thirdly, Japanese business enterprises have been rushing into the Asian markets to enhance their international competitiveness by combining the factors of production in the most efficient way especially since the Plaza Accords in 1985. They have been establishing production networks around the region. However, the Japanese enterprises faced various defects of industrial infrastructure which obstructed the establishment of region-wide production networks for enhancing international competitiveness. Therefore, enhancing industrial foundation through regional co-operation was expected to contribute to further promoting an international division of labour, thereby enhancing the economic strength of Japanese enterprises as well as those of the developing countries.

In the Asia-Pacific context, two purposes had to be realized simultaneously; to reduce the trade deficit of the United States (to decrease Asia's dependence on the US market) and to maintain a steady increase of exports of the Asian economies to sustain economic growth. To realize both purposes simultaneously, Japan had first of all to enhance its capacity to absorb exports from other Asian economies. And, with the increasing enhancement of economic foundation of the Asian economies, their capacity to absorb exports especially from the US had to be enhanced. In this regard, it was vitally important to improve the industrial infrastructure of the Asian economies.

---

[13] Minister's Office, MITI (ed.), *Nihon No Sentaku* [*Japan's Options*] (Tokyo: Tusyo Sangyo Chosakai, June 1988), pp. 18–25.
[14] The trade deficit of the United States with Asia reached its historic peak in 1988.

Thus, MITI took the initiative in establishing networks for the 'horizontal division of labour' in the Asia-Pacific region, through its integrated use of ODA, trade and investment. This policy manifested itself in the so-called New Asian Industrial Development (AID) Plan. As the 1988 MITI White Paper pointed out, Japan's role was to promote the horizontal division of labour in Asia and to reduce Asia's dependence upon the US market.

The New AID Plan called on Japan to recycle its huge financial surplus to the Asian developing countries in the form of investment, to open the Japanese market to Asian exports, and to extend more aid and technical co-operation to its Asian neighbors to enhance their industrial infrastructures. The initiative reflected Japan's growing awareness that it had to strengthen regional co-operative efforts, to promote the construction of the region-wide production networks which were expected to enhance the industrial foundation of the Japanese enterprises operating in the region. The New AID Plan also reflected the view that Japan had to be prepared to meet the double challenge of the world's continuing drive toward globalization and Japan's need to move to higher value-added production.[15]

The rising feeling of crisis in late 1980s prompted Japan to tackle with those issues at the ministerial level. The ministerial forum for regional co-operation was also expected to serve as a regional framework to contain US unilateralism, such as the threat of retaliation under the Super 301 of the 1974 Trade Act, through putting a regional constraint on US behaviour.[16]

Japan's idea of enhancing regional co-operation through a ministerial forum was in a sense coloured by the traditional policies of its successive administrations which had emphasized the aspects of development co-operation with the rest of Asia. But the idea suggested that Japan viewed ASEAN and NIEs as one integrated economic entity, requiring a region-wide comprehensive perspective on aid, trade and investment. Japan began to seek to take on a more prominent role in regional economic integration through establishing Japan-based regional networks of production.[17]

---

[15] Peter Katzenstein and Martin Rouse, 'Japan as a Regional Power in Asia', in Jeffrey A. Frankel and Miles Kahler, *Regionalism and Rivalry: Japan and the United States in Pacific Asia* (University of Chicago Press, 1993), pp. 229–230.

[16] Trade policy disputes will continue to occur. Accordingly, there is an urgent need for a more rational approach to settling disputes. The idea of setting up an APEC Dispute Mediation Service which was contained in the Osaka Action Agenda reflected Japan's concern about trade disputes.

[17] The Foreign Ministry responded to the MITI's idea negatively. The Foreign Ministry could not accept the idea that only trade ministers would represent respective governments. The US Secretary of State Baker's speech in June 1989 in New York, which expressed its willingness to join a more institutionalized governmental forum for regional co-operation, greatly contributed to the changes of the attitudes of the Foreign Ministry. Baker's speech was more acceptable to the Foreign Ministry in which the role

Japanese Approach to APEC

Stalemate of the GATT Uruguay Round of Negotiations and the Emergence of Regional Arrangements

Since the first ministerial meeting in 1989 in Canberra, Australia, Japan has taken a cautious attitude so as not to create confrontation between the developed and developing countries within APEC, given the scepticism expressed by the ASEAN countries toward APEC as symbolized in the so-called Kuching Agreement.

The Japanese approach to APEC has been characterized by its emphasis on development co-operation to establish more stable economic foundations in Asian developing countries. In fact, from the beginning of APEC, Japan has tried to put forward an agenda relating to development co-operation, into the APEC processes which seemed to be more acceptable to the developing countries, especially to ASEAN. Most of the issues taken by the respective APEC work programmes are those in which the developing countries have common interests.[18]

Since its establishment, APEC has been concentrating on those issues in which member economies stood the best chance of co-operation. To prevent polarization, members have adopted a decision-making process based upon consensus. Indeed, APEC has placed a higher priority on creating an atmosphere of co-operation ('habit of co-operation' and 'institutionalized dialogues') and on promoting confidence-building among the members, than on solving the immediate economic problems. As an international institution, APEC accords an unprecedented level of discretion and independence to its members. Generally speaking, these processes suited the Japanese preference for confidence-building and development co-operation as the most important agenda for regional co-operation and steady progress towards institutionalization.

In spite of the bureaucratic rivalries within the Japanese government in the APEC processes, there has existed a common understanding in Japan concerning the basic modalities of regional co-operation. In fact, for example, the report of the Round Table on Japan and the Asia-Pacific Region in the 21st Century commissioned by then Prime Minister Kiichi Miyazawa pointed out that for the region to continue to enjoy economic growth, in line with the MITI's New AID Plan, Japan had to continue, by persisting in its efforts to increase imports of manufactured goods, to promote a horizontal division of labour among the regional

---

[18] of the Foreign Ministry was more appreciated, and that broad issues not necessarily specifying only in trade and investment-related ones were presented as possible agenda of regional co-operation.
Asahi Shinbun (11 November 1989).

countries, and to further expand direct investment and technology transfer to them.[19]

In the meantime, the GATT Uruguay Round Negotiations has failed several times to meet the deadline for a settlement. The stalemate in the GATT's negotiations and ensuing anxieties about the future of the multilateral free trading system had been pushing many countries in the direction of economic regionalism. It was feared that the GATT might be less effective than in the past.

Although Japan supported the idea that APEC would demonstrate collective willingness and determination to complete the Uruguay Round as soon as possible, Japanese basic attitudes toward economic regionalism did not change. That is, given the fact that the Asian economies are dependent upon the European and American markets, Asia could not alone have a completly self-contained regional economic system with an appropriate division of labour. It was therefore clear that any attempt to build walls to isolate Asia from the rest of the world is inherently ill-suited to the region.[20]

Thus, it was commonly conceived that Japan should not consent to any regionalism if it were to incorporate discriminatory measures against the outside. Any attempt to introduce regionalism to this region should adhere to the following basic principles: it should be non-exclusive, non-discriminatory, and free in nature; it should be compatible with the GATT; and it should not harm the interests of countries outside the region.[21]

In this context, APEC has been regarded as an important forum not for deeper institutional regional integration but for looser policy co-ordination at the regional level through the exchange of views and information on structural adjustment, economic co-operation, technology transfer and so forth.

Japan, Institutionalization and the Concept of 'Open Regionalism'

The APEC ministerial and informal Summit meetings, held in Seattle (US) and Bogor (Indonesia) in 1993 and 1994 respectively, marked significant milestones as APEC moved to transform itself from a loose consultative body into an organization with concrete goals and timetable. Both meetings indicated a move by APEC towards institutionalizing Asia-Pacific co-operation, or a shift in priority from the dialogue process itself to actual policy implementation, tackling with pressing trade and investment issues.

---

[19] *The Round Table on Japan and the Asia-Pacific Region in the 21st Century*, 'Japan and the Asia-Pacific Region in the 21st Century – Promotion of Openness and Respect for Plurality' (25 December 1992).
[20] *The Round Table Report* (December 1992), p. 17.
[21] *The Round Table Report*, ibid., p. 18.

In spite of these developments, however, the basic rationale of APEC for Japan has not changed in this period. We would point out that there has been a fairly strong consensus among government, business and academic circles in Japan about how APEC should develop in the future.

First, it should be institutionalized gradually, paying due attention to the sensitivities of the smaller developing countries. For the time being, at least, it should be a consultative body, not a formalized regional integration scheme. No political, business and academic leaders have insisted that APEC should become a more formalized regional economic arrangement such as a free-trade agreement or customs union with external discrimination.

The rapid economic development of Asian countries has been carried out without any region-wide institutional framework of economic liberalization. Asian economies liberalized their economies mainly on a voluntary basis. Therefore, many Japanese experts have argued that the 'natural' market mechanism, as opposed to an institutional framework, should be an essential factor in Asian development, and that it would be counter-productive to institute such a framework for economic liberalization, particularly if it would jeopardize the voluntary liberalization efforts and distort the market mechanism.[22]

Some Japanese experts even have argued that customs unions and free-trade agreements would be for those nations that have lost economic dynamism and vitality.[23] They have also pointed out that through international structural changes of the last decade some mechanisms to promote voluntary liberalization have been built in the region, particularly in the developing countries. Therefore, some 'competition for liberalization' to enhance their international competitiveness would be continued in this region without any institutionalized regional framework. There has been a firm belief that, given a relatively high rate of protection in the Asian economies and their pressing need to attract foreign direct investment, there remained much room for further unilateral liberalization in the Asian economies. Thus, a concept of the 'Open Economic Association' presented by one Japanese economist has been more acceptable in Japan than more formalized regional economic integration schemes.[24]

Second, APEC should maintain its guiding principle of 'Open Regionalism'. This means that liberalization measures taken within APEC should be unconditionally applied to non-APEC members. APEC should avoid taking

---

[22] Toshio Watanabe, 'Ajia-Taiheiyou ni okeru Boueki-Tousi no Sin-Choryu [New Trends of Trade and Investment in Asia and the Pacific]', paper delivered at the symposium organized by the Japan Forum on International Affairs, 1994.
[23] The Policy Recommendations on 'The Future of Regionalism and Japan', Tokyo, June 1994, The Japan Forum on International Relations.
[24] On the Open Economic Association (OEA), see Ippei Yamazawa, 'On Pacific Economic Integration', *The Economic Journal*, 102:415 (November 1992).

discriminatory measures not only regarding its members but also regarding non-members. The Japanese ministers who attended the successive APEC ministerial meetings have emphasized this point explicitly. There have been few in Japan who have supported the argument that discriminatory regional liberalization measures be used as bargaining instruments to put pressure on other regional arrangements to take a more outward-oriented position.

Third, development co-operation should be one of the major agendas of APEC, given the fact that many of the regional countries were suffering from the lack of industrial infrastructure and human resources.[25] The major Japanese aim has not been the market access pushed by the private sector. Japan has not been so aggressive in accessing markets, basically due to its huge trade surplus vis-à-vis most of the APEC economies.

These Japanese basic attitudes were summarized in the remark made by the Japanese Foreign Minister Tsutomu Hata at the 1993 Seattle ministerial meeting.[26]

Regionalism as a Supplement to Globalism

In spite of its continued concerns about discriminatory regional trading arrangements, through their experiences in dealing with regional arrangements such as APEC, NAFTA and AFTA, the Japanese government now recognizes the importance of regional approach as a supplement to a global approach, and as a regional instrument to enhance global arrangements. The Japanese Diplomatic Bluebook of 1996 emphasized, for the first time in an extensive way, the importance of regional mechanisms such as APEC and ARF (ASEAN Regional Forum) in enhancing the global mechanisms such as the United Nations and GATT/WTO. It also suggested that multiplex and multi-layered mechanisms including bilateral, regional and global ones will provide basic foundations for global peace and stability.[27] The 1996 annual report of the MITI also pointed out the importance of APEC to further promote trade and investment liberalization as

---

[25] This was reflected in the fact that the APEC-related matters have been taken care of by the division in charge of the developing economies within the Economic Bureau of the Japanese Foreign Ministry.

[26] They were (i) due attention to the different stage of development and diversity; gradualism with consensus, (ii) consultation rather than negotiation, (iii) consistent and complementary with GATT, (iv) Open Regionalism; unconditional provision on a MFN basis, and (v) intensive consultation and dialogue with non-members. Speech by Foreign Minister Tsutomu Hata at the APEC Ministerial Meeting in Seattle, Ministry of Foreign Affairs of Japan.

[27] *Gaikou-Seisyo* [*Diplomatic Blue Book*] 1996, Vol. 1 (Tokyo: Ministry of Foreign Affairs), pp. 11–21.

well as development co-operation.[28] In a sense, the APEC meetings held in Bogor and Osaka played the role of catalyst to consolidate Japan's basic position toward APEC's goals; liberalization, facilitation and co-operation.

Today, many begin to recognize that regional economic arrangements are in many ways more effective than GATT or the WTO in promoting free trade and investment because of their flexibility in collective actions. Regional arrangements could also act as negotiating labouratories for new issues that have not yet advanced on the multilateral trade agenda. Regional arrangements could broaden and deepen GATT or WTO trade reform, and in so doing provide useful models to strengthen multilateral disciplines. Furthermore, regional co-operation has also been expected to address the central question facing Japan: whether Japan could achieve a radical deregulation of its domestic economy in order to cope with economic globalization and mega-competition. This recognition is also shared by an increasing number of government officials as well as business leaders and academics.

By combining with development and technical co-operation, APEC could promote, as a result, liberalization more than the WTO could do. In order to further promote liberalization at the APEC level, it is vitally important for the APEC liberalization to contribute to further liberalization at the WTO level. And further liberalization at the WTO level is expected to encourage further liberalization at the APEC level. Both processes have to proceed hand in hand. Mutual enforcing processes have to be established.[29]

APEC as a Regional Economic Regime

APEC as a regime can be described in the following way. The principles – the most important goals of APEC – are liberalization, facilitation and economic co-operation, even though the weights among them have shifted over years and have been perceived differently depending upon individual members. The basic norms – the rules of behaviour – are that APEC is a consultative body based upon voluntarism (concerted unilateral action), not through hard negotiations, that its aim is confidence-building, and that it should be based upon the concept of 'Open Regionalism' and be GATT/WTO consistent. The set of principles which were declared at the Osaka meeting such as compatibility, comprehensiveness and so

---

[28] *Tsuusho Hakusyo* (Annual Report of MITI) 1996 (Tokyo: Ministry of International Trade and Industry), pp. 59–90.
[29] 'Ippei Yamazawa, Eipekku Manira Koudou-keikaku to AjiaTaiheiyou no Keizai Titujyo [The APEC Manila Action Program and a New Economic Order in the Asia-Pacific]', *Sekai Keizai Hyoron* (February 1997), pp. 20–31.

forth can be considered a set of concrete norms or rules, particularly for liberalization in trade and investment.

The actual outputs of the regime are the individual commitments of liberalization and facilitation measures and varied projects of economic and technical co-operation. Since one of the basic principles of APEC is voluntarism, there is not a strong mechanism either to promote the basic goals or to enforce commitments. Constant review among the members and peer pressure by both governmental and private sectors are the major mechanisms.

Japanese interests in APEC were, at least at the beginning, reactive in the sense that Japan tried to utilize APEC as a means to avoid, or solve, the external pressures arising from its huge external surplus, and at the same time, to maintain the stability of the economic order in the Asia-Pacific region as well as in the entire global economy.

Japan has also pursued the traditional policies of economic co-operation (provision of official development assistance) within the APEC context. The basic characteristics of Japanese style in forging APEC has been rather low key and modest due partly to historical legacies resulting from World War II. The major Japanese aim, at least on the surface, has not been the market access pushed by the private sector, even though Japan appreciated the trade and investment expansion in the region. Japan could not be so aggressive in market access, basically due to its huge trade surplus *vis-à-vis* most of the APEC member economies. However, we may argue that Japan, as a result, has been successful in penetrating and expanding its economic presence in the APEC region through varied means taken by the APEC process. In a sense, while Japan has took a low-key approach so as not to create a North–South confrontation, it has been successful in economic expansion in this region.

We argue that the above-mentioned characteristics of APEC as a regime have been consistent with Japanese basic interests and that Japan has been contributing to establishing such a regime, as exemplified by the five principles for co-operation presented by Foreign Minister Tsutomu Hata in Seattle.

The Asian Financial Crisis and Japan's Response: IMF vs. Asian Monetary Fund

The rolling Asian financial and economic (and political in some cases) crisis has posed a challenge to Japan over the way to respond to it, given the fact that Japan has much involved in the troubled countries in terms of investment, loans and ODA.

Unlike the earlier emphasis on import substituting investment in East Asia, the Japanese investment served to develop a dynamic division of labour in the region, especially since the mid-1980s. In the 1990s, Japanese affiliates in the region have actively expanded their sales in the extra-regional markets, along with a greater reliance on the region as a source of production units. In addition, most of the local profit of the Japanese affiliates in East Asia was reinvested in the region. The Japanese companies operating in East Asia sought 'self-containment' of their business activities within the East Asian networks by looking within the region for their sales and purchasing and reinvesting their profits there. Furthermore, encouraged by the liberalization of the capital markets of the Asian economies, the Japanese financial institutions provided huge amounts of loans to the East and South-East Asian countries in the 1990s. In most of the countries in the region, the Japanese banks were listed as the largest financial contributors.

Given its huge political and economic stakes in Asia, it was quite natural for Japan to take an initiative to cope with the crisis. Japan's responses can be divided into two categories: one is through the IMF and the other through bilateral dealings with the trouble countries. Although initially Japan contributed trough the international financial institutions such as IMF, recently Japan enhanced its dealings with the rest of Asia on a bilateral and multilateral (regional) basis as was shown in the so-called 'Miyazawa Plan' and Japan–ASEAN industrial co-operation forum.

As the largest investor in Thailand, the Japanese government played the key role in forming the rescue package led by the IMF to Thailand. Japan, as an individual contributor, promised to contribute the largest amount of loans to the troubled countries. In addition, the Japanese government (especially the Ministry of Finance – MOF) tried to respond to the crisis by establishing a so-called 'Asian Monetary Fund'. Although the background to the idea is not yet clear, it was reported that given huge amounts of loans and credit of the Japanese financial institutions in South-East Asia, the MOF hoped to have a regional monetary fund able to respond to the crisis quickly. There might be some concern to the undue intervention of the US-dominated international financial institutions like the IMF which would ignore the unique characteristics of the Asian economies. Critical of universal approach of the IMF, it was reported that they hoped to establish a regional monetary fund carrying 'Asian' character.[30]

---

[30] In my understanding, the MOF's idea of establishing an Asian Monetary Fund is closely connected with Japanese domestic politics. Under the political disputes over administrative reform, the issue of separation between budget and finance is one of the hottest ones. A large number of politicians who are expressing concerns about the existence of the too big and too powerful Ministry of Finance are demanding that matters under the jurisdiction of MOF be divided and that the jurisdiction in dealing with financial matters be transferred from MOF to the newly established independent agency. The MOF has a strong feeling of crisis of this being realized. The Asian

The MOF's idea faced both strong support and opposition externally and internally. Most of the Asian governments responded to the idea favourably. They might have expected the proposed regional fund to give the respective recipients more policy freedom and autonomy, worrying about strong intervention of the IMF in economic management which are closely related to the governance structure of the countries concerned. China and the US were suspicious of the idea. They might have seen it as a expression of Japanese willingness to dominate Asian monetary issues under the strong Japanese financial leadership. The US especially seemed to fear that Asian financial issues would be taken care of within a Japan-dominated regional framework in which the US would not have a dominant voice. Within the Japanese government, other ministries such as the Ministry of Foreign Affairs responded negatively to the idea, paying careful attention to the negative reactions from Washington.

Although there still remain voices to establish an Asian Monetary Fund in both in Japan and the rest of Asia,[31] the Japanese government has taken the official position that support be provided under the framework of international support built upon on the core of the IMF, as was clearly announced in the statement of the Japanese Prime Minister Hashimoto at the Japan–ASEAN summit meeting in Kuala Lumpur in December 1997.[32] Asian countries including ASEAN, China and South Korea also accepted the central role of the IMF, although some countries have sought to diminish the role of the IMF because of the stringent austerity measures it imposes as a part of bailouts. Malaysia likened the intervention of the IMF to a 'return of colonialism'.

Thus, Japan's proposal to set up an Asian Monetary Fund failed to obtain support from the major powers and finally resulted in the so-called Manila Framework in September 1997 which included measures to strengthen the capacity of the IMF to respond more quickly to the financial crisis and to set up a cooperative financial arrangement to supplement the IMF funds. As a result, different from the rescue package to Thailand in which Japan's financial contribution was being allocated to Thailand together with the IMF, Japan's financial stake in the rescue efforts to Indonesia and South Korea was limited in a 'second line of defence', which would be tapped only if all other aid was exhausted. Japan followed the scheme provided by the US. When the IMF assembled rescue packages for Indonesia in September and South Korea in November 1997, the US

---

[31] Financial crisis gives a golden opportunity to justify their arguments that jurisdiction in dealing with both budget and finance be maintained under the MOF.
At the Japan–Korea meeting held in November 1998, South Korean Prime Minister Kim Jong Pil proposed an Asian Monetary Fund on the scale of $300 billion.

[32] It was reported that Hashimoto implicitly rejected Malaysia's call for Japan to intervene in place of the IMF. *Japan Times*, 17 December 1997.

government limited its financial stake in the rescue efforts to participation in a 'second line of defense' and demanded other contributors to follow the scheme.

In spite of its failure to establish an Asian Monetary Fund, together with participation in the IMF-led rescue packages, Japan has enhanced its bilateral co-operation with the ASEAN which was demonstrated in Japan's offer of a package of measures at the Japan–ASEAN Summit meeting in December 1997. The package included lowering the standard interest rate on yen loan, inviting trainees to Japan under the new human resource development initiative, the provision of an $18.5 billion trade insurance credit line and the pledge to apply more preferential loan interest rate for across-the-border infrastructure projects. Japan and the ASEAN also agreed on the establishment of two new mechanisms – one to enhance development co-operation and the other to promote industrial co-operation.

Furthermore, Japan promised to allocate $30 billion as financial support for Asia (the so-called 'Miyazawa Plan') at the APEC annual meeting held in Kuala Lumpur in November 1998. The plan has played an important role to ameliorate the burden of the crisis. Industrial co-operation between Japan and the rest of Asia has also been enhanced. The first meeting of the ASEAN Economic Ministers and Japan's Minister of MITI (AEM–MITI) Economic and Industrial Co-operation Committee was held in November 1998 in Bangkok. The Committee will take various measures to stimulate the real sector and to restructure ASEAN industries on a long-term basis in order to revitalize and improve the efficiency, productivity and international competitiveness of these industries.[33] These new policy measures taken by the Japanese government will contribute to further enhancing Japan–ASEAN economic relations, in spite of various criticism against Japan that Japan has not done enough to support the badly hit Asian economies.

Japan's new relations with the rest of Asia is also seen in the recent remarkable development in Japan–South Korea relations. The Korean economic crisis has promoted and enhanced bilateral consultation and co-operation between Japan and Korea. Although this has been mainly resulted from Korea's immediate necessity to obtain financial support from Japan, the resultant close co-operation and consultation has a long-term implication for bilateral relations.

Korea introduced various reform measures including the full market opening for Japanese-made products under the direction of IMF. Foreign investment liberalization measures were also introduced. These reform measures will make a contribution to further integration both economies, thereby opening a new era in bilateral relations.

---

[33] *Co-Chairs' Summary of the First Meeting of AEM–MITI Economic and Industrial Co-operation Committee*, 23 November 1998, Bangkok, MITI, Japan.

The state visit of Korean President Kim Dae-Jung in October 1998 was a milestone in this context. Both leaders of Japan and Korea agreed to promote more balanced and enhanced co-operation between two countries in such broad areas as politics, security, economics and cultural exchanges.[34] Furthermore, at the bilateral ministerial meeting held in December 1998 both governments agreed to conduct a joint research on a Japan–Korea Bilateral Free Trade Agreement.

If further economic integration takes place between two countries, Korean will participate in the production networks led by Japanese multinational corporations and find better market penetration world-wide. A free trade arrangement with Korea will provide Japan, which has been suffering from economic difficulties and facing a sudden collapse of business networks extending other parts of Asia, with new business opportunities. Japan can also have an easy access to highly-skilled workers in Korea.

A successful conclusion of a bilateral FTA will make a great contribution to strengthening the foundation of their respective economic diplomacy at the multilateral forums such as GATT/WTO and APEC in this era of regionalization of the world economy. A bilateral FTA will also put the bilateral relations on more stable political foundation, thereby contributing to peace and stability in Northeast Asia.

The Financial Crisis and the Future of Asia-Pacific Regionalism

The financial and economic turbulence facing the Asia-Pacific region have had grave impacts on the process of developing regionalism. The recent developments have clearly shown that APEC has not yet developed or matured enough to tackle the crisis. In fact, the rescue packages for Thailand, Indonesia and South Korea have been established under the leadership of the IMF. The G7 also played an important role in these processes. APEC just conformed to the central role of IMF, as was shown in the APEC Vancouver statement in November 1997. Although APEC agreed to study appropriate regional mechanisms to enhance financial monitoring of the regional economies at the APEC meeting in November 1998, concrete steps have not yet been taken seriously. How will Asia-Pacific regional co-operation, especially APEC, develop in the coming years ? Several scenarios might be presented.

---

[34] *Joint Declaration on New Japan–ROK Partnership for the 21st Century*, 8 October 1998, Tokyo.

Stalemate of APEC to be Caused by Domestic Opposition and Turmoil

The crisis, first of all, has had a grave impact on political legitimacy, stability and succession in Asia. For many Asian countries, political legitimacy has been based upon an implicit social contact by which the general public support their governments in exchange for a steadily growing prosperity. To the extent that people could no longer count on getting rich, the results are not easy to predict. In addition, trying to force reforms within the string deadline, however legitimate, may only invite chaos, failure and resentment, leading to nationalistic response to the international society. Indonesia is critical in this regard. The continued domestic instability has greatly constrained the capability of the government to further promote regional co-operation.

Furthermore, serious trade disputes may emerge between the US and Asian economies, including Japan, if Asian countries try to expand exports to the US market by the enhanced international competitiveness which was obtained by the drastic depreciation of the Asian currencies.

We have witnessed the increase of the US trade deficit in its trade with Asia in the recent past. This might send the politically sensitive US trade deficit to politically dangerous heights. In fact, the US government has already sent a strong warning to the Japanese government that it would not be acceptable for the US that Japan has compensated the reduce domestic demand for the increase of export to the US. Given the possible sharp decline of domestic consumption, Asian manufactures have had no option but to depend upon export earnings. However, a surge of exports to the US market has further increased the US trade deficit. This strengthened protectionist forces in the US, thereby demanding the US government to take a much tougher position toward Asia. The rising deficit has also strengthened the power of isolationist forces in the US Congress, which was shown in their refusal of giving a fast-track authority to start the negotiation of the FTAA. (Fears that the US would turn inward after the end of the Cold War have been replaced by worries that it may retreat into economic isolationism. Concern has been heightened by President Clinton's failure to win fast-track authority in November 1997 and warnings that a rise in the US trade deficit due to Asia's financial crisis risks triggering a protectionist backlash.)

The crisis has also posed serious challenges to the unity and co-operation of the ASEAN. The development of the ASEAN's unity has been one of the basic foundations to promote region-wide economic regionalism in the Asia-Pacific region.

Indonesia is critical in this regard. Indonesia's continued drift with economic turbulence and political unrest have had a grave impact on the other ASEAN countries, thereby having adverse impacts on the unity and co-operation of ASEAN.

The ASEAN countries themselves have tried to strengthen their co-operation to reverse the current economic trends through the ASEAN summit meeting and the meeting of the ASEAN finance ministers. However, the recent developments have indicated that the ASEAN failed to find a solution to the difficulty. The ASEAN as an institution has showed little fresh to boost confidence in their sagging economies, just urging major economic powers to do more.

The ASEAN has developed into one of the most successful regional organizations, overcoming deep-seated mutual suspicion and regional political turbulence in the last decades. However, it is still to be seen whether the ASEAN could unify themselves with keeping regional common agenda, overcoming narrowly-defined national interests. In this context, it is critically important whether the ASEAN could develop a regionally acceptable way to jointly intervening in economic management of the other members, overcoming the ASEAN's long-held common code of conduct of not intervening in domestic affairs of the other member countries.

Toward Deeper Integration

On the one hand, economic hardship such as the rise of unemployment in the troubled Asian economies has created strong domestic political opposition to the further liberalization of their economies which may further hit the devastated economies. In fact, there are strong voices in various parts of the region to the effect that the financial crisis took place because of the too-quick opening of the financial markets of the countries concerned. The governments became more inward-looking and vulnerable to the domestic opposition to further liberalizing their economies, which have had a negative impact on the regional liberalization.

On the other hand, however, the strong intervention of the IMF in economic and financial management of some of the Asian economies has forced further liberalization of the economies, thereby contributing to deeper economic integration of the region. In order to overcome the economic difficulties, Asian countries had to obtain confidence of international investors in their economic management by implementing various reform measures demanded by the international financial institutions in spite of domestic unpopularity. These measures included various reforms of internal regulatory systems and interventionist industrial policies. This has made the economic and financial systems of the Asian economies more transparent, accountable and compatible to the rest of the world, thereby further promoting deeper integration of the region and strengthening institutional structure of APEC. In fact, in spite of the continued economic turbulence in Indonesia, Thailand has been moving to fulfil the WTO agreement to open the financial sector to foreign institutions and has been ahead of schedule on trade liberalization measures agreed to by ASEAN. It has been legislating stricter bank regulations to try to prevent in the future the kind of slipshod banking that sparked off the currency crisis. The South Korean government also has implemented various reform measures to further open its economy.

Sector by Sector Co-operation

There has been some concern among some of the APEC economies (including Japan) that liberalization based upon the principle of voluntarism was apt to produce the minimum common liberalization, not enough to maintain economic dynamism of the region. They see some possibility of negotiations taking place among the like-minded economies on specific issues.[35] This implies that the APEC liberalization process will eventually take a form of 'APEC minus X'. The ITA (Information and Technology Agreement) of 1996 demonstrates this example.

The developed countries of the APEC support this formula. However, there remains strong opposition to the sectoral liberalization on the part of the developing countries in APEC. They have argued that sectoral liberalization would obstruct across-the-board liberalization which is one of the basic principles of APEC liberalization.

'Harmonization' has become an important topic to be co-ordinated at APEC. The crisis has shown interconnectedness among the financial institutions and between Asian and the global financial systems. Policies deemed 'unwise' in which one state engages had a grave impact on the overall function of the global financial system. The crisis also taught that domestic financial systems which lack transparency, proper prudential supervision and sensible market-oriented criteria for lending have a quick negative spill-over effects on the others. The APEC could provide an useful forum for the regional countries to discuss regional harmonization and surveillance. The Manila Framework in 1997 and the 'Chaingmai Initiative' for currency swap taken at the ASEAN+3 (Japan, China and Korea) Finance Ministers' meeting in May 2000 are quite important steps in terms of enhancing regional financial architecture.

More Emphasis on Development Co-operation

Under the IMF-led prescription, Thailand, Indonesia and South Korea have been forced to implement numerous economic reforms. One change being aggressively pursued was the implementation of the opening of Asia's highly protected markets and industries to foreign participation. Increased competition from foreign

---

[35] Speech by Mr Toshinori Shigeie, Deputy Secretary-General, Economic Affairs Bureau, MFA, on 2 December 1996, *Sekai Keizai Hyoron* (February 1997), p. 15.

competitors has put pressures on firms to upgrade efficiency and the quality of their products or services. The IMF has also strongly demanded that the governments should not intervene to keep alive weak enterprises. The IMF has argued that these weak enterprises should be allowed to fail, so that their assets would be redeployed into more productive sectors. Any resulting unemployment should be theoretically temporary, as workers move to new enterprises. However, this process of 'creative destruction' destroyed more than it was creating. Job creation was stalled owing to the inability or unwillingness of local and foreign banks to finance capital investment in new firms. Even if such financing was available, weak domestic demand did not justify expansion of productive capacity. Continued success of the region's export-led growth still depends upon foreign demand, coupled with the capacity to upgrade the quality of products. However, neither condition is assured. Product upgrading was difficult because most of the troubled countries did not have enough skilled workers, and did not have the money to invest in education and training.

Thus, enhancing development co-operation will still be one of the pressing tasks of APEC. However, there have been strong reluctance on the part of the developed countries for APEC to become an organization mainly dealing with development co-operation.

External Factors – Inter-regional Relationships: Asia, Europe and the US

Whether APEC can maintain its basic principle of 'Open Regionalism' depends to a large extent on the external factors, especially the response of the EU. It is still to be seen whether APEC could sustain its principle of 'Open Regionalism', when the non-members do not offer *de facto* reciprocal liberalization to the APEC economies. Given a high protection level of the most of the APEC economies, 'open regionalism' based upon voluntarism may work for the next few years. Asian economies have much room to be further liberalized. In addition, in order to attract foreign direct investment and foreign capital, they have to liberalize their economies much more actively. For the next few years, therefore, the APEC economies may allow the non-members to enjoy a free ride. Thereafter, however, if the non-members continue to enjoy free-riding without reciprocal liberalization, APEC may face difficulties in sustaining the concept of 'Open Regionalism'.

The EU's role will be crucial in this context. If the APEC and EU could agree to the overall mutually acceptable reciprocal liberalization measures through intensive inter-regional dialogues (APEC–EU dialogue), it will make a great contribution to the APEC's sustaining 'Open Regionalism'. In addition, global liberalization may be realized through the consultation and negotiations between APEC and EU.

Today, Asia, America and Europe are playing an interesting game in which different combinations of two exclude the third. Asia and America forms APEC excluding Europe. Asia and Europe started the ASEM excluding America. Europe and America agreed to talk about the TAM (Transatlantic Market) idea, excluding Asia. The APEC–EU dialogue and consultation framework including all these three major economic entities will be a more appropriate one in terms of the strengthening of the global trading system.

In the context of the inter-regional consultation and negotiation, the future of the EU–US relations will have a critical impact on the future development of the APEC. It was reported that the US and the EU were considering a new drive to sweep away barriers to transatlantic trade and investment.[36] The purpose of the strengthening of transatlantic relations was reportedly to help rebuild political support in Washington for further trade liberalization, after President Clinton's failure to win fast-track authority in November 1997. Both Washington and Brussels were reported to hope to use the transatlantic initiatives as a springboard for a world trade round. Although the results of the consultation are to be seen, if the EU and US fail to convince other governments that any liberalization they agree will be extended to the rest of the world on a MFN basis, the adverse impacts of the agreement on Asia (APEC) will be enormous.

Asian economic development and state formation for the last decades have entered a new stage. The so-called 'globalization' has directly caused Asia to move to this new stage. The current economic and political difficulties signify that the Asian nations, which have become deeply woven into the global market system, are facing the need to adjust their own internal systems so that they can fully respond to external requirements. Economic development in Asia during the past decades had pushed each nation to the point where the reorganization of the internal order in these countries was required. In a sense, the economic crisis was caused by the maturity of the domestic conditions of the Asian nations to push Asian economics and politics into the new stage of development. Japan, which had successfully penetrated into the region and contributed to economic welfare of the region, is now tackling this new challenge. Japan is facing a difficult task. However, contrary to the popular view, Japan has actively and skilfully engaged in joint endeavours with the regional countries to enhance their economic foundation for the last few years. Contacts between Japan and the rest of Asia in both government and private sectors have been enhanced. Concrete steps to rectify the economic troubles have been steadily taken between Japan and the rest of Asia. Japan's political and economic commitment to Asia has been constantly enhanced after the crisis. Therefore, although Japan is facing serious challenges internally and externally, this will promote Japan to establish a more stable and firm regional

---

[36] *Financial Times* (2 February 1998).

framework within which Japan's power and interest will be well addressed. The 'ASEAN+3' formula for cooperation which was established after the financial crisis is a first step in this direction.

Chapter Ten

Pacifism and the Japanese Attitude toward the United Nations

Matake Kamiya

I

The attitude of the Japanese people toward the United Nations has long been characterized by two contradicting faces: faith in the United Nations (*Kokuren Shinko*) and reluctance to participate in UN peace operations. Both of these faces are the consequences of the same unique characteristic of post-World War II Japanese society, namely, a deep pacifist orientation among the Japanese people.[1]

This orientation has its roots in collective Japanese memories of the country's militarist past and runs deep in Japanese elite and mass culture. The memory of World War II, and a sense of guilt over their nation's role in that war, has produced among the post-war Japanese an unwavering determination that they must transform their country into a 'nation of peace' (*heiwa kokka*) that should never again wage war. When the current 'Peace Constitution' (*heiwa kenpo*) was written under American occupation, this determination was clearly embodied in the Preamble and Article 9. In the Preamble, there is a sentence that reads:

> We, the Japanese peoples, desire peace for all time and are deeply conscious of the high ideals controlling human relationship, and we have determined to preserve our security and existence, trusting in the justice and faith of the peace-loving peoples of the world.

Then Article 9, known as a 'no-war clause' (*fusen joko*), provides:

> Aspiring sincerely to an international peace based on justice and order, the Japanese people forever renounce war as a sovereign right of the nation and the threat or use of force as a means of settling international disputes.
> In order to accomplish the aim of the preceding paragraph, land, sea, and air forces, as well as other war potential, will never be maintained. The right of belligerency of the state will not be recognized.

---

[1] On Japan's post-war culture of anti-militarism, see Thomas U. Berger, 'From Sword to Chrysanthemum: Japan's Culture of Anti-militarism', *International Security*, 17:4 (Spring 1993); and Peter Katzenstein and Nobuo Okawara, 'Japan's National Security: Structures, Norms, and Policies', *International Security*, 17:4 (Spring 1993).

The determination of the post-war Japanese people never to wage war again has been strongly buttressed by the extremely negative image of the military shared in post-war Japanese society – another aspect of post-war Japanese pacifism. In pre-war Japan, the structure of the state under the Meiji Constitution of 1889, the strong links between the military and civil society, and social and legal norms all favoured the military.[2] It enjoyed broad popular support and exercised enormous influence over the Japanese politics during that period. In the 1930s, the Japanese military had virtually got out of any form of effective civilian control and frequently intervened in political affairs. Under the strong political influence of the military establishments, the Japanese government made a series of reckless decisions, which led to Japan's disastrous defeat in World War II. Until 1945 when the American occupation forces landed in Japan, in more than 1,300 years of recorded history, the Japanese had never experienced surrender of their home islands to any foreign enemy. The catastrophe of the war, unconditional surrender and the following American occupation were therefore such traumatic experiences for the Japanese people that their perception of the military changed dramatically after the end of the war. Disgusted with the follies of their own military leaders since the beginning of the 1930s, the Japanese people developed a deep distrust of the military, which led to the total elimination of its influence over national policy in post-war Japan.

Since the end of the war, great skepticism about the legitimacy and usefulness of military power has been widely shared among the Japanese people. They have in fact consistently viewed anything even remotely connected with the military with a degree of wariness that borders on total rejection. There has been a strong aversion to military solutions to the problems of national security and world peace, because they are seen as contradictory to the ideal of peace embodied in Japan's Peace Constitution. Because of the strong public abhorrence of anything military-related as a tool of external policy, even including policy for the defence of Japan, the security issue has been one of the most sensitive issues in post-war Japanese domestic politics.

Such a mood in post-war Japan has militated so strongly against any commitment abroad which might lead to military involvement with other nations that successive Japanese Prime Ministers until the late 1970s avoided using the word 'alliance' to describe the relationship existing between Japan and the United States. They carefully described the bilateral relationship as a 'partnership' or 'friendship' instead, before Masayoshi Ohira, who was in office from December 1978 until his death in June 1980, consciously started to use verbally the word 'alliance.' In a written form, the Joint Communique issued after the summit

---

[2] Peter J. Katzenstein, *Cultural Norms and National Security: Police and Military in Post-war Japan* (Ithaca and London: Cornell University Press, 1996), pp. 53–57.

meeting between Zenko Suzuki and Ronald Reagan on 8 May 1981 was the first occasion in which the Japanese Prime Minister officially used the word 'alliance'.[3]

II

Such a deep pacifist orientation is the root of an overriding faith of the post-war Japanese in the United Nations that is perhaps unparalleled in the world. Throughout the post World War II era, the Japanese people have held a very rosy picture of the United Nations. A mirage-like view of the United Nations as the embodiment of the ideal underlying Japan's Peace Constitution – maintenance of peace by the justice and faith of the peace loving nations of the world – has been widely shared. The reality of the United Nations as a gathering of individual sovereign states with their respective national interests has tended to be neglected. The Japanese have tended to view the United Nations as a representative of international opinion, and to believe that the organization should someday develop into a panacea for the problems of war and peace in the world.

In post-war Japanese society, such a faith in the United Nations has been shared not only among people on the street but also by political elites to a considerable extent. When the Ministry of Foreign Affairs published the first edition of the Diplomatic Blue Book in September 1957, nine months after Japan was accepted as a UN member, it listed 'UN centered diplomacy', together with 'maintenance of Japan's position as a member of Asia' and 'cooperation with other liberal countries', as the 'three fundamental principles of the Japanese diplomacy'.

The Cold War environment, however, did not allow Japan to adopt the United Nations as a cornerstone of its foreign policy. The efficiency of the United Nations was seriously limited under the East–West confrontation, particularly in the field of international peace and security. This reality forced Japan to pursue its security policy entirely within a dominant-bilateral context, that is, the alliance with the United States, and made the relations with the United States the real cornerstone of Japanese foreign policy. The Diplomatic Bluebook in fact started to emphasize the limitations of the United Nations in 1961. In 1969, it stated that 'the relations with the United States is more important than relations with any other countries' for Japan.

Despite such realities of Japanese foreign policy, faith in the United Nations survived in the minds of most of the Japanese people. Among the Japanese political elites today, faith in the United Nations is quite widely shared,

---

[3] In the Joint Communique issued after the summit meeting between Prime Minister Zenko Suzuki and President Reagan, the relationship was stated as the 'alliance between the United States and Japan', Joint Communique, 8 May 1981.

transcending differences of political ideology or belief. One needs only to list the names of current influential Japanese political leaders who argue strongly that the UN collective security system must be strengthened considerably. The list is a very long one, including such top leaders as Kiichi Miyazawa, Ichiro Ozawa, Naoto Kan, Yukio Hatoyama, and Tsutomu Hata.

When the Japanese government somewhat timidly started to consider assuming wider international security roles beyond Japanese territory during the Gulf Crisis, it had to enact legislation which would enable the Self-Defense Forces to join the multilateral forces in a constitutionally sound manner. It should be noted that the bill submitted to the Diet in October 1990 was carefully named the UN Peace Cooperation Bill. After the failure of this bill to pass the Diet, the government submitted another bill in September 1991, which was eventually approved by the Diet in June 1992. The bill was entitled the Bill Concerning Cooperation for the UN Peacekeeping Operations and Other Operations. These bills actually limited the scope of Japan's international security role to participation in UN peacekeeping operations. The very fact that the government introduced such bills indicates how favourably the Japanese citizens view the United Nations even today. In fact, 'making a contribution for the sake of the United Nations' sounds very nice to the ears of the most Japanese people, because of the still prevalent image among them of the United Nations as a shrine of peace. One former top-ranking diplomat even suggested that the concept of Japan's contribution to international security might not be accepted by the Japanese people unless the scope of Japan's contribution was not limited within the UN framework.[4]

III

Nothing is more ironic than the fact that a deep pacifist orientation in post-war Japanese society, which has brought about an overriding faith of the Japanese in the United Nations, has long represented the most fundamental obstacle to active Japanese participation in UN peace operations.

According to the official interpretation of the constitutional provisions by the Japanese government, which has been widely supported by the public, the Constitution prohibits Japan from participating in the UN operations whose purposes and duties entail the use of force. According to the government's interpretation, Article 9 of the Constitution does not deny Japan the right of self-defence as an inherent right of a sovereign state. The exercise of the right of self-

---

[4] Yoshio Okawara and Younosuke Tanaka, 'New Realities, New Focus: Can Japan Shoulder the Responsibility of a New Role in the UN and Global Community?', *By the Way*, 3:4 (July/August 1993), 6.

defence is, however, allowed only to the extent minimally necessary to repel aggressors. Beyond such minimal exercise of the right of individual self-defence, the Constitution does not allow Japan to use military force. According to the government's interpretation of the Constitution, therefore, Japan is banned from exercising the right of collective self-defence even if its allies are attacked. Japan is also banned from dispatching the Self-Defense Forces to other countries' territories, territorial waters or territorial spaces for any military purpose, because such dispatch is interpreted to exceed the minimal exercise of the right of the self-defence.

Such interpretation of the constitutional provisions by the government has a direct bearing on the question of whether the Constitution allows Japan to participate in UN peace operations. Since the use of force other than minimal exercise of the right of individual self-defence and the dispatch of the Self-Defense Forces overseas for any military purpose are both interpreted as unconstitutional, the logical conclusion must be that Japan is constitutionally banned from participating in the UN missions if their purposes and duties entail the use of force. This in fact represents the position of the Japanese government on the relationship between the constitutional provisions and the possibility of Japan's participation in UN peace operations.

According to this interpretation, however, there is theoretically a room for Japan's sending of the Self-Defense Forces to the UN missions whose purposes and duties do not entail the use of force, such as in the case of traditional UN peacekeeping operations. Until the Gulf Crisis, however, this possibility had not been seriously considered by the Japanese government at all. The government fully recognized the fact that the Japanese people would strongly object even to the dispatch of the Self-Defense Forces overseas for non-combat purposes.

As was emphasized before, the image of the military in post-war Japanese society has been extremely negative. The Japanese people have tended to view the use of armed forces for any purpose more or less contradictory to the ideal of peace embodied in their Peace Constitution, and have been far from enthusiastic about using the Self-Defense Forces on any occasion. For example, when a massive earthquake hit the Kobe area on 17 January 1995, and killed more than 5,000 people, '[t]he ghost of Japan's militarist past delayed crucial decisions to send in the army to rescue victims', one foreign journalist reported. The Governor of the disaster-hit Hyogo Prefecture, the only authority who could call in the Self-Defense Forces under Japan's post-war regulations, failed to do so for more than four hours after the earthquake hit Kobe, while the central government was reluctant to dispatch the military forces without a formal request by the Governor.[5]

---

[5] Eugene Moosa, 'Japan: Ghost of Japan's Militarism Hinders Quake Relief', Reuters News Service (on Reuters Business Briefing) (23 January 1995).

The politicians evidently felt uneasy about mobilizing military forces even to help the rescue effort.[6]

In addition, the Japanese media until very recently tended to warn the public that the dispatch of the Self-Defense Forces abroad for any purpose would invite the most unwelcome criticism for Japan from its East Asian neighbours, who still harboured some lingering doubts about Japan's future intentions, that Japanese militarism might be reviving. Besides, in Japan there was a haziness about the distinction between UN peacekeeping operations and enforcement actions taken under the United Nations Chapter VII. The vast majority of the Japanese people simply did not know the difference between peacekeeping and peace-enforcement.

Consequently, until the spring of 1991, public opinion in Japan was negative to sending the Self-Defense Forces to any UN operations, including traditional peacekeeping. The inaction of the Japanese government as to Japan's participation in the UN peace operations was mainly due to such public sentiment.

IV

The Gulf War represented a watershed in the Japanese attitude toward overseas commitments. The Iraqi invasion of Kuwait and the events that followed activated the debate in Japan about Japan's contribution to UN peace operations. The majority of the Japanese seemed to agree that Japan should do something. No consensus was reached, however, as to what that something was. In October 1990, the Japanese government suddenly submitted to the Diet the UN Peace Cooperation Bill, which would authorized the participation of Self-Defense Forces personnel in non-combat roles not only in UN peacekeeping operations but also in UN-authorized enforcement operations. The bill, however, was severely criticized by the public as well as the opposition parties and did not pass even the House of Representatives where the ruling Liberal Democratic Party commanded the majority. Various public opinion polls showed that less than a third of the Japanese supported the bill. The bill was so unpopular, because it would have authorized the participation of Self-Defense Forces personnel in UN missions whose purposes and duties entailed the use of force – which many Japanese felt would be unconstitutional.

Consequently, Japan's contribution to the Gulf War was limited only to the financial support and the sending of a small number of civilians, in spite of the strong American pressure to do more. In fact, Japan provided some US$13 billion to support the multilateral operation against Iraq, but received no thanks, only strong criticism from other countries that it had not done anything more than

---

[6] A comment by Makoto Momoi. *Yomiuri Shinbun* (22 January 1995).

contribute money. Above all, the Japanese were shocked when the Kuwaiti government placed a big advertisement in the *Washington Post* and other major US newspapers to record its appreciation to about thirty countries which contributed to the Gulf War. The name of Japan was not even mentioned. One Japanese commentator called this incident 'Japan's defeat in the Gulf War'.[7] Consequently, Japan woke up rather abruptly to the fact that other countries viewed it as a nation unwilling to shoulder the political and security responsibilities that go with its economic power. For the first time since 1945, a majority of the Japanese people came to share the understanding that their country must fulfill an obligation to participate more actively and visibly in the maintenance of world peace and must take on greater political and security responsibility, in order to be a respected member of international society.

Since then, the Japanese government has somewhat timidly started to assume wider roles in regional and global security, including dispatch of the Self-Defense Forces overseas to work with other countries in non-combat operations. In this process, the United Nations has provided a convenient shelter under which Japan can justify its more active international security roles beyond its territory and which helps to allay the lingering domestic and international opposition to Japan's assuming such roles. First, in a somewhat belated effort to silence international criticism of Japan for its failure to contribute more than cash to the allied military efforts in the Gulf War, the government sent four minesweepers and two support ships to the Gulf in April 1991. This time, the Japanese public supported the sending of the Self-Defense Force ships to the Gulf. Despite Tokyo's initial concern that the mission might alarm the Asian countries, in the end most of them responded favourably to the mission.

In September 1991, the government submitted to the Diet the Bill Concerning Cooperation for the UN Peacekeeping Operations and Other Operations, which would authorize the participation of Self-Defense Forces personnel in UN peacekeeping operations and UN humanitarian relief operations. After a long and intense debate, and with a number of revisions, the bill finally passed the Diet in June 1992. In October 1992, under the new UN Peacekeeping Law, an engineering battalion of Japan's Ground Self-Defense Forces was sent to join the UN Transitory Authority in Cambodia (UNTAC). This marked the first time that Japanese troops had participated in UN peacekeeping operations. While on duty for about a year, the battalion repaired 100 km of highway and some forty bridges. It won wide praise.

Since then the domestic opposition to the participation of the Self-Defense Forces in the UN peacekeeping operations has ebbed. The decision to send a small number of military personnel to be a part of the UN peacekeeping operation in

---

[7] Ryuich Tejima, *1991-nen Nihon no Haiboku* (Tokyo: Shincho-sha, 1993).

Mozambique (the United Nations Operation in Mozambique, or UNUMOZ) in May 1993 provoked barely any protest.

A sea change in the Socialist Party policy took place not long after Tomiichi Murayama became in June 1994 the first Socialist Prime Minister since 1948. The Socialists had cherished an extremely pacifist policy of unarmed neutrality for over forty years (they had argued that Japan should abolish the unconstitutional Self-Defense Forces and abandon the Japan–US Security Treaty), and had bitterly opposed the dispatch of the Self-Defense Forces abroad for any purpose. Soon after Murayama assumed the premiership, however, the Socialist Party started to signal that Japan was ready to play a bigger international peacekeeping role under the auspices of the United Nations, including dispatch of the Self-Defense Forces for non-combat purposes.

The success of a Self-Defense Forces mission to help Rwandan refugees in Zaire from September to December 1994 further encouraged the Japanese people. This was a watershed mission for Japan, because it represented the first time since the end of World War II that Japan had sent Self-Defense Forces abroad under its own flag. While on duty, in the eastern Zairian town of Goma, medical staff of the Self-Defense Forces treated the sick while Japanese soldiers repaired sewers and provided drinking water amid misery and chaos. A Reuters correspondent in Zaire reported on 5 December that the Japanese mission 'is winding up to plaudits from aid workers and local people', because of their politeness, efficiency and teamwork.[8]

From February 1996 to the present, Japan has also been participating in the United Nations Disengagement Observer Force (UNDOF) in the Golan Heights.

The Japanese people have been gradually learning through these experiences that Japan's active participation in the UN peacekeeping and humanitarian relief operations can contribute effectively to world peace and win high esteem internationally. They have been gradually acquiring confidence that the dispatch of Japanese peacekeepers overseas does not automatically alarm Japan's neighbours. Now the vast majority of the public supports Japan's active participation in the UN peacekeeping and humanitarian relief operations including dispatch of the Self-Defense Forces abroad.

V

Thus, the contradiction between the overriding faith of the Japanese people in the United Nations and their reluctance to participate in the UN peace operations has

---

[8] Vincent Tsas, 'Zaire: Japanese Rwandan Mission Ends to Plaudits', Reuter News Service (on Reuter Business Briefing) (5 December 1994).

been resolved to a great extent. But the residue of the contradiction still remains. The Japanese people seem to be satisfied with Japan's record of participating in the UN operation under the UN Peacekeeping Law so far, and are quite reluctant to give support to more active contributions by their country.

Under the current UN Peacekeeping Law, the so-called 'core functions' (*hontai gyomu*) of peacekeeping forces are still 'frozen'. The 'core functions' of peacekeeping forces means the missions which are usually carried out by armed troops, such as monitoring disarmament, stationing and patrolling in buffer zones, and inspection of the carrying in and out of weapons. Consequently, possible contributions by the Self-Defense Forces to UN peacekeeping operations are now limited only to logistical support, including medical care, sanitary measures, transportation, communication, and construction. This restriction was introduced by the Komeito Party during the long, bitter debate in the Diet over the Bill Concerning Cooperation for the UN Peacekeeping Operations and Other Operations in order to hit upon a compromise between the Liberal Democratic Party, the Democratic Socialist Party, and the Komeito Party. At that time, it might have been a necessary restriction so that the bill could pass the Diet, but now, the 'freeze' of the 'core functions' of the peacekeeping forces imposes a serious limitations on Japan's security role within the UN framework.

In addition, the Japanese guideline on the use of weapons by peacekeepers prescribed by the UN Peacekeeping Law shows a subtle but significant divergence from UN practice. Both Japanese law and UN practice restrict the use of weapons by peacekeepers to the purpose of 'self-defence'. The concept of 'self-defence' embodied in the Japanese law, however, is different from the UN concept.

According to UN practice, 'self-defence' includes not only the protection of lives of the peacekeepers themselves against armed attacks, but also the removal of situations hindering the carrying out of UN missions. Under the current Japanese law, however, 'self-defence' is limited only to the former. The use of weapons is allowed only to protect the lives of the Japanese peacekeepers. Among the Japanese public, consensus has not been reached over whether the use of weapons by Japanese peacekeepers to remove situations hindering the carrying out of UN missions would be constitutional, because many Japanese think that the use of weapons by Japanese peacekeepers for any purpose beyond protection of their own lives exceeds the minimal exercise of the right of self-defence. Consequently, Japanese peacekeepers currently are not allowed to use weapons in order to protect peacekeepers from other countries nor members of NGOs, Japanese or foreign. This fact also limits Japan's security role within the UN framework.

The public, however, are not very enthusiastic about 'thawing' of the 'core functions' of peacekeeping forces so that Japan can participate in UN peacekeeping operations in a full-fledged manner. They are even more reluctant to allow Japanese peacekeepers to use weapons beyond the purpose of protection of their own lives, and strongly against the idea of Japan's participation in more forceful actions under UN auspices. This attitude of the Japanese public reflects the facts that the pacifist sentiment is still quite strong among the Japanese people today, and that their image of the military is still considerably negative. As Reinhard Drifte points out, '[m]ilitary power is still more associated with direct use and the invasion of other countries, whereas in other Western countries military power is more perceived as a deterrence, and as an additional and legitimate means to influence other countries'.[9]

Reflecting these attitudes of the Japanese people, the government still maintains the traditional interpretation of the Constitution that Japan's participation in the UN operations whose purposes and duties entail the use of force at all is unconstitutional. This means that if an event similar to the Gulf War occurs again, Japan will find itself in deep trouble, because Japan is still prohibited from sending its troops to participate in UN-sponsored multilateral actions even for logistical support, let alone collective enforcement actions.

Even if the public attitude mentioned above does not change and the government maintains the traditional interpretation of the Constitution, it is still possible to 'thaw' the 'core functions' of the peacekeeping forces. It can make an important difference: for example, such a change could have made it possible for the Japanese government to dispatch the Self-Defense Force to the peace operations in East Timor. In reality, Tokyo could not send any peacekeeper to East Timor, although it dispatched three civilian police officers to United Nations Transitional Administration in East Timor (UNTAET) from July to September 1999 and more than 100 personnel of the Air Self-Defense Force to West Timor from November 1999 to March 2000 to contribute to the evacuation operation in East Timor. Japan has also provided a huge financial contribution to help the East Timorees; but all this without more fundamental change, however. But under such conditions, Japan cannot go any further. In the last few years, Japan has made remarkable progress in the field of participation in the UN peace operations, from the total non-existence of Japan's participation to its limited participation in traditional UN peacekeeping operations. There still remains, however, a contradiction between the overriding faith of the Japanese people in the United Nations and such a limited manner of Japan's participation in the UN peace operations. If Japan's bid to become a permanent member of the UN Security Council is a serious one, this contradiction must be resolved totally. The key questions here is how and when the Japanese people can find a way to modify their pacifism so that Japan's unlimited participation in the UN peace operations will become possible.

---

[9] Reinhard Drifte, *Japan's Foreign Policy in the 1990s: From Economic Superpower to What Power?* (New York: St Martin's Press, 1996), p. 26.

Chapter Eleven

Looking Forward – Prospects for Multilateralism: Implications for Japan[1]

Reinhard Drifte

Japan's gradual involvement in multilateral diplomacy has been promoted by various pressures and incentives which have increased since the end of the superpower confrontation and which are related to Japan's economic superpower status:

- pressures from allies and other members of the international community to accept more burden-sharing commensurate with its economic importance;
- a realization in Japan that the country's global economic interests are increasingly dependent on conditions which are affected by international co-ordination and international organizations;
- a realization that the heavy if not often exclusive focus on bilateralism with the US in the past is no longer sufficient for safeguarding the country's national interests;
- a realization that it is in Japan's interest to counteract to American policies (for example, withholding of assessed contributions to the UN; leaving certain international organizations) which tend to weaken international organizations;
- and a growing national self-confidence and urge for international recognition and prestige.

These five major factors have created institutional and bureaucratic pressures and incentives which further enhance involvement in multilateral diplomacy. Multilateral diplomacy offers, for example, many ministries and agencies of the Japanese government opportunities to enhance or maintain their prestige and budgetary allocations, an important consideration in times of budgetary restraint and economic crisis. Once a part of the bureaucracy is linked to an international organization, an institutional momentum is created. The ministry with the greatest

---

[1] The author gratefully acknowledges the receipt of a Japan Foundation Fellowship (May 1997 – February 1998) and a grant for relief from teaching and administration from the Konishi Foundation in 1997–98 and Urenco Ltd. in 1998–99 which made the research possible. The research was published as *Japan's Quest for a Permanent Security Council Seat*, by Macmillan Publishers/St Antony's Series in 1999 (in Japanese with Iwanami Shoten).

stake in multilateral diplomacy is, of course, the Ministry of Foreign Affairs which has to juggle between keeping its role as a co-ordinator of these growing links between other ministries and international agencies, and creating an internationally interested 'constituency' within Japan which has a vested interest in multilateral diplomacy. The Ministry of Finance is a close second with its power over the purse strings and its responsibility for international financial organizations. It is increasingly also trying to influence foreign policy.[2]

These pressures and incentives are, however, checked by lack of political leadership, conflicting interests resulting from Japan's close alliance with the US, bureaucratic infighting and a general reluctance to get involved in global affairs beyond the economic field.

This chapter cannot deal with all these aspects and instead will concentrate on Japan's quest for a permanent Security Council seat to present some findings which are of general relevance to Japan's multilateral diplomacy and its future. The quest for permanent Security Council membership has been a long-pursued goal of certain parts of the bureaucracy and the political leadership to regain what they would call Japan's proper status in the world community as an economic superpower. At the same time it is the more recent result of heeding outside pressure to assume more international burden-sharing. As we will see, this ambition for a permanent Security Council seat epitomizes the gulf between those trying to involve their country in more than just international economic matters and getting in turn a fair recognition for these endeavours, and those who want to leave high international politics and security issues to other countries or make only a minimal contribution.

Background

Membership of the UN corresponded very much to the aspirations of most Japanese and when Japan finally joined in 1956, it symbolized the re-admission of their country to the civilized world. Many thought that UN membership would prevent a recurrence of past Japanese aggression in the Asia-Pacific region and that the UN with its peace-keeping functions would eventually provide for Japan's security and make rearmament unnecessary. The initially announced UN-centred diplomacy (*kokuren chushin shugi*) gave soon way to the realities of Japan's US-centred diplomacy, and Japan's UN diplomacy turned out to be rather quiet and uninspired. This changed in the 1980s when more issues dealt with in UN organizations started to impinge on Japan's interests, and calls were made on Japan to contribute more to the maintenance of the international system. Another important factor was Japan's rapidly increasing ODA which has been channelled to a large extent through international organizations.

---

[2] See e.g. the report 'Japan's national interests defined. Global strategies for the new millennium' (April 1997) by the Foundation for Advanced Information and Research, an organization affiliated with the Ministry of Finance.

When Japan joined the UN, many Japanese political observers and policy-makers with pre-war experience were aware that Japan had been a permanent member of the Council of the League of Nations, and for the more nationalistically-minded among them, Japan would only regain its former status once it had been admitted as a permanent Security Council member to the UN. Very soon after 1956, Japan joined those members who were interested in revising the Charter. The most immediate reason was the deletion of the so-called 'enemy clauses' of the UN Charter (Articles 53, 77 and 107) which allow, for example, actions without UN authorization against any state which, during World War II, was an enemy of any signatory of the Charter. Since Japan was also interested in improving the ability of the UN to maintain peace and international stability in order to reduce its reliance on the US and to prevent being drawn into international dispute as an alliance partner of the US, it became apparent over the years that some Charter revision might be necessary (and the Japanese government pressed this point) to improve this peace function of the UN (emphasized since the 1960s). These endeavours had to aim in the first place at the Security Council whose main task that is. In addition the Japanese policy-makers had always sympathized with the dissatisfaction of many other member states concerning the composition of the Security Council and its modus operandi (that is, the veto power).

At the end of the 1960s, growing economic success had raised Japan's self-confidence, and Foreign Minister Aichi suggested indirectly in his speech at the UN General Assembly in 1969 and 1970 that Japan should become a permanent Security Council member. The reasons given then in public and in press background talks (which were very explicit) resemble very much those mentioned today as well:

- the convenient opportunity: the twenty-fifth UN anniversary in 1970;
- the country's economic strength (for example, overtaking Germany's GNP in 1969; membership in the OECD);
- the high assessed share in the UN budget (sixth largest in 1969);
- improving the representation of the Security Council;
- Japan as a spokesman of Asia;
- Japan as a non-nuclear power among the nuclear P5 (at that time Taiwan was, however, still representing China);
- Japan as a country which could keep an eye on the peacekeeping activities to be not one-sided but fair and impartial.

Under the circumstances of the Cold War, however, there was no chance of Japan being elevated to the status of a permanent Security Council member. Apart from the Soviet Union, France and Britain also opposed Security Council reform. The Third World was not keen on another industrialized country becoming a permanent Security Council member, and in particular a close ally of the US like Japan. Although the US from the beginning of the 1970s supported Japan's bid, it can only be interpreted as a mere pat on the shoulder of a loyal ally. Given the circumstances of the Cold War, US support could rather be interpreted as a death knell for Japan's bid. Moreover, politicians like Aichi did not energetically pursue the matter due to other foreign policy objectives, Japan's entrenched bilateralism and the single-issue focus of the Ministry of Foreign Affairs. However, since the end of the 1960s there had always been in the Ministry an influential group of diplomats which continued to keep the bid in mind. A general consensus was formed around a policy which would reinforce Charter revisionist tendencies among the UN membership, promote in various ways Japan as a major UN member and strengthen the UN function of keeping world peace. This policy was general enough to get the support of most policy-makers in the Ministry as well as in the ruling party, since its implementation had to rely on a whole range of implementory policies which were dear to or at least acceptable to a number of policy-maker constituencies. The policy was also flexible enough to allow variable momentum or the pursuit of only some of the implementory policies at a given time, depending on external circumstances or even on the enthusiasm of individual policy-makers. At the same time this general policy did not imply any deadline, while leaving open the goal of a permanent Security Council seat.

The following implementory policies were adopted for this consensual policy:

— mentioning of UN reform in most annual UN speeches by the Japanese foreign minister;
— active co-operation in the UN committee which has been dealing with UN and Security Council reform since 1970;
— seeking election as a non-permanent member of the Security Council and of other important UN bodies as often as possible;
— attempts to encourage more personnel involvement in PKO rather than mere financial contributions;
— making proposals to strengthen the peace functions of the UN.

Among these five tactics, Japan was most successful with being elected to a non-permanent member seat on the Security Council, achieving this eight times so far, which is only equalled by Brazil. However, this achievement has sometimes been in the past a rather narrow victory due to dissatisfaction with Japan's policies, seen to be too closely linked with the US (for example on apartheid and the international economic order), as well as racial slurs by leading Japanese politicians, and has always demanded a huge mobilization of foreign policy resources. One reason for pursuing a permanent Security Council seat has therefore become the desire to avoid the considerable effort involved in getting elected to a non-permanent seat.

In order to get elected and to please the Third World which has an overwhelming majority in the UN General Assembly, Japan has undertaken considerable efforts to reconcile notably the African block, the biggest voting block in the General Assembly with fifty-three votes, by using its growing ODA in a focused manner. When the Chairman of the LDP's Policy Board, Fujio Masayuki asked Indonesia in 1985 for support for its bid for a permanent Security Council seat, he had been firmly rejected.[3] Today Indonesia, which is the recipient of the second highest ODA allocation in Asia after China, supports Japan's bid. In the case of Africa, the Tokyo International Conference on African Development (TICAD) of October 1993 and October 1998 and its many related activities at bilateral and multilateral level are a good example of the linkage of interest in the development of Africa with the government's wish to create a positive atmosphere for Japan's bid for a permanent Security Council seat.[4] Other Japanese initiatives in the area of new development strategies can also be seen in this light. The main motive for Japan's emphasis on economic development has been, of course, its desire to be seen to make international contributions in the non-military field as well as to support its economic expansion. As a result, financial and increasingly conceptual inputs in the area of development have become a major agent in involving Japan in multilateral diplomacy.

At the same time, as a result of its phenomenal economic growth, Japan's UN budgetary assessment has kept increasing, and the government has reinforced the impact by substantial voluntary contributions to many international organizations and active participation in Committee V (finances and administration) of the General Assembly. In 1973 Japan's assessed contribution to the UN budget increased from the orginal 2.19 per cent at the time of joining in 1956 to 7.15 per cent, thus making Japan the third biggest contributor and leaving behind the permanent Security Council members France and the UK. In 1986, Japan became the second biggest contributor to the UN budget after the US. Japan became the second largest contributor to the UNHCR in 1979, the UN Environment Programme in 1981, the UN Development Programme in 1984 and the World Bank in 1985.

Japan's non-financial contribution to UN policies has been rather unremarkable. An exception was in the middle of the 1980s when the Japanese government became concerned about the growing rift between the US and the UN which threatened the financial viability of the UN system in general. At that time, the US, followed by Britain, even left UNESCO. Some of the reasons had to do with the bureaucratic inefficiencies of the UN, while others were related to policy differences like the growing politization and Third World leaning tendencies of some UN work. This Anglo-Saxon reaction was perceived as a threat to Japan's growing interests in multilateral diplomacy. Foreign Minister Abe Shintaro proposed in September 1985 the establishment of a 'Wisemen's Group' to recommend reform of the UN's administrative and budgetary process. It was jointly tabled by twelve countries at Japan's initiative, and adopted unanimously at the General Assembly on 18 December 1985. Developing countries were at first opposed to the Group's establishment because they feared a paring of the UN's budget and structure. To accommodate these concerns Japan had to increase the

---

[3] Jakarta papers attack Japan's bid for UNSC, *Japan Times* (9 May 1985), p. 3.
[4] Morikawa, Jun. Japan and Africa. *Big Business and Diplomacy* (Africa World Press: Trenton, NJ, 1997) p. 206.

number of the members from twelve to eighteen.[5] The Group was set up in February 1986 and after four meetings submitted a report with seventy-one recommendations in August of the same year.[6] The subsequent reforms in the UN led the US administration approving a payment of $100 million to the UN and recommending Congress to revise the Kassebaum amendment which threatened to cut US contributions to the UN. Robert Immerman, a former State Department official in Tokyo and in New York, called it Japan's most notable UN initiative.[7]

The most difficult tactic to advance Japan's qualification as a permanent Security Council member was the attempt at more personnel involvement in PKO. It has been obvious to Japan's policy-makers for a long time that personnel contribution to PKO is generally seen as a necessary political condition for Japan's bid, although the permanent five Security Council members have not all been major PKO contributors. China started to contribute personnel to PKO only in 1989. The US started with UNIKOM (UN Iraq–Kuwait Observation Mission) in 1991 although it was involved in a small role a while back in two other peacekeeping operations. However, after the UN PKO debacle in Somalia, it opposes putting US soldiers under UN command.[8]

When the Ministry of Foreign Affairs submitted to the public in 1983 a report on strengthening Japan's contribution to the UN which included also personnel contribution, it was forced to withdraw that particular recommendation.[9] After a long and tortuous debate, Japan finally passed the International Peace Cooperation Law in 1992 which allowed the participation of its military in only logistical and other support functions of PKO. Since then the Self-Defense Forces have been deployed in various PKO missions, the longest and still ongoing one being on the Golan Heights (forty-five personnel, thus making Japan ranking on forty-third place among altogether seventy-one countries). However, it is doubtful whether

---

[5] 'UN Wise Men's Council', *Daily Yomiuri* (23 December 1985).
[6] MOFA, *Diplomatic Bluebook 1987*, p. 178.
[7] Robert M. Immerman, 'Japan in the United Nations', in Craig C. Garby and Mary Brown Bullock (eds), *Japan. A New Kind of Superpower?* (Washington, D.C.: Woodrow Wilson Center Press/ Johns Hopkins University Press, 1994) p. 189.
[8] The US was involved in a small role in UNTSO (United Nations Treaty Supervision Organization), 1948 to date and UNMOGIP (United Nations Military Observer group in India and Pakistan), 1949–1954). For details see Trevor Findlay (ed.), *Challenges for the New Peacekeepers* (Oxford: Oxford University Press, 1996). See also Edward F. Bruner, 'US forces and multinational commands: PDD-25 and precendents', Congressional Research Service Report for Congress, 29 August 1996, p. 3–4. China decided in November 1989 for the first time to dispatch five military observers to serve in the United Nations Truce Supervision Organization (UNTSO) in the Middle East and twenty Chinese civilians to serve as members of the UN Transitional Assistance Group (UNTAG) to help monitor the independence process of Namibia. In April 1992, China dispatched 47 military observers and 400 military engineers to join the UN Transitional Authority in Cambodia (UNTAC). Based on Samuel S. Kim, 'China and the United Nations', in Michael Oksenberg and Elizabeth Economy (eds), *China Joins the World - Progress and Prospects* (New York: Council on Foreign Relations Press, 1998).
[9] John Michael Peek, 'Japan and the United Nations: International cooperation and world order', Ph D thesis (University Microfilm International: Ann Arbor 1985), pp. 267–268.

this restricted deployment would be acceptable to the US Congress if a bill on UN enlargement reached Congress. Indicative of this mood is a US Senate resolution (initiated by Sen. William Roth) passed on 15 July 1994 as part of a broader bill which demanded that Japan should only be admitted as permanent Security Council member if it is 'capable of discharging the full range of responsibilities accepted by all current permanent members of the Security Council', comparing Japan's position unfavourably with that of Germany.[10]

Since the enlargement of the Security Council is dependent on the revision of the UN Charter, Japan worked actively in the Special Committee on the Charter of the United Nations and on the Strengthening of the Role of the Organization (Res. 3499 [XXX]) which still meets briefly each year.[11] However, the work in this Committee only achieved a new impetus with the end of the Cold War. There was an attempt during the era of Prime Minister Nakasone, a keen promoter of Japan's permanent Security Council seat and of the deletion of the so-called enemy clause, to circumvent a proper Security Council reform by elevating Japan to the status of a quasi-permanent Security Council member, but this effort, despite being supported by the US, did not lead anywhere.[12] At that time Japan was again a non-permanent Security Council member (1987–88) and was actively involved in 1987 in drafting a UN resolution which led to a ceasefire in the Iraq–Iran war.

A New Momentum in UN Security Council Reform

With the end of the Cold War the composition and secretive working practices of the United Nations Security Council became even more intolerable to the majority of UN members. In December 1992 the General Assembly passed resolution 47/62 asking the Secretary-General to invite member-states to submit written comments on Council reform by June 1993. In September 1992 Foreign Minister Kinkel announced to the General Assembly that Germany would like to be considered a candidate for a permanent Security Council seat in case the Security Council's composition was to be reconsidered. In December 1993 the General Assembly adopted Resolution 48/26 which was introduced by India and co-sponsored, among others, by Japan, setting up the Open-Ended Working Group on the Question of Equitable Representation on and Increase in the Membership of the Security Council and other Matters Related to the Security Council. Another favourable condition for Japan's chances to become permanent Security Council member was Clinton's support for Japan's candidature since his election campaign in 1992.

However, Japan's official application for a permanent Security Council seat has been rather muted and conditional. In 1992 Prime Minister Miyazawa had veiled

---

[10] Amendment of 15 July 1994, provided by the office of Sen. Roth.
[11] For the background see A/52/100 of 15 July 1997, pp. 223–224.
[12] 'Nihon o jun Joninkoku atsukai ni' (Japan wishes to be treated as associate Permanent Security Council member), *Yomiuri Shimbun* (7 June 1987).

his country's bid in the demand for reforms of the UN which should take the new international circumstances into account. The top representatives of the Ministry of Foreign Affairs were much more forthcoming in 1992, reflecting the impatience of the Ministry. The Japanese ambassador to the UN, Hatano Yoshio, told interviewers that Japan hoped to have a permanent seat on the UNSC in five years' time while the Ministry's spokesman, Hanabusa Masamichi, was quoted as hoping to achieve this goal by 1995, the UN's fiftieth anniversary.[13] In September 1993 Prime Minister Hosokawa declared in the UN General Assembly on Security Council reform: 'It is important that those countries having both the will and the adequate capacity to contribute to world prosperity and stability be actively engaged in that effort ... Japan is prepared to do all it can to discharge its reponsibilities in the United Nations reformed with the previous three points taken into account.'[14] These three points related to reform of peacekeeping, the structure of the Security Council and UN administration and finance. The conditionality of this cloaked bid had to do with the power struggle of the new parties which temporarily had managed to exclude the LDP from power and form a coalition government. It betrayed the ignorance of the leading politicians about UN matters in demanding a 'reformed UN' as a precondition for a Japanese permanent Security Council membership since the mere enlargement of the Security Council would never have found a consensus with the majority of the UN members without the reform of the UN in general and the working procedures of the Security Council in particular. But the statement also reflected the doubts of many policy-makers about Security Council membership and the fear that permanent membership would increase pressure to make more PKO contributions, leading to a stronger seurity policy. At the same time, leading diplomats, notably the UN ambassador in New York (Hatano Yoshio was followed by Owada Hisashi) supported strongly and clearly their country's bid and actively participated in the debate of the new Open-Ended Working Group.

The Reasons for Security Council Membership

In the following I want to discuss the reasons advanced for Japan's permanent Security Council membership and see what they might tell us about Japan's willingness and ability to enhance its multilateral diplomacy.

UN Budgetary Share

Japan's assessed share of the UN budget is the second highest, considerably more than the third largest contributor, Germany, and moved from a share of 17.981 per cent in 1998 to 20.573 per cent in the year 2000 (Germany's share moved from

---

[13] *Japan Times* (1 March 1992); *Financial Times* (1–2 February 1992).
[14] Statements delivered by Delegates of Japan during the 48th Session of the General Assembly of the United Nations (Ministry of Foreign Affairs: Tokyo 1994).

9.630 per cent to 9.857 per cent) before declining to 19.629 per cent in 2001. Many Japanese supporting Japan's bid for a permanent Security Council seat have mentioned this high share as the main reason, speaking of 'No taxation without representation'.[15] In 1994 a senior Japanese diplomat was even quoted as saying: 'The UN question is basically a question of money. We'll be raising our contribution soon from 12.4 per cent to 15 per cent – and that should give us a right of entry.'[16] In the 1997 discussions about the assessed contribution to the UN budget for the next three years, Japan argued that more contribution should go with more responsibility, obliquely referring to the ongoing Security Council reform discussions. Former UN Ambassador Hatano gave an interesting twist to the financial argument by saying that Japan has a lot of things to say, but without being a permanent Security Council member, it cannot speak but only provide money.[17] But this budgetary argument, together with the use of ODA to win support from the Third World, has led to criticism that Japan is trying to buy a seat and is not willing to contribute also through policies, ideas and personnel.

Japan's Position and Prestige in the World

There are many statements which clearly indicate that prestige ranks very high among bureaucrats and politicians, and the high budgetary contribution is closely linked to this point. Already in 1971 Akashi Yasushi, commenting on the bid for permanent membership by Foreign Minister Aichi, referred to the 'almost pathological concern of the Japanese with the international status of their country'.[18] Owada Hisashi, while still Vice Foreign Minister, is quoted as saying: 'The choices of Japan for a course ahead are either whether it wants to become a "normal country" like Europe and the US which includes participation in military activities, or to become a "handicapped country" which pays more than three times in non-military areas' (*gunji igai no men de yoso no san bai no gisei o harau*).[19]

Access to Information

The experience of the Gulf War in 1990–91 was for many Japanese diplomats traumatic. They felt excluded from the deliberations of the Security Council, but

---

[15] See e.g. UN ambassador Hatano mentioning it in the official discussions of Security Council reform. Statement by H.E. Mr Yoshio Hatano, Permanent Representative of Japan, at the fifth meeting of the open-ended working group on Question of Equitable Representation on and increase in the Membership of the Security Council, in: Ministry of Foreign Affairs, UN Policy division, Security Council Reform, Basic Documents, 23 January 1996.

[16] *Far Eastern Economic Review* (25 August 1994) p. 23.

[17] Ampori Joninriiri (Membership in the Security Council) Dialogue between Kamo Takehiko and Hatano Yoshio, *Nikkei Shimbun* (25 September 1994).

[18] Yasushi Akashi, 'Japan in the United Nations', *Japanese Annual of International Law*, vol. 15 (1971), p. 25.

[19] 'Saki isogu Gaimusho ni ayausa' (The danger of the Gaimusho of moving fast forward) *Asahi Shimbun* (15 July 1993), p. 7.

were forced to contribute $13 billion to the war without getting proper recognition.[20] Former UN Ambassador Hatano even argues that had Japan had a seat on the Security Council during the debate on handling the Gulf crisis, it could have helped put together a package of action that would have reduced criticism of its actions.[21]

Public Opinion

The proponents point out that polls indicate that a majority supports Security Council membership. According to the latest poll by the Prime Minister's Office published in January 2001 and conducted in October 2000, 67.1 per cent agree to Japan becoming a permanent member, only 9.9 per cent are against, and 22.0 per cent don't know. The major newspapers are predictably split, the *Asahi Shimbun* and the *Mainichi Shimbun* being reluctant, and the *Yomiuri Shimbun* and the *Sankei Shimbun* in favour. However, the real meaning of these polls is not as unambiguous as the figures might indicate. As we will see, there is still great concern that Security Council membership will mean more involvement in PKO. It is therefore not surprising that the failure of Security Council reform in December 1997 did not give rise to any strong disillusionment or harsh counter-reaction to the UN.

International Opinion

The Japanese government mentions that Japan has been voted a record eight times as a non-permanent member of the Security Council, which it interprets as a vote of confidence for Japan's bid and general recognition. Permanent membership, however, is a different matter, and there are also other issues not related to Japan's qualification as a permanent member which influence the UN member-states in their attitude on Security Council enlargement. There is concern that Japan is still following the American line too much, leading some to conclude that a permanent Security Council seat would only give the US a second veto.[22] But the government expresses the belief that a majority of UN member countries are at least in principle in favour of Japan becoming a permanent member. Only one country, North Korea, has explicitly turned down Japan's quest. But two of Japan's immediate neighbours, China and South Korea, have made it clear unofficially that they are also not supportive of Japan's bid.

---

[20] Yoshikatsu Suzuki, 'Ampori kamei. Gaimusho no shoso' (Joining the Security Council. Impatience of the Gaimusho) *Bungei Shunju* (November 1994).
[21] Asahi-NewsPaper-enews (18 December 1996).
[22] Yasuhiko Yoshida and Terumasa Nakanishi, 'Kokuren Gari kozo to Nihon no moso' (The concept of Ghali and Japan's foolish imaginings), *Shokun* (April 1993), p. 127.

Asian Countries

Japan's membership would enhance the Asian voice in the UN and contribute to a better reflection of the demographic reality of Asia. The South-East Asian countries may welcome Japan counterbalancing China. However, because of its economic position and its Western inclination, Japan is not an ideal Asian voice. China is reluctant to let Japan represent Asia because it considers this its own role. It is also a big question to what extent Japan would side with the South-East Asian countries against China, its biggest neighbour which is also one of its top economic partners.

Non-Nuclear Status

Since all other permanent members of the Security Council are nuclear powers, it is often pointed out that its non-nuclear status gives Japan's bid a particular legitimacy.[23] However, this argument is not convincing to all member-states given Japan's mixed record in the discussions on nuclear disarmament, the American nuclear umbrella over Japan, and its growing plutonium stockpiles. On the other hand, the post-Cold War period has strengthened the opponents of nuclear weapons even in the US military establishment and thus frees Japan from some of its diplomatic constraints *vis-à-vis* its nuclear alliance partner. However, the French and British diplomats let it known at the beginning of the Security Council debate in the 1990s that nuclear power status has something to do with the qualification for a permanent Security Council seat.[24]

PKO

Japan takes great pride in now providing SDF for peacekeeping operations, and the government is making the most of it in convincing international opinion that Japan is doing its fair share of burden-sharing. Conscious of the reservations by many Japanese people, it is often argued that the UN Charter does not impose PKO contributions. The cooling down of the PKO fever in the immediate post-Cold War period is taken as a comforting sign that PKO is no longer that important. Shinyo Takahiro, an active proponent of Japan's permanent Security Council membership, suggests that Japan should therefore agree to co-operative security (not collective security) which would not require constitutional revision.[25] Given the high costs or

---

[23] Takahiro Shinyo, Shin Kokuren ron. 'Kokusai heiwa no tame no Kokuren to Nihon no yakuwari', *Osaka Daigaku Shuppankai* (Osaka, 1995), pp. 55-56. See also 'Kokuren Ampo sho Rijikai no kaikaku' (Reform of the UN Security Council), Ministry of Foreign Affairs, UN Policy Division, 3 July 1996, p. 3.

[24] Patrick A. McCarthy, *Positionality, Tension and Instability in the UN Security Council*, EUI Working Paper RSC No. 97/12 (European University Institute: Florence 1997), pp. 12–13.

[25] Shinyo Takahiro, 'Kyoryokuteki anzenhosho no susume' (In favour of cooperative security), *Toyo Keizai* (May 1996), p. 198.

rather reluctance of the major countries to finance PKO, former UN ambassador Hatano recalls that he stressed at his time in New York 'peace with justice' rather than 'peace at any price', asking his Security Council colleagues (1992–93) always to consider the costs for each decision to use force, and rather opt for peaceful means.[26] But others may ask, what is to be done if non-coercive measures do not work? It has also to be asked whether Japan's evasion of fully-fledged PKO responsibilities will not continue to cause frictions with the US (as it did during the Gulf War in 1991), and whether it is acceptable or even healthy for the UN that one country, based on its high assessment ratio and other financial contributions (including economic aid related to conflict prevention), can participate in PKO by flouting the rules of the UN's General Guidelines for Peace-Keeping Operations of October 1995. As a senior official of the UN Department of Peace-keeping Operations put it to the author:

> We bend backwards for Japan because Japan is an important country. The negotiations for the Golan Heights deployment lasted two years. The rules are halfway met. In addition the Japanese soldiers are very spoiled: if a soldier writes home that the food is bad and its gets into the press, it is immediately picked up. The reality has to adapt to Japan, and not the other way round.[27]

Public support in Japan of PKO has in the meantime improved. Between 1991 and 1994, the support for Japan's participation in PKO increased from 45.5 per cent to 48.4 per cent, those opposed fell from 37.9 per cent to 30.6 per cent (Prime Minister's Office polls 1991 and 1994).

Conclusions

Certain conclusions about Japan's attitude and potential for multilateral diplomacy can be drawn from the above overview of Japan's bid for a permanent Security Council seat. Ultimately the major issue is the understanding of the role of multilateralism in Japan's foreign and security policy, and the institutional and political support to implement it. Moreover, concerning the chances of achieving the bid, it has to be acknowledged that a consensus in the UN on Security Council enlargement is to a large extent an independent variable. It is doubtful, however, that the General Assembly will soon find such a consensus because of fundamental differences in interest. After the hopes for a breakthrough in 1997 were dashed, the General Assembly has been extending the mandate of the 'Open-Ended Working Group' each year as happened with its predecessor.

---

[26] Interview on 17 July 1997.
[27] Interview with a senior official of the UN Department of Peace-Keeping Operations, 8 May 1998.

The reasons given for Japan's bid for a permanent Security Council seat often reflect a bureaucratic perspective, like access to information and ending the costly efforts of gaining non-permanent membership.

Very few promoters give strategic reasons or mention what Japan could do better as a permanent Security Council member. An exception is, for example, a 1996 document of the Ministry of Foreign Affairs which mentions that membership would help Japan to promote dialogue with North Korea and that Japan's contribution to the establishment of peace through an active foreign policy in Cambodia was possible only because Japan was at the time a non-permanent member.[28]

One of the main reasons for the preponderantly bureaucratic perspective is the lack of open support for the bid by politicians. Only few politicians express public support, and even fewer are able and willing to provide a convincing case which goes beyond mentioning Japan's budgetary contribution. Given the background of an ongoing process of political realignment and power struggles, it is not deemed advantageous to get involved in an issue which is still rather controversial. The same would also apply to any major issue in international politics. A group of parliamentarians in support of more contributions to the UN, including permanent Security Council membership, was established in May 1997, but its main leaders are young Dietmembers without much political clout.[29]

Given the distance from international politics by most politicians, this should not come as a surprise. This passive and hands-off approach has been aptly criticized by Professor Ito Kenichi in the case of the bid for a permanent Security Council seat:

> If proponents of the passive approach understood just how much decision-making authority the UN wields when dealing with important international problems ... and if they understood just how arbitrarily those on the Security Council (particularly the permanent members) tend to formulate UN policies, they would see that no scenario in which Japan is excluded from permanent Security Council membership could possibly work in favor of Japan's national interests.[30]

The proponents of the bid seem more often to be motivated by bilateral concerns, such as improving Japanese–American relations, soothing American demands for more international burden sharing and/or deflecting American demands for more military contributions within the scope of the bilateral security alliance. This strong bilateralism is enhanced by Japan's overreliance on American support for its bid. This is understandable to a certain degree, given the close comprehensive alliance and the US's position in the Security Council. But it reinforces with many

---

[28] Ministry of Foreign Affairs, UN Policy division, 3 July 1996, 'Kokuren Ampo sho Rijikai no kaikaku', p. 3.
[29] *Yomiuri Shimbun* (13 May 1997).
[30] Ito, Kenichi. 'A rightful place. Why Japan should push to become a permanent member of the Security Council', *Look Japan* (February 1997), p. 3.

member-states the impression that a Japanese Security Council membership would only enhance the American position, and not that of the UN as the major institution of multilateralism. Moreover, over-reliance on US support has considerably curtailed Japan's ability and willingness to contribute more constructively to the whole Security Council reform debate. In the debate about Security Council reform, Japan has shown great interest and impatience with its slow progress, but compared with Germany, its contribution has been less concrete and constructive. There is a tendency to play it safe, to rely more on bilateral back-stage operations and to defer to US positions. In some ways, pursuing the bid for a Security Council seat (including a non-permanent seat) has even reinforced Japan's bilateral bias. Contributions to other multilateral issues tend to be either budgetary or procedural. As usueful as these may be, they are not on a par with Japan's international power and aspirations. When a major issue erupts, Japan's multilateral diplomacy is often reduced to either a monetary contribution and/or the proposition of a conference of all relevant countries in Japan rather than some compelling policy input or the use of 'shuttle diplomacy'.

This ignorance of and distance from multilateral diplomacy is reflected in public opinion although it is improving. The quest for a permanent Security Council seat has a rather narrow active supporter base despite the positive opinion polls. It is this lack of active popular support not expressed in the opinion polls which is most worrisome for Japan's ability to sustain an active diplomacy as a permanent Security Council member. As long as issues are not too high-profile or do not involve directly or visible (for public opinion) Japan's national interests, Japanese diplomats will be able to make useful contributions which will be, however, limited to procedural and atmospheric manoeuvres. Political leaders will be very reluctant to involve in shuttle diplomacy.

The budgetary argument used by the government and many proponents of the bid is a rather double-edged tactic for the future of the country's multilateral diplomacy, since the failure of Security Council enlargement could seriously erode public support for the UN and multilateral diplomacy in general. This risk is enhanced by the cut of ODA from Fiscal Year 2001 which has fallen mainly on multilateral aid, in contrast to bilateral ODA which is considered politically too useful to sacrifice.

In the end, it comes down to two alternative approaches towards the legitimacy of Japan's quest for a permanent Security Council seat. There is one which is based on a judgement about Japan's qualification as a permanent Security Council member. For example, many Japanese academics and intellectuals oppose the bid because they deem Japan not yet ready to take up the responsibility of a permanent Security Council member although there are often also other reasons behind this judgement. Only once Japan has achieved this qualification – the concrete conditions are never made clear – should it become a permanent Security Council member.

The other approach can either share this negative judgment or not, but in both cases it comes to the conclusion that if Japan is given the opportunity as a permanent Security Council member, it will be forced to acquire the necessary qualification, and that Japan can be trusted to be able to do so. One of the most proliferic promoters among Japan's diplomats, Shinyo Takahiro, asserts that Japan would learn more about international problems by being forced to make its position clear.[31] Tadokoro Masayuki, a professor of the Defence Academy, speaks of Japan's suppressed nationalism and 'legitimacy' deficit, which has tended to take the form of isolationist and pacifist anti-Americanism. He considers it therefore 'both wasteful and somewhat dangerous to keep the Japanese mentally inward looking'.[32]

The first approach is too passive, and would only reinforce Japan's entrenched passivity and isolationism while endangering relations with its Western partners. The second approach is based on hope, and in any case its outcome will be very gradual. However, more Japanese are now understanding the need for multilateral diplomacy in an age of declining American power. The present economic crisis has demonstrated how interdependent the country has become. More responsibility in the UN would accelerate the process of international burden sharing. Although the Security Council debate has been insufficient in clarifying the future role of Japan's multilateral diplomacy, it has at least advanced it.

---

[31] Takahiro Shinyo, Shin Kokuren ron, 'Kokusai heiwa no tame no Kokuren to Nihon no yakuwari', *Osaka Daigaku Shuppankai* (Osaka 1995), pp. 55–56.
[32] Masayuki Tadokoro, 'A Japanese view on the restructuring of the Security Council', in Bruce Russett (ed.), *The Once and Future Security Council* (Macmillan: Houndsmills 1997), p. 131.

Bibliography

Ahaka, Tsuneo and Langdon, Frank (eds) (1993), *Japan in the Posthegemonic World*, Lynne Riener.
Barnhart, Michael A. (1995), *Japan and the World since 1868*, London; New York; E. Arnold.
Buckley, Roger (1992) *US-Japan Alliance Diplomacy, 1945-1990*, Cambridge; New York; Cambridge University Press.
Curtis, Gerald L. (ed.) (1993), *Japan's Foreign Policy after the Cold War*, Armonk, M.E. Sharpe.
Dauvergne, Peter (1998), *The Rise of an Environmental Superpower? Evaluating Japanese Environmental Aid to Southeast Asia*, Canberra; Australian National University, School of Pacific and Asian Studies, Working paper no. 3.
Drifte, Reinhard (1996), *Japan's Foreign Policy in the 1990s: From Economic Superpower to What Power?*, New York; St Martin's Press.
Drifte, Reinhard (2000), *Japan's Quest for a Permanent Security Council Seat: A Matter of Pride or Justice?*, Houndmills; Macmillan, New York; St Martin's Press.
Frankel, Jeffrey A. and Kahler Miles (1993), *Regionalism and Rivalry: Japan and the United States* in *Pacific Asia,* Chicago; University of Chicago Press.
Garby, Graig C. and Brown Bullock M. (eds.) (1994), *Japan, a New Kind of Superpower?*, Washington D.C.; Johns Hopkins University Press.
Hall, Ivan P. (1997), *Japan's New Cultural Push toward Asia: Partner, Hegemon, or Perpetual Outsider?*, University of San Francisco, Center for the Pacific Rim, Pacific Rim report no. 3.
Hunsberger, Warren S. (ed.) (1997), *Japan's Quest: The Search for International Role, Recognition, and Respect*, New York; M.E. Sharpe.
Inoguchi, Takashi (1991), *Japan's International Relations*, London; Pinter; Boulder; Oxford; University Press.
Inoguchi, Takashi (1993), *Japan's Foreign Policy in an Era of Global Change*, London; Pinter.
Inoguchi, Takashi and Stillmann, Grant B. (eds) (1997), *North-East Asian Regional Security: The Role of International Relations*, Tokyo; United Nations University Press.
Katzenstein, Peter (1996), *Cultural Norms and National Security: Police and Military in Post-War Japan*, Ithaca and London; Cornell University Press.

Katzenstein, Peter et al. (2000), *Asian Regionalism*, Ithaca; East Asia Program, Cornell University.
Lake, David and Morgan, P. (1997), *Regional Orders*, University Park, Pennsylvania State University Press.
Newland, Kathleen (ed.) (1990), *The International Relations of Japan*, London; Macmillan.
Pollard, Vincent Kelly (1999), *Globalization, Democratization and Leadership: Domestic and International Politics of Foreign Policy Making in Asia*, Harvard University Library Political Research Online.
Pyle, Kenneth (1992), *The Japanese Question: Power and Purpose in a New Era*, Washington D.C.; AEI Press.
Russett, Bruce (ed.) (1997), *The Once and Future Security Council*, Houndmills, Macmillan.
Tow, William T. and other authors (2000), *Asia's Emerging Regional Order: Reconciling Traditional and Human Security*, Tokyo; United Nations Press.
Unger, Danny and Blackburn, Paul (eds.) (1993), *Japan's Emerging Global Role*, Georgetown; Lynne Rienner Publications.
Yamahuda, Michael (1996), *The International Politics of the Asia-Pacific (1945–1995)*, London; Routledge.
Yamamoto, Yoshinobu et al. (1997), *Emerging Pluralism in Asia and the Pacific*, Hong Kong; Chinese University of Hong Kong, Institute of Asia-Pacific Studies.
Yamamoto, Yoshinobu and Kikuchi, Tsutomu, *Japan's Approach to APEC and Regime Creation in the Asia-Pacific*, in *Asia-Pacific Cross-roads: Regime Creation and the Future of APEC*, New York; St Martin's Press.
Yoshitsu, Michael M. (1984), *Caught in the Middle East: Japan's Diplomacy in Transition*, New York; Macmillan.

Index

Abkhazia 102, 105–111, 125
Abu Saud 57
Acheson, Dean 147
ACSA agreement 24
Afghanistan 118
Agenda for Peace 104
Agenda 21 56
aid programmes 74, 158
Albania 90, 127
Albright, Madeline 25
Algeria 43
alienation of states 10, 14
alliance, use of term 176–177
alliances 10, 19–20, 24
'American syndrome' 149–150
Amnesty International 81
Amsterdam Summit (1997) 132
Annan, Kofi 85
Ardzinba, Vladislav 111
Armenia 103, 106–112 *passim*, 120
arms-control regimes 8–9, 21, 35, 46, 100
Asia Europe Meeting (ASEM) 59–61, 91, 95, 173
Asia Pacific Economic Co-operation (APEC) 91, 153, 156, 170–173
  Japanese involvement with 159–164, 167–168
  as a regional economic regime 163–164
Asian Development Bank 80
Asian financial crisis 52, 54, 57, 65, 80, 94, 143, 164–166, 169–170
Asian Monetary Fund, proposed 165–167
Association of South East Asian Nations (ASEAN) 13, 60, 91, 94, 153, 158, 169–170
  'ASEAN plus 3' formula 60, 174
  ASEAN Regional Forum (ARF) 3, 13–16, 22, 34, 91, 94, 123–124, 162
  'ASEAN way' 13
Atomic Energy Commission 35

ATT card 72–73
Azerbaijan 103–104, 112, 120

Bailes, Alyson 131
balance of power systems 7–10
banking, Islamic 56–57
Barcelona Process 133, 137
Baring's Bank 66
Barnett, Michael 43–45
Baruch Plan (1946) 84
bilateralism 24, 27
biological weapons 15
'Black Monday' (1987) 157
Bocelli, Andrea 54
Bosnia 36, 88–92
'Bottom-up Review' (1993) 22
Brassed Off 76
Braudel, Fernand 140–141
Bretton Woods regime 149
Brookings Institution 78
Brzezinski, Zbigniew 130
burden-sharing 185, 195, 199
Burley, Anne-Marie 30
Bush, George 77

Cable News Network *see* CNN
Cambodia 181, 197
Canada–US Free Trade Agreement (1989) 157
Canberra Commission (1997) 89
capital flows 65
Cattaul, Maria Livanos 71
Caucasus, the 101–109, 116, 119–125
Central Asia Liaison Office (CALO) 116
Central Asian Republics 118–119, 124
Central Intelligence Agency (CIA) 70, 147
Chiangmai Initiative 171
Chechnya 101
chemical weapons 15–16
Chemical Weapons Convention 24, 35
Chibirov, Ludvig 109

China 10, 23–24, 50–58, 84, 88, 93–96, 166, 194–195
  as a world-economy 143–146
Chirac, Jacques 132
Christopher, Warren 59
civil society 30, 117
Clinton, Bill 39, 77, 169, 173, 191
CNN (Cable News Network) 72
'CNN effect' 44
coalitions of nations 7–8
Cold War, ending of 22, 34, 69–70, 87–88, 91, 136, 191
collective security systems 14–15, 18
commercial peace 14
Commonwealth of Independent States (CIS) 102
concert systems 12–15, 18–21
Conference on Security and Co-operation in Europe (CSCE) 3, 9, 91, 99–100
confidence-building measures 8, 12, 18, 21, 34, 99, 101, 109, 153, 159, 163
conflict management 101–115
Congo 85
contagion 65–66
co-ordination games 16
Council of Europe 128
Cox, Robert 28, 30–31
'creative destruction' 172
crisis management 134–137
Cyprus 36

Dayton peace agreement 127
decolonization 85
defection from regimes 9
democratic peace thesis 15
deregulation 50, 52, 163
Deutsch, Karl 14–15
dialogue process 133, 160
disarmament 35, 46; *see also* arms-control regimes
Drifte, Reinhard 184
Drucker, Peter 67
drugs trade 72

East Asia Strategic Initiative 22
East Asian Economic Caucus 60
East Timor 184
Ecology Action 55
The Economist 54, 130
El Salvador 41
electoral processes 42–43, 120

Elysée treaty 94
embedded liberalism 30–31
environmental protection 54–55, 73, 118
ethnic cleansing 36, 104, 107, 130, 137
ethnic minorities 106–107, 118
euro, the 92, 95, 132
Euro-Atlantic Partnership Council 133–134
Eurofor and Euromarfor 135
European Commission 59
European Union 42, 79, 124, 172
  enlargement of 126, 131–133, 137
  foreign and security policy 90–91
  monetary union 132; *see also* euro, the
  relations with the United States 173
exclus 75–76
externalities of regimes 4–5, 9–10, 13, 20

Falkland Islands 78
Forces Answerable to the WEU (FAWEU) 129
foreign direct investment (FDI) 69, 71, 74–75, 155
France 45, 65, 134
free-riding 11
Freundenschuß, Helmut 44
Fukuyama, F. 54

G7/G8 88, 168
Gaddis, John Lewis 95, 132
Gamsakhurdia, Zviad 107
Garton Ash, Timothy 132
GATT (General Agreement on Tariffs and Trade) 4, 49, 58, 77–78, 154–157, 160, 163, 168
genocide 44–45, 107, 130
Genscher, Hans-Dietrich 91
Georgia, Republic of 101–111
Germany 88
globalization 65–79, 140, 142, 173
  concerns about 70–73
  polarization of 74–75
  victims of 76
Golan Heights 182, 190, 196
governance, alternative conceptions of 32
Great Depression 143
Greater East Asian Coprosperity Sphere 147, 149
Greenpeace 81

guanxi 56
Gulf War 79, 178–181, 193–194

Habyarimana, Juvénal 42
Haiti 42
Hammarskjold, Dag 85
harmonization 171
Hashimoto, Ryutaro 166
Hata, Tsutomu 162, 164, 178
Hatano, Yoshio 192–196
Hawke, Bob 156
Hegel, G.W.F. 54
hegemony 11, 77–78
Helsinki Final Act 99
Hideyoshi, Toyotomi 144
Higuchi report (1994) 23
Hisashi, Owada 192–193
Hotoyama, Yukio 178
hub-and-spoke system of alliances 14, 86
human rights 73, 99–100, 117, 120
humanitarian relief operations 181–182
Hussein, Saddam 39, 77

idealist aspirations 32
Immerman, Robert 190
imperialism 27
India 84
Indian Ocean trade 143
Indonesia 43, 92–93, 166, 169, 188–189
information technology 67, 72
Information and Technology Agreement (1996) 171
institutions, importance of 29
interest rates 57
International Atomic Energy Agency (IAEA) 35, 84, 89
International Chamber of Commerce 71
International Monetary Fund (IMF) 52, 54, 66–67, 71, 92, 94, 165–172 *passim*
internationalisation as a subversive force 51
Iran 113
Iraq 38–39, 77–78, 84, 88, 180
Ishihara, Shintaro 76
Israel 38
Italy 128–129, 135

Jackson, Robert 46
Jakobsen, Peter 44
Japan
  alliance with the United States 22–24, 176–177, 197–198
  bilateral relations in general 167–168
  and the Bretton Woods regime 149
  contribution to international institutions 80–81
  insularity 79–80, 199
  involvement with APEC 159–164, 167–168
  Ministry of Finance (MOF) 165–166, 186
  Ministry of Foreign Affairs (MOFA) 166, 177, 185–192 *passim*, 197
  Ministry of International Trade and Industry (MITI) 156, 158, 162, 167
  and multilateralism 48–50, 96
  and OSCE 121–123
  and *Pax Americana* 79
  as part of a world-economy 143–147
  Peace Constitution 175–179, 184
  possible membership of UN Security Council 88, 92–93
  regional co-operation activities 154–158, 162–163
Jeavons, John 55
Judt, Tony 76
JUSCANZ grouping 61

Kan, Naoto 178
Kassebaum amendment 190
Kazakhstan 117, 119
Kenichi, Ito 197
Kennedy, John F. 84
Kennedy, Paul 70
Keynes, J.M. 57
Khujand-Kulyab coalition 112
Kim Dae-Jung 94, 168
Kinkel, Klaus 191
Kirgyztan 117
Kissinger, Henry 52
Kiyoi, Mikie 80
Kobe earthquake (1995) 179
Kohler, Josef 50

Kojima, Kiyoshi 155
Korea (North and South) 22–23, 51, 93–94, 121–124, 144, 146, 166–168, 171, 194, 197
Korean peninsula Energy Development Organization (KEDO) 94
Korean War 148
Koskenniemi, Martii 33, 37, 46
Kosovo 37, 44, 130
Krugman, Paul 140
Kuching Agreement 159
Kurds 38
Kuwait 78, 180–181

land mines 24
Le Pen, Jean-Marie 76
League of Nations 25, 187
Levy, Marc A. 13
liberal internationalism 129–130, 137
liberal interventionism 27, 33–34
liberalization 155
    opposition to 170–171
    voluntary 161, 171
Libya 37
Lipset, Seymour 59
Lockerbie disaster 37

McDonald-ization 65
Mahathir, Muhammad 60, 71
Malaysia 166
Manchuria 148
Manila Framework (1997) 166, 171
Manila Treaty (1954) 86
Masamichi, Hanabusa 192
Masayuki, Fujio 188–189
Masayuki, Tadokoro 199
MCI telephone card 72–73
Mediterranean Co-operation Group 133
Meinig, Donald 149
Mexican debt crisis 65
military power, Japanese attitudes to 176, 179–180, 184
Milosevic, Slobodan 130
Minsk Group and Minsk process 101–105, 108, 111
Missile Technology Control Regime 10
mixed-motive games 9
Miyazawa, Kiichi 159, 178, 191–192
Miyazawa Plan 165, 167
Mobutu Sese Seko 70
Morocco 41
most-favoured nation (MFN) treatment 4, 173

Mozambique 181–182
Mubarak, Hosni 37
multilateral security institutions 136
multilateralism 78–79, 94, 143, 185–186, 196, 199
    attitudes to 25–26, 29–30
    beneficiaries of 44
    'critical' understanding of 28
    definitions of 27–28
    future development of 46–47
    norms and principles of 27
    as a product of the Cold War 48
    as a product of Western thinking 49
'multilateralism in principle' 4–5
multinational companies 71, 168
Murayama, Tomichi 182

Nagasaki 145
Nagorno-Karabakh 101–112 passim, 125
nation-building 42
nationalism 105, 107, 199
NATO (North Atlantic Treaty Organization) 10, 37, 44, 82, 86–89, 94, 127–137
    enlargement of 90, 95, 126, 131–132
    Mediterranean Dialogue 133
'natural' market mechanism 161
nature, views of 54–56
NEC (company) 69
neo-liberalism 27
neo-realism 27, 130–131
New AID (Asian Industrial Development) Plan 158–159
'93 + 2' programme 89
non-governmental organizations (NGOs) 73, 81
non-proliferation regimes 3, 10–11, 21, 35, 84
North Atlantic Assembly 130
North Atlantic Treaty Organization see NATO

Office for Democratic Institutions and Human Rights (ODIHR) 115–121
Ogata, Sagata 81
Ohira, Masayoshi 154, 176
Okita, Saburo 155
omnilateralism 48, 54, 58–61
Open Regionalism 161, 163, 172
Operation Alba 127–129

Operation Lifeline 41
Opium Wars 146
Organization of American States (OAS) 42
Organization for Economic Co-operation and Development (OECD) 50
Organization for Security and Co-operation in Europe (OSCE) 3, 42, 91, 100–128, 137
    Japan's relations with 121–123
    Stability Pact 134
Ozawa, Ichiro 178

pacifism 175–178, 182, 184, 199
'paradox of the state' 46
Paris, Roland 130
Partnership for Peace programme 133–134, 137
Pax Americana 70, 77–79
peace enforcement 137, 180;
    see also United Nations Charter: Chapter VII
peacekeeping operations (PKO) 24, 26, 35–36, 43, 108
    Japanese involvement in 178–184, 190, 195–196
Perry, Commodore 146
Petersberg Declaration 133
Pfaff, William 51
Plaza Accords (1985) 157
pluralistic security communities 14–15
Polanyi, Karl 30, 139
pop music 54
Portugal 145
power relations 28–30
prisoners' dilemma 8–9, 11, 16
prohibition regimes 15–16, 20–21
propiska system 120

Ramazotti, Eros 54
rationalism 27
rationalist multilateralism 40
Reagan, Ronald 70, 177
realism 28
recycling 55
regimes, definition of 4
'regionalism by declaration' 153
regions 141–142, 150
    definition of 139

renga tradition 56
Ricupero, Rubens 73
Risse-Kappen, Thomas 44
Roth, William 191
Rubin Doctrine 52
Ruggie, John 4, 25, 30–31
Russia 10, 95–96, 108–109, 113
Rwanda 37–38, 41–42, 44–45, 87, 182
Ryukyu Islands 144–145

Samuelson, Paul 57
Schumpeter, Joseph 143
SEATO (South East Asia Treaty Organization) 86
security, threats to 7, 130–131
security regimes
    based on generalized multilateralism 12–17
    characteristics and functions of 6, 9, 19–22
    objectives of 12
    types of 7–12
Segal, Gerald 74, 77
self-defence
    for peacekeepers 183
    for states 32, 178–179
self-interest of states 29
Serbia 90, 130
Shanghai 73–75
Shevardnadze, George 109
Shintaro, Abe 189
shuttle diplomacy 198
social contract 169
social purpose of international society 29–30
Somalia 40–41, 88
South Ossetia 101–110 *passim*, 125
South Sea Bubble 143
sovereignty 32–33, 44, 47, 88
    restoration of 41
Soviet Union 83–84
Spain 135
stag hunt game 16–18
standard of civilization 33
state formation 126
strategic alliances 60
'strong harmony' 16
structural liberalism 136
suasion games 8, 11

Index

Sudan 37, 41
superpower co-operation 84–85
Suzuki, Zenko 177
Sweden 69

Taiwan 148
Tajikistan 112–114, 119
Takahiro, Shinyo 195, 199
Tawain Strait incident (1996) 23
territorial integrity of states 103–104
terrorism 37–38
Thailand 165, 170–171
Thatcher, Margaret 78
Tokyo International Conference on African Development (TICAD) 189
'Tote-Board diplomacy' 13
Transatlantic Market (TAM) concept 173
Treaty of Rome 94
tributary trade 144–145
tulip mania 143
Turkmenistan 119
'2 + 4' treaty 88

United Nations
　accountability of 41
　great powers' abandonment of 36–37
　Japanese attitudes to 175, 177–178, 182–184
　Japanese contributions to budget of 189, 192–193
　reform of 92–93, 192, 198
　see also peacekeeping operations
United Nations Charter
　Article 1 32
　Article 2 46, 88
　Chapter VII 26, 37–39, 42, 83, 180
　Chapter VIII 104
　'enemy clauses' 187, 191
United Nations Conference on Trade and Development (UNCTAD) 71
United Nations General Assembly 32, 34–35, 191
United Nations Security Council 32–40, 44–46, 79, 85, 88
　membership of 45, 88–89, 92–93, 184–199
　Resolution 687 93
　Resolution 688 38, 88
　Resolution 794 38, 88
　Resolution 853 104

United Nations Security Council (cont.)
　Resolution 884 104
　Resolution 940 42
　use of veto 83, 187
United States
　alliance with Japan 22–24, 176–177, 197–198
　bilateral relations in general 86
　fast-track authority for trade talks 169, 173
　as global hegemon 77–78
　military presence in East Asia 23
　relations with the European Union 173
　relations with the Soviet Union 84
　trade deficit 157, 169
　see also 'American syndrome'
Uniting for Peace resolution (1950) 34–35
Uruguay Round 77–78, 160
Uzbekistan 116–117

Vietnam War 77
Voluntary Restraint Agreements 49

Wall Street Journal 72
war crimes tribunals 37–38
Washington Post 181
Wassenar Agreement 10
Western Sahara 41
Westphalian state system 40, 42
Western European Union (WEU) 90, 127–129, 133–136
　Forces Answerable to 129
Williams, Michael 36
'winnability' of international operations 45
Wisemen's Group (on UN administrative and budgetary processes) 189–190
Wolf, Martin 77
'world-economies' 140–143
World Trade Organization (WTO) 68, 73, 77, 163, 168
Worldwatch Institute 56

Yasushi, Akashi 193
Yoshimitsu, Ashikaga 144
Yugoslavia 37–39, 41, 127–128

Zaire 182
Zelikov, Philip 136
zero-sum games 7–9